THOMAS HARDY

A Critical Biography

J. I. M. Stewart

In a masterpiece of literary dissection a distinguished scholar of English literature analyzes the art and craft of Victorian England's greatest novelist and one of her greatest poets of all ages. Dr. Stewart probes the private life and intellectual background of his subject and relates them to the prose and poetry that he wrote: fourteen novels including such landmarks of English fiction as *The Return of the Native* and *Tess of the D'Urbervilles,* as well as over nine hundred short poems.

Hardy is represented by Dr. Stewart's incisive analysis as a full-blown artist who could re-create in his writings the passions of his whole experience. This portrait of the author and his work will serve both as a superb introduction to one of the great men of letters as well as an enlightening revelation to the reader already an admirer of the vision and art of T

His publications inclu *Motive in Shakespear Writers* (the final volu mental *Oxford History* ture), *Rudyard Kipling, Joseph Conrad,* and a series of novels. Under the pseudonym of Michael Innes, Dr. Stewart is the author of a number of witty and erudite novels of suspense.

Thomas Hardy

A Critical Biography

Also by J. I. M. Stewart

CHARACTER AND MOTIVE IN SHAKESPEARE

EIGHT MODERN WRITERS

RUDYARD KIPLING

JOSEPH CONRAD

Thomas Hardy

A Critical Biography

J. I. M. Stewart

Longman

LONGMAN GROUP LIMITED LONDON

Associated companies, branches and representatives throughout
the world
© J. I. M. Stewart 1971
Second impression 1972

First published 1971

ISBN 0 582 11783 6

Printed in Great Britain by
Lowe & Brydone (Printers) Ltd., Thetford, Norfolk

23094

Contents

1 Hardy's Autobiography 1
2 Private Life 16
3 Intellectual Background 31
4 Early Writing 47
5 *A Pair of Blue Eyes* 63
6 *Far from the Madding Crowd* 74
7 *The Return of the Native* 91
8 *The Mayor of Casterbridge* 108
9 *The Woodlanders* 127
10 Minor Fiction 147
11 *Tess of the d'Urbervilles* 162
12 *Jude the Obscure* 184
13 *The Dynasts* 204
14 Hardy's Major Poetry 219
Chronology 234
Bibliography 237
Index 241

Acknowledgements

We are grateful for permission to reproduce copyright material to the Trustees of the Hardy Estate, Macmillan Canada, Macmillan London and Basingstoke and the Macmillan Company of New York for extracts from the works of Thomas Hardy.

1
Hardy's Autobiography

HARDY DIED ON 11 JANUARY 1928, AND WITHIN THREE WEEKS
there had been despatched to Macmillan the manuscript of a book
which they published on 2 November with the following title-
page:

THE EARLY LIFE OF / THOMAS HARDY / 1840-1891 / COMPILED
LARGELY FROM / CONTEMPORARY NOTES, LETTERS, DIARIES, AND /
BIOGRAPHICAL MEMORANDA, AS WELL AS FROM / ORAL INFORMA-
TION IN CONVERSATIONS EXTENDING / OVER MANY YEARS / BY /
FLORENCE EMILY HARDY

The volume is dedicated 'To the dear Memory', and the first
sentence of a *Prefatory Note* is: 'Mr Hardy's feeling for a long
time was that he would not care to have his life written at all'.
On 29 April 1930 there was published:

THE LATER YEARS OF / THOMAS HARDY / 1892-1928 / BY /
FLORENCE EMILY HARDY

This entire enterprise is described by Professor Richard Purdy,
Hardy's incomparable bibliographer, as an 'innocent deception',
the fact being that only the four concluding chapters of the second
volume—chapters which cover the last ten years of Hardy's life—
are by Mrs Hardy. Elsewhere, in Purdy's words, 'her work was
confined to a few editorial touches, and the writing is throughout
Hardy's own'. The bibliographical evidence makes it clear, moreover, that both Hardy and Mrs Hardy took considerable pains to
ensure that their deception should remain a secret. Hardy destroyed his manuscript as fast as Mrs Hardy completed a typescript,
and when he subsequently made alterations in the typescript it was
in a calligraphic hand which he must have somewhat guilelessly
supposed capable of baffling the perspicacity of scholars in a
future time.

The *Life* (as we may call the two volumes together) is largely a compilation from old letters, diaries, notebooks, and the like; and in the context of so much obfuscation as attended its making we are unsurprised to learn that almost everything of the kind which Hardy did not select for his biographical purpose he there and then destroyed. We have no business whatever to be indignant or resentful about this. Every man, and therefore every artist, has some right to privacy, and to guard this it is surely fair that exceptional means should be taken by those whom eminence exposes to exceptional curiosity. Moreover, a man's standards and actions here may properly be judged only in the light of what is held seemly and decorous in his time. Different times assert different views as to where the lines of privacy should be drawn. Today, for example, it is possible to take quite literally Yeats's presumably metaphorical remark that 'there's more enterprise in walking naked': not long ago I read of a citizen of the United States who judged his rights and liberties under the Constitution of his country to have been violated when the police insisted on his putting on a pair of pants before they arrested him.

It is not quite self-evident, moreover, that an extreme communicativeness in relation to our private affairs is our best means of guarding against the risk of being judged boring. There is always some sort of mean to be observed, and we may now feel that the Victorians (except for disreputable ones, such as Frank Harris) had rather too enlarged a notion of what is no business of ours. Many of them (Matthew Arnold, for example) took great pains to 'cover up' this or that. In what is called 'public life' there are in England, to this day, well-understood conventions designed to protect what are regarded as a man's private affairs. But it so happens that among writers and artists this tradition has become a good deal attenuated—largely, I suppose, owing to the influence of theories which see their creative work as radically determined by matters which a man would more naturally take to his psychiatrist than his publisher. The Victorians failed to view poems and novels and paintings in quite this genetic way. It is possible to maintain, indeed, that they lived in a kind of innocence which prevented them from seeing how *suspicious* we were going to be. It does not really follow that when a man shrinks from being made the subject of a biography there must be matter of an intriguingly unedifying sort to be dug up about him. Thus, one of Hardy's younger contemporaries, Rudyard Kipling, hated the idea of somebody writing his life. He thought to forestall such a formal biography by preparing for posthumous publication an autobiographical memoir accurately entitled *Something of Myself*, and he wrote a poem (slightly reminiscent of the lines incised on Shakespeare's tomb) which he called 'An Appeal':

> If I have given you delight
>   By aught that I have done,
> Let me lie quiet in that night
>   Which shall be yours anon:
>
> And for the little, little, span
>   The dead are borne in mind,
> Seek not to question other than
>   The books I leave behind.

It would be foolish to conclude from this that Kipling had anything very notable to sweep under the rug. And so with Thomas Hardy. He may, as has lately been maintained, have had a son by a cousin who later and rather unfortunately turned out actually to be a niece—although I judge it, indeed, to be extremely improbable. But assuredly the strong sentiment of privacy and reticence that produced such an oddity as the *Life* is poor evidence when arguing anything of the kind.

The *Life*, we must still admit, *is* an oddity. How should we feel about Boswell's *Life of Samuel Johnson, LL.D.*, if nine-tenths of it proved to have been written by Samuel Johnson, LL.D., himself? It is worth remarking here that a lot of Boswell's *Johnson*, indeed, *is* by Johnson: 'a series of his epistolary correspondence', and so on, as the title-page tells us. Still, the fact remains that Hardy was, so to speak, his own Boswell, and hoped to pass undetected as such.

Strictly regarded, indeed, the *Life* must be acknowledged as full of fibs, and of fibs which Hardy clearly enjoyed fabricating and insinuating into the record, as when we are told in it of 'his absolute refusal at all times to write his reminiscences', or that 'many of the details . . . which Hardy himself did not think worth recording, have been obtained from diaries kept by the late [i.e. first] Mrs Hardy'. Hardy always relished ingenuity; we encounter it in phrases like 'so he once remarked' and 'so far as is remembered by the present writer'. Yet it cannot have been for the sake of thus laughing up his sleeve at us that Hardy undertook the labour of being his own biographer. So why, in fact, did he do so?

Purdy answers this question obliquely when he remarks of the book: 'The conditions of Hardy's birth and childhood are idealized. The bitterness of his struggle for an education and a profession and the suffering of his first marriage find no reflection.'

There are really two distinct considerations here, although both
can be brought under the general head of that Victorian sense of
reticence and decorum which I have mentioned. First, Hardy must
have been aware that, in the regard alike of the large middle class
for whom he wrote his novels and of the smaller upper class which
he had come a good deal to frequent, his origins would appear to
be simply those of a Dorset peasant. But such a view would be
inaccurate in two particulars. Among the common people there
are gradations of substance, manners, cultural tradition, even
education which tend to be little regarded when viewed even from
a not very considerable social remove; and it was of enormous
significance in Hardy's early life that his own people were for the
most part high up on this small social scale. Again, Hardy had
come to believe that, not many generations back, his forbears had
been gentlefolk, and that he himself was to be most authentically
viewed as of an exhausted patrician, or at least squirarchal, stock.
This persuasion (which was the mainspring of his greatest novel)
has been, for what the point is worth, substantiated by recent
research. At the same time, there is no doubt that Hardy's immediate relations must have thought and felt and comported
themselves as simple people. In all this there worked, we may say,
a complexity of motives and attitudes which Hardy was unwilling
to leave the portrayal of to anybody else. Much of the softening
and blurring of his early social situation which the *Life* exhibits is
to be attributed less to any sort of snobbery than to an instinct for
what must be called artistic truth. It connects with what I hope
presently to exhibit: a strong artistic impulse at work in what
appears casually as a very inartificial performance.

With the suppression of what Purdy calls 'the suffering of his
first marriage' we come to something rather different. It is partly,
no doubt, the Victorian reticence, which was never more nearly
absolute than when matters with a sexual element were in question.
But much more, I think, it is loyalty and compassion and remorse
that are at work. And again there may be a component of artistic
feeling: a conviction that there exist regions of experience the
truth about which can be rendered only in poetry:

> Woman much missed, how you call to me, call to me,
> Saying that now you are not as you were
> When you had changed from the one who was all to me,
> But as at first, when our day was fair.

In some ways Hardy *was* much a peasant: stingy with his
sixpences, building in 1885 a substantial yet mean-looking dwelling,

Max Gate, which remained without a bathroom forty years later. Yet he was gentle in the old-fashioned sense of being a man capable of chivalrous instincts and fine feelings.

2

When we learn that the *Life*, launched with such posthumous promptitude, is in fact Hardy's own venture sailing under false colours we are inclined to think, as we read, in terms of censorship and distortion. But it is really more useful to consider the book as a great piece of luck, something reflecting Hardy's personality and vision in a manner which would otherwise be lacking to us. Received in this way, it can be an illuminating prelude to the novels and poems. It can be this because it itself exhibits certain of Hardy's instincts, and even actual formulations, in the field of aesthetics.

It is in the *Life*, indeed, that most of the formulations come. 'Art consists in so depicting the common events of life as to bring out the features which illustrate the author's idiosyncratic mode of regard.' 'I prefer late Wagner, as I prefer late Turner, to early (which I suppose is all wrong in taste), the idiosyncrasies of each master being more strongly shown in these strains.' 'Art is a changing of the actual proportions and order of things, so as to bring out more forcibly than might otherwise be done that feature in them which appeals most strongly to the idiosyncrasy of the artist.' This emphasis upon the value of a uniqueness of vision is of cardinal importance in understanding Hardy's art. But—we must be very clear—he is far from believing that the idiosyncrasy of the artist is a matter of amusing or sensational aberration. On the contrary, Hardy's theory of art is eminently vatic. The artist's idiosyncrasy—at his farthest extension, his uniqueness—is revelatory in its effect. But what is thus revealed must, since it is novel, appear to *us*, at least upon a first reception, as distortion and incongruity. 'My art is to intensify the expression of things, as is done by Crivelli, Bellini, etc., so that the heart and inner meaning is made vividly visible.' Hardy's fondness for the macabre and the bizarre, so constantly illustrated in the *Life*, is chiefly prompted by a sense of the power of incongruity 'to intensify the expression of things' in a manner enforcing basic if uncomfortable truths of the human situation. Thus in 1882 'the Hardys attended Ambulance-Society lectures—First-Aid being in fashion just then'. And Hardy notes:

A skeleton—the one used in these lectures—is hung up inside the window. We face it as we sit. Outside the band is playing, and the children are dancing. I see their little figures through the window past the skeleton dangling in front.

This is, as he would say, a moment of vision, and its shock-value is in its oddity. Hardy knew that it was important to him as an artist that he could 'notice such things' even as he could notice how 'a crossing breeze cuts a pause' in the 'outrollings' of a passing bell. It is true that he would sometimes seem to notice the macabre side of life rather obsessively and repetitively: the English children dancing behind the skeleton are answered eight years later by the *cancan* dancers of the Moulin Rouge, 'grimacing at the men', while through windows behind them could be seen 'the cemetery of Montmartre . . . the last resting-place of so many similar gay Parisians silent under the moonlight'.

One idiosyncrasy of the *Life* consists in its affording an astonishing anthology, or necrology, of mortuary occasions. Hardy holds a candle at an autopsy; inspects with Lord Portsmouth 'a bridge over which bastards were thrown and drowned'; recalls for the benefit of Mr and Mrs John Galsworthy 'what his mother had said about the Rush murder when he was about the age of six'; 'looks through a slit' at the coffin of Lord Warwick, whom he had long delayed to visit, and murmurs 'Here I am at last, and here are you to receive me!' (This last occasion, Hardy assures us, 'made an impression . . . which he never forgot'.) Some of these cherished anecdotes are pointless, as when we hear of a grave, commissioned by telegram, which was unclaimed and had to be filled up again. Others are merely gruesome: 'T. Voss used to take casts of heads of executed convicts. . . . There was a groove where the rope went'. Most have some more or less entertaining quirk or twist to them, after the fashion of the following:

> Holder as a young man was a curate in Bristol during the terrible cholera visitation. He related that one day at a friend's house he met a charming young widow, who invited him to call on her. With pleasant anticipations he went at tea-time a day or two later, and duly inquired if she was at home. The servant said with a strange face: 'Why, Sir, you buried her this morning!'

Other stories deal with grim or grotesque or absurd incidents not concerned with mortality. There are public floggings as well as public hangings. Three wooden-legged men used to dance a three-handed reel at Broadmayne. A girl who bore an illegitimate child to a parish doctor with a squint 'hung a bobbin from the baby's cap between his eyes, and so trained him to squint likewise'. A former lover's abandoned watch starts ticking when a girl marries his supplanter. Some eels come half-way upstairs in the night.

One cannot imagine such a proliferation of queer and often quite inconsequent anecdotage being put into a life of Thomas Hardy except by Thomas Hardy. And they are certainly very deliberately deployed from his memory and his notebooks as a means of exhibiting 'the author's idiosyncratic mode of regard'. They do not, perhaps, much succeed in surprising us if we happen to have read the novels and short stories and poems. What is much more unexpected is the space given up, year after year, to the chronicling of polite social occasions.

As soon as he could afford it, this simple countryman, austere philosopher, and inspired chronicler of rural England pertinaciously 'did' the London season every spring and summer. His first novel, *The Poor Man and the Lady*, had been a sweeping and uninformed satire upon the upper classes; we are told that he 'constitutionally shrank from the business of social advancement' and that he 'did not think worth recording' 'his adventures in the world of fashion at dinner-parties, crushes, and other social functions'. But in fact he transcribes into the *Life* a great deal about a 'customary round of picture-viewing, luncheons, calls, dinners, and receptions'. 'Hardy', he records of himself, 'does not comment much on these society-gatherings, his thoughts running upon other subjects'—such as (we immediately read) its being the 'becoming' of the world that produces its sadness. But in fact he *does* quite often comment. Sometimes it is in a sparely caustic way:

> With E. to lunch at Lady Stanley's (of Alderley). Met there Lord Halifax, Lady Airlie, Hon. Maude Stanley, her brother Monsignor Stanley, and others. An exciting family dispute supervened, in which they took no notice of us guests at all. . . .
> In May or June he paid a few days' visit to Lord Curzon at Hackwood Park, where many of the house-party went into the wood by moonlight to listen to the nightingale, but made such a babble of conversation that no nightingale ventured to open his bill.

Frequently, however, social occasions are recorded at which nothing whatever of interest is noted as having transpired—and the recording voice, moreover, seems to accept the convention that anybody met two or three times in a lifetime is a 'friend' or an 'old friend'. Hardy, the celebrant of local pieties, presents himself as a man who knows everybody in England.

The formation of these social habits may have been due initially
to the first Mrs Hardy, who was very conscious of her own natural
affinity with people of superior social station. But in fact she often
remained in the country when Hardy went to town. We shall later
find incontrovertible evidence that she became increasingly jealous
of her husband's frequentation of aristocratic drawing-rooms and
dinner-tables. Hardy enjoyed moving in society much more than
the *Life* admits, and it is clear that well-bred, beautiful, and clever
women appealed to him very much.

3

Nor is Mrs Hardy (although pious in a blurry way) accountable
for another of Hardy's at first perplexing attitudes—the church-
iness (as he accurately calls it) which he managed to combine with
his radical and indeed obsessive agnosticism. One gets the impression, indeed, that he did a good deal of his church-going, as he
did his party-going, when actually getting away from his wife. His
consciousness of incongruity here is pleasantly expressed in a letter
written in his eightieth year:

> I almost think that people were less pitiless towards their
> fellow-creatures—human and animal—under the Roman Empire
> than they are now; so why does not Christianity throw up the
> sponge and say, I am beaten, and let another religion take its
> place?
> I suddenly remember that we had a call from our Bishop and
> his wife two or three days ago, so that perhaps it is rather shabby
> of me to write as above. By a curious coincidence we had
> motored to Salisbury that very day, and were in his cathedral
> when he was at our house.

But anything which could conceivably be described as the
development of Hardy's religious (or philosophical) opinions
comes to us in the *Life* only piecemeal and in the most disjointed
way. As a child he was delicate, intellectually precocious, of an
'ecstatic' temperament, and fond of wrapping himself in a sheet
and delivering sermons; it is evident that when 'everybody said
that Tommy would have to be a parson' it was not entirely by way
of a joke. When, at the age of sixteen, his father's trade connection
as a builder brought him the opportunity, too favourable to be
turned down, of pupilage to a Dorchester architect, we are told
that Hardy 'cheerfully agreed' although his inclination was for
something more bookish and 'he had sometimes, too, wished to

enter the Church'. He and a fellow-pupil were later much exercised
over the question of adult baptism—Hardy seeking light on the
matter, but without much success, in Hooker's *Ecclesiastical
Polity*. Many of the friends he made as a young man had a clerical
background. One of them, Horace Moule, who certainly (despite
disclaimers by Hardy) stood to him in the same mentor's and
patron's relationship as does another 'reviewer and essayist',
Henry Knight, to the young plebeian architect, Stephen Smith, in
A Pair of Blue Eyes, was interested in the relationship of religion
and science. But we are not told anything material about Moule's
views here, nor is there any reason to suppose that the depression
which eventually induced him to commit suicide was precipitated
by any crisis of faith. We learn that Moule admired Newman's
Apologia and that Hardy therefore tried to admire it too but had
to judge its reasoning not securely based. This was when Hardy
was twenty-five, and it was at about the same time that, although
he had 'formed the idea of combining poetry and the Church',
he had to decide that he could not go to Cambridge (although
'not altogether hindered going') owing to 'his discovery that he
could not conscientiously carry out his idea of taking Orders'.
There is some evidence, however, although not in the *Life*, that
Hardy's academic aspirations were in fact 'hindered' and indeed
snubbed on account of his birth and station. His conscientious
scruples, therefore, may have been in part a salve to wounded
pride. On the same page on which he records them we read that he
stayed to the Sacrament at morning service in Westminster
Abbey.

We are not positively told in the *Life* that he ever ceased being a
communicant member of the Anglican Church. Certainly he
remained an intermittent church-goer all his days, chiefly, no
doubt, because of his sentimental attachment to that tradition of
church music which had been so prominent in his family for
generations, and which he celebrates so splendidly in the story of
the Mellstock Quire in *Under the Greenwood Tree*. But in middle-
age, at least, he would note (of St George's, Hanover Square) that
'the electric light and old theology seem strange companions; and
the sermon was as if addressed to native tribes of primitive
simplicity, and not to the Nineteenth-Century English'. It is on the
page preceding this note that he records: 'I have been looking for
God 50 years, and I think that if he had existed I should have
discovered him'. He remarks, about the same time, that at Bow
Church in Cheapside the rector and curate appear glad ' that you
have condescended to visit them in their loneliness'. But words as
well as music could move him. At Salisbury: 'Passages from the

first lesson (Jer. vi) at the Cathedral this afternoon. E. [Emma
Hardy, his first wife] and I present. A beautiful chapter, beautifully
read by the old Canon.'

Of intellectual influences upon Hardy's progress to agnosticism
we learn very little. 'As a young man he had been among the
earliest acclaimers of *The Origin of Species*.' But Charles Darwin
had been buried, after all, in Westminster Abbey, and this particular note is part of Hardy's recording that he attended the
solemnity. In 1860 he was much impressed by *Essays and Reviews*.
But few people were not. Far more important, clearly, was the
'deep influence' of Leslie Stephen, which affected him—Hardy
explicity states— 'more than that of any other contemporary'. In
1875 he acted as witness to Stephen's signing 'a deed renunciatory
of holy-orders under the act of 1870'. Stephen had been ordained
at the age of twenty-three, as Hardy, we may reflect, would almost
certainly have been had he too had Eton and a Cambridge tutor-
ship behind him. Stephen—a dominating personality, professional scholar, down-to-earth editor, and up-the-Schreckhorn
mountaineer—was not at all like Hardy, who was a poet. But his
agnosticism was of a high-minded and ethically somewhat oppressive sort which the younger man perhaps found both reassuring
and edifying.

Long before he met Stephen, however, he was of a divided mind
before the spectacle of institutional religion, and when not under
the influence of his particular kind of churchyard piety he enjoyed
spotting the various incongruities which may attend it. He records
that 'modern Christianity' was one of the objects of his satire in
The Poor Man and the Lady, and he goes on:

> One instance he could remember was a chapter in which, with
> every circumstantial detail, he described in the first person his
> introduction to the kept mistress of an architect . . . the said
> mistress adding to her lover's income by designing for him the
> pulpits, altars, reredoses, texts, holy vessels, crucifixes, and
> other ecclesiastical furniture which were handed on to him by
> the nominal architects who employed her protector—the lady
> herself being a dancer at a music-hall when not engaged in
> designing Christian emblems.

This joke is reflected, in a less juvenile form, in Sue Bridehead's
early employment in *Jude the Obscure*, and in the scandal which
later attends her helping Jude's journeyman-work in a church. In
Jude, too, there is a long and inconsequent anecdote about
inebriated workmen renovating the Ten Commandments to very

shocking effect which echoes records in the *Life* expressive of a similar humorous irreverence. Thus:

G. R. —— (who is a humorist) showed me his fowl-house, which was built of old church-materials bought at Wellspring the builder's sale. R.'s chickens roost under the gilt-lettered Lord's Prayer and Creed, and the cock crows and flaps his wings against the Ten Commandments. It reminded me that I had seen these same Ten Commandments, Lord's Prayer, and Creed, before, forming the side of the stone-mason's shed in that same builder's yard, and that he had remarked casually that they did not prevent the workmen 'cussing and damning' the same as before. . . . A comic business—church restoration.

And here, from later in the *Life*, is a related passage—but longer and of more substance, so that we may be a little reminded of the imagination at work in the stage-directions of *The Dynasts*:

A service at St Mary Abbots, Kensington. The red plumes and ribbon in two stylish girls' hats in the foreground match the red robes of the persons round Christ on the Cross in the east window. The pale crucified figure rises up from a parterre of London bonnets and artificial hair-coils, as viewed from the back where I am. The sky over Jerusalem seems to have some connection with the corn-flowers in a fashionable hat that bobs about in front of the city of David. . . . When the congregation rises there is a rustling of silks like that of the Devils' wings in Paradise Lost. Every woman then, even if she had forgotten it before, has a single thought to the folds of her clothes. They pray in the litany as if under enchantment. Their real life is spinning on beneath this apparent one of calm, like the District Railway-trains underground just by—throbbing, rushing, hot, concerned with next week, last week. . . . Could these true scenes in which this congregation is living be brought into church bodily with the personages, there would be a churchful of jostling phantasmagorias crowded like a heap of soap bubbles, infinitely intersecting, but each seeing only his own. The bald-headed man is surrounded by the interior of the Stock Exchange; that girl by the jeweller's shop in which she purchased yesterday. Through this bizarre world of thought circulates the recitative of the parson—a thin solitary note without cadence or change of intensity—and getting lost like a bee in the clerestory.

We may feel that this is a partial view of a devotional occasion. Or we may feel that it is very much a matter of 'art' as we have seen

Hardy defining it: 'Art consists in so depicting the common events
of life as to bring out the features which illustrate the author's
idiosyncratic mode of regard'. Here at St Mary Abbots he is
precisely 'changing the actual proportions of things' in order to
'bring out more forcibly than might otherwise be done that feature
in them which appeals most strongly to the idiosyncrasy of the
artist'.

Hardy is aware that his sort of church-going must represent, to
some extent, an involvement in a false position. 'We repeat the
words from an antiquarian interest in them, and in a historic sense,
and solely in order to keep a church of some sort afoot—a thing
indispensible.' But we perceive that none of the congregation
recognizes our motive, so 'we are pretending what is not true; that
we are believers'. And 'This must not be; we must leave. And if we
do, we reluctantly go to the door, and creep out as it creaks com-
plainingly behind us.'

To the end of his days it was reluctantly that Hardy went to the
door. His critics, he said, called him an atheist and a pessimist, but
they might much more plausibly have called him churchy—'not in
an intellectual sense, but in so far as instincts and emotions ruled'.
Towards the end of his life he appears to have lost his grip on
what was probable or possible in the way of 'rationalizing' the
English Church. When there was talk of a revised Liturgy 'his
hopes were . . . raised by the thought of making the Established
Church comprehensive enough to include the majority of thinkers
of the previous hundred years who had lost all belief in the supernatural'. But when the new Prayer Book appeared 'he found that
the revision had not been in a rationalistic direction, and from
that time he lost all expectation of seeing the Church representative
of modern thinking minds'. Yet only two years before his death,
while noting that 'unfortunately there appears to be a narrowing
instead of a broadening tendency among the clergy of late', he
thought that 'if a strong body of young reformers were to make a
bold stand' something might still be done. Thus did Hardy's mind
reflect to the end what, long before, he had called his 'infinite trying
to reconcile a scientific view of life with the emotional and spiritual'.

There is no doubt something lugubrious about the spectacle of
Hardy in senescence, obsessively occupied with the mortuary
husks of the Christian faith. His favourite walk was to the churchyard at Stinsford where all his family were buried. He regularly
took visitors there—for example Walter de la Mare, who 'was
much interested in hearing about the various graves'. On particularly solemn occasions of this sort he carried a black walking-
stick which had belonged to his first wife.

He last heard an Anglican service with the aid of the wireless. It was on 11 November 1927, two months before his death. The second Mrs Hardy records it: '*Armistice Day*. T. came downstairs from his study and listened to the broadcasting of a service at Canterbury Cathedral. We stood there for the two minutes' silence.' Hardy had no intimate loss to mourn. But 'he said afterwards that he had been thinking of Frank George, his cousin, who was killed at Gallipoli'. Frank George was, in fact, a second cousin's son. And at the time of Gallipoli Hardy had made a note of him: 'Frank George, though so remotely related, is the first one of my family to be killed in battle for the last hundred years, so far as I know. He might say *Militavi non sine gloria*—short as his career has been.'

I do not know whether I am right in finding extremely moving the spectacle of this old gentleman thus listening to a distant cathedral service with the aid of a recently invented scientific contraption, and then standing—as Christians and agnostics alike were doing all over the British Isles—for 'the two minutes' silence'. But certainly the scene epitomises much that was essential in Hardy's situation.

4

One may sum up on the *Life* by saying that one puts it down with a strong sense of having received, through means more artful than is immediately apparent, a vivid impression of the personality of Thomas Hardy. This, I believe, Hardy intended to give. But to admit the reader to anything which could be called his intimate life was no part of his plan. Nor is there the slightest pretence that the book attempts anything of the kind.

He was a child—we are told in the first chapter—of ecstatic temperament, but we are afforded virtually no impression of what legacy this left the man. 'A clue to much of his character and action throughout his life'—the second chapter says—'is afforded by his lateness of development in virility.' But the clue is not really followed. His twenty-fifth birthday finds him 'not very cheerful'. A little later he writes down some 'cures for despair' (beginning with 'Read Wordsworth's "Resolution and Independence" ') but the occasion is given as 'in all likelihood . . . mental depression over his work and prospects'. A little later again we are told of his marking in his copy of *Hamlet*: 'Thou wouldst not think how ill all's here about my heart: but it is

no matter!', and six months later of his doing the same with
Macbeth:

> Things at their worst will cease, or else climb upward
> To what they were before.

There are other similar notes here and there: 'In a fit of depression, as if enveloped in a leaden cloud'. But there is no hint of an
explanation connected with his marriage. He once regrets its
childlessness, but the only passage markedly carrying that note of
sexual pessimism which is percurrent in the novels and poems was
written down nearly ten years before his marriage took place:

> There is not that regular gradation among womankind that
> there is among men. You may meet with 999 exactly alike, and
> then the thousandth—not a little better, but far above them.
> Practically therefore it is useless for a man to seek after this
> thousandth to make her his.

Hardy's reticence over his sexual life needs no explaining. It is
perhaps more surprising that the *Life* offers hardly any chronicle
of that sort of acute travail of the spirit confronted by new
intellectual persuasions which so many eminent Victorians experienced and judged it not unbecoming to avow. We can be quite
sure that Hardy came through very bad times here, but I believe I
am right in saying that, within the bounds of the *Life*, we receive
chiefly the impression of a man very little prone to be thrown off
balance, or into acute distress, by the astronomers and geologists
and biologists. What may be called here Hardy's rocky tone is well
illustrated in his brief exchange with A. B. Grosart in February
1888:

> In the latter part of this month there arrived the following:
> 'The Rev. Dr A. B. Grosart ventures to address Mr Hardy on
> a problem that is of life and death; personally, and in relation to
> young eager intellects for whom he is responsible. . . . Dr
> Grosart finds abundant evidence that the facts and mysteries of
> nature and human nature have come urgently before Mr Hardy's
> penetrative brain.'
> He enumerated some of the horrors of human and animal
> life, particularly parasitic, and added:
> 'The problem is how to reconcile these with the absolute
> goodness and non-limitation of God.'

Hardy replied: 'Mr Hardy regrets that he is unable to suggest any hypothesis which would reconcile the existence of such evils as Dr Grosart describes with the idea of omnipotent goodness. Perhaps Dr Grosart might be helped to a provisional view of the universe by the recently published Life of Darwin, and the works of Herbert Spencer and other agnostics.'

This is as much as Grosart deserved, but it is scarcely communicative. And there is nowhere in the *Life* any extended discussion of an intellectual position. Hardy comes nearest to anything of the kind when referring to *The Dynasts*, which he seems willing to regard as in part philosophic statement. 'That the Unconscious Will of the Universe is growing aware of Itself,' he says, 'I believe I may claim as my own idea solely'; and he adds, with characteristic oddity: 'I believe, too, that the Prime Cause, this Will, has never before been called "It" in any poetical literature, English or foreign'. But much more frequently his references to the supposed philosophical or doctrinal implications of his own work are by way of disclaimer. Such 'views' as his writings exhibit are properly to be regarded as being 'mere impressions that frequently change'; and moreover he insists that it is illegitimate to assume that he himself subscribes to beliefs and persuasions exhibited by characters in his novels or similarly in dramatic and personative form in his poetry.

One consequence of this rather defensive attitude in the *Life* is that we have to look elsewhere for any substantial view of Hardy's work considered in relation to the thought of his time.

2
Private Life

PARTICULARLY AS A POET, BUT ALSO IN A VARYING DEGREE AS A
novelist, Hardy is an unmistakably personal writer. His own
fortunes and his emotional reactions to his fortunes go largely
into his work. They are, of course, transformed in various ways.
His purpose is artistic, not confessional, and he shapes his material
accordingly. Moreover the material, even when it comes from
private experience, often comes from private experience far back
in his life, so that there has been at work upon it the transmuting
operation of time. This last seems to me an important consideration. He speaks of his possessing a power which we ourselves
particularly associate, perhaps, with Wordsworth, but which
Hardy does not regard as being exceptional:

> I believe it would be said by people who knew me well that I
> have a faculty (possibly not uncommon) for burying an emotion
> in my heart or brain for forty years, and exhuming it at the end
> of that time as fresh as when interred.

He immediately goes on to illustrate this by saying that his poem
'The Breaking of Nations', written in 1915, 'contains a feeling'
that had moved him during the Franco-German war of 1870.
But if we were to take literally the 'forty years' of this note and
count back from it, we should arrive at the first years of Hardy's
marriage. And those years, as it happens, were 'exhumed' by
Hardy, very nearly forty years after being painfully 'interred',
with the result that he produced some of the greatest love-poems
in the language. We are really obliged to find out what we can
about Emma Lavinia Gifford, who was born in the same year
as Hardy and married him shortly before her thirty-fourth
birthday.

It may be useful, however, to begin with somebody else—a girl
whom Hardy certainly knew long before he met Emma. It may be
useful, I think, as prompting us to a certain caution in the whole

business of relating aspects of Hardy's personal life to aspects of his work.

Hardy was nearly thirty when he first met Miss Gifford, and it is unlikely that a man whose work was to show him so keenly susceptible to the charm of women had not already been in love. He had certainly written numerous love-poems. Several early attachments are mentioned in a decorous way in the *Life*; but one appears to have been admitted to the record only obliquely and through inadvertence, and it has attracted a good deal of curiosity as a result. On 5 March 1890 Hardy made the following note:

> In the train on the way to London. Wrote the first four or six lines of 'Not a line of her writing have I'. It was a curious instance of sympathetic telepathy. The woman whom I was thinking of—a cousin—was dying at the time, and I quite in ignorance of it. She died six days later. The remainder of the piece was not written till after her death.

The poem referred to is called 'Thoughts of Phena at News of her Death', and these are its first two stanzas:

> Not a line of her writing have I,
> Not a thread of her hair,
> No mark of her late time as dame in her dwelling, whereby
> I may picture her there;
> And in vain do I urge my unsight
> To conceive my lost prize
> At her close, whom I knew when her dreams were upbrim-
> ming with light,
> And with laughter her eyes.
>
> What scenes spread around her last days,
> Sad, shining, or dim?
> Did her gifts and compassions enray and enarch her sweet
> ways
> With an aureate nimb?
> Or did life-light decline from her years,
> And mischances control
> Her full day-star; unease, or regret, of forebodings, or fears
> Disennoble her soul?

The name of the cousin whom Hardy here describes as his 'lost prize' was Tryphena Sparks; she was eleven years younger than he; she married a certain Charles Gale, a book-keeper and superior publican, three years after Hardy's own marriage;

shortly after her death, which occurred twelve years later again at
the age of thirty-nine, Hardy and his brother Henry paid a call on
her family after laying a wreath on her grave.

Nothing more is securely known about Hardy's relationship
with Tryphena. Nor does the poem itself take us very far. It
carries the strong individual stamp of Hardy's style, but apart
from this is somewhat conventional in suggestion; guesses about
the unknown fate of a former sweetheart are common in Victorian
verse; Matthew Arnold, for example, indulges in them when
celebrating his mysterious Marguerite.

Arnold, as it happens, has his niche in Tryphena Sparks's story—
at least to the extent that he inspected that Plymouth Public Free
School of which she became headmistress at the strikingly early
age of twenty. But another girl who takes charge of a school when
scarcely 'husband-high' is Fancy Day in *Under the Greenwood
Tree*, so may not Fancy's character be based upon Tryphena's?
And may not Sue Bridehead's training college in *Jude the Obscure*
reflect the training college which Tryphena attended at Stockwell—
even although, indeed, Hardy's sister Mary attended a similar
place and we know that one of her exploits there gets into the same
novel?

The case for Tryphena as an important influence in Hardy's life
is supported in part upon a hunt through the prose and poetry for
such correspondences, and in part upon the reminiscences of a
daughter of Tryphena's, communicated (between her eighty-first
and eighty-seventh years) to a pertinacious enquirer. The old lady
was in no doubt whatever that her mother and Tom Hardy had
been engaged for a number of years, and that her mother had
broken the engagement under the persuasions of Charles Gale,
whom she eventually married. Of the full truth even of this it is
impossible to be confident. The Gales were simple people, and
Thomas Hardy died as a famous man and was buried in Westminster Abbey. Under such circumstances, and as decades pass,
family legends are not unlikely to be stretched into family facts.
But at the end this ancient informant went further. She was shown,
in her mother's—Tryphena's—photograph album, a small portrait
of an unidentified boy. She said: 'That was Hardy's boy'. She
said this, we are told, 'four or five times'. Later, she said:
'That was Rantie', and agreed that *Rantie* had perhaps been
Randy and that *Randy* had perhaps been short for *Randolph*.
Later still, she was asked whether another unidentified photograph
in the album was that of the same boy grown up, and she replied
with apparent certainty that it was.

That Tryphena Sparks may have borne her cousin, Thomas

Hardy, an illegitimate son who was called Randolph by no means ends conjecture about this girl. For various circumstances make it possible to believe that her birth was not what it was supposed to be. She was perhaps not Hardy's cousin but his niece.

What we are required to subscribe to is the following hypothetical recasting of the Hardy family records:

As an unmarried girl of sixteen, Hardy's future mother, Jemima Hand, bore a daughter to some unknown man, perhaps the local squire. This child, called Rebecca, was passed off as the daughter of Jemima's elder sister Maria, who was respectably married to one James Sparks, a cabinet-maker. Rebecca in her turn had an illegitimate daughter, probably by the lord of the manor. This child, called Tryphena, was also passed off as Maria's daughter; as the sister and not the daughter, that is to say, of her true mother. Being Rebecca's daughter and Jemima's granddaughter, Tryphena Sparks, so-called, was Thomas Hardy's niece. Hardy's postulated sexual relations with Tryphena, therefore, were in fact, although not in law, incestuous. Rantie, Randy, or Randolph (who it is suggested, incidentally, may have been sent by his father, become a successful novelist, to Harrow) was thus the issue of an unholy, as well as an irregular, union. Hardy's belated discovery of the truth darkened his remaining days.

There are several points to be made about *Providence and Mr Hardy*, the book in which all these conjectures are set forth. The writers, Miss Lois Deacon and Mr Terry Coleman, have made some attempt to distinguish between fact and speculation. At the same time, their manner of unfolding and documenting their case, although entertaining, is not such as would be wholly commended either by scholars or in a court of law. One instance may be given. Their informant, Mrs Bromell, was only eleven when her mother—Tryphena Gale, *née* (or not *née*) Sparks—died, and in her eighties was recalling supposed family events of close on a century before. By the time that she 'positively identified the boy' ('That was Hardy's boy', four or five times reiterated) she was 'confused, and wandering in her thoughts' as often as not. In these circumstances, the photographs may be regarded as crucial. If Mrs Bromell were to be proved wrong about them—if they turned out to be from a studio, of a date, with a provenance rendering her statements chronologically or otherwise impossible—her credibility as a witness would largely lapse, and we should know precisely as much about Hardy and Tryphena as 'Thoughts of Phena at News of her Death' tells us. If, on the other hand, enquiry turned up facts *not* incompatible with her claims, the case for it would be a little strengthened. But although the provenance of the photographs could probably be investigated in various ways, the proponents of the Tryphena-theory record no attempt of the kind in *Providence and Mr Hardy*.

The tone of this book seldom hints at much awareness of what literary critics judge hazardous in squeezing a large and important corpus of imaginative writing in the interest of biographical detection. In its argument, moreover, there are three radical weaknesses. The first is chronological. The relationship postulated between Hardy and Tryphena—whether it were a liaison or a formal engagement—is supposed to have come to an end in 1873, coincidentally with the appearance in Tryphena's life of the personable publican, Charles Gale. But by then Hardy had been much in love with Miss Gifford for something like three years. This is so deeply written into the record as to be undeniable. The sensible conclusion would seem to be that Tryphena, although Hardy's first love and one whom he was poignantly to remember, was supplanted by Miss Gifford and had to make do with Mr Gale. Hardy, in fact, was quite as much Tryphena's 'lost prize' as she was his. Hardy married just as soon as marriage to an upper-class woman became economically feasible. Tryphena appears to have spent four years thinking about Gale, who was in prosperous if socially undistinguished circumstances from the first.

The second weakness is psychological. There is far less likelihood that a man will develop a temperamental bias as a consequence of things happening to him at twenty-seven than that things will happen to him at twenty-seven as a consequence of a temperamental bias as near innate as makes no matter. Compulsions lying deep in our natures surely match blind chance in determining what befalls us. Hardy's thirty-eight years of unhappy marriage, moreover, are likely to have borne more heavily upon him than did the memory of his love-affair with his cousin—even if she was capable, in the last week of her life, of occasioning that 'curious instance of sympathetic telepathy'. And that Hardy was destined by nature to bring a melancholic temper to the experience of love perhaps sufficiently appears in a poem entitled '1967' and dated 1867. (It could thus belong only to the earliest phase of his acquaintance with Tryphena.) The poet looks forward to a time, a hundred years on, when nothing shall be left of his sweetheart and himself 'beyond a pinch of dust or two', and concludes:

> I would only ask thereof
> That thy worm should be my worm, Love!

The third weakness in the argument is historical. This will be borne in upon us if we simply spend a little time reading in Hardy's *Collected Poems* at random:

> The night-hawk stops. A man shows in the obscure:
>   They meet, and passively kiss,
> And he says: 'Well, I've come quickly. About this—
>   Is it really so? You are sure?'
> 'I am sure. In February it will be.
> That such a thing should come to me!
> We should have known. We should have left off meeting.
> Love is a terrible thing: a sweet allure
>   That ends in heart-out-eating!' . . .

> 'Twill be brought home as hers. She's forty-one,
> When many a woman's bearing is not done,
>   And well might have a son.' . . .

In this poem, called 'A Hurried Meeting', the woman is 'haughty-hearted' and comes from 'the marble mansion of her ancient race', whereas of the man it is noted: 'inferior clearly he'. In 'The Christening' a child is being baptized in what appear to be entirely blameless circumstances, until to the scandal of the congregation its true mother, this time a village girl, bursts into the church and declares herself, asserting that the father is 'in the woods afar', and that he comes to her only 'in lovelike weather . . . just now and then'. 'Now if the mother were Jemima—' *Providence and Mr Hardy* begins to comment. But this is absurd. The forsaken women, bastard children, brutal or smooth-spoken or arrogantly high-born seducers of popular fiction and balladry have their true genesis only in the immemorial experience of the folk. Consider another poem, 'On a Heath', which is again about an uncovenanted child:

> I could hear a gown-skirt rustling
>   Before I could see her shape,
> Rustling through the heather
>   That wove the common's drape,
> On that evening of dark weather
>   When I hearkened, lips agape.

> And the town shine in the distance
>   Did but baffle here the sight,
> And then a voice flew forward:

'Dear, is't you? I fear the night!'
And the herons flapped to northward
In the firs upon my right.

There was another looming
    Whose life we did not see;
There was one stilly blooming
    Full nigh to where walked we;
There was a shade entombing
    All that was bright of me.

It is conceivable that we are here being presented with Hardy and
Tryphena, meeting on Egdon Heath at a spot from which one can
see the Dorchester 'town shine' down in the valley, and still in
ignorance of the future young Harrovian already 'stilly blooming'
in the womb. But the situation in this and other ballad-like poems
is so authentic to the whole social context in which Hardy was
nurtured that we are left with no positive warrant for supposing
that an intimately personal experience must be reflected in them.
And this would continue to hold had he written, whether in prose
or verse, of a woman whose daughter was brought up as her niece,
and whose son slept with, and begot a child on, that daughter's
daughter, who had herself been brought up as her mother's sister.
Ignorance, poverty, and an oppressive morality produced such
confused and degraded situations frequently enough in the rural
England of the nineteenth century. Hardy was to declare in old age
that, in this respect, his writing was very far from darkening the
picture. Had he presented a fully candid description of village
life, 'no one would have stood it'.

2

If Tryphena Sparks is a hypothesis, Emma Gifford is a fact. She
was a daily fact in Hardy's life from 1870 when he first met her to
1912 when she died. Her memory haunted him for the rest of his
days. Among the nine-hundred odd poems he wrote there is only
one the connection of which with Tryphena is more than conjectural, whereas there are scores that demonstrably take their
origin in his relationship with his wife. Yet here, too, we find that
we have to be cautious. There turn out to be poems, identically
toned with some of the finest related to Emma and commonly
thought of as prompted by his estrangement from her, which there
is good reason to suppose were occasioned by a later attachment
to which I shall presently come. What we have to remember is that

there may flow into a poem, the conscious focus of which is one
relationship, an emotional charge generated by another. Love
poems are not very satisfactory evidence in a divorce court.

> When I set out for Lyonnesse,
>   A hundred miles away,
>   The rime was on the spray,
> And starlight lit my lonesomeness
> When I set out for Lyonnesse
>   A hundred miles away.
>
> What would bechance at Lyonnesse
>   While I should sojourn there
>   No prophet durst declare,
> Nor did the wisest wizard guess
> What would bechance at Lyonnesse
>   While I should sojourn there.
>
> When I came back from Lyonnesse
>   With magic in my eyes,
>   All marked with mute surmise
> My radiance rare and fathomless,
> When I came back from Lyonnesse
>   With magic in my eyes!

There is no doubt about this one. It is 1870 and Hardy is thirty.
His first novel, *The Poor Man and the Lady*, has been rejected and
Desperate Remedies begun. But he is still working, in a not very
promising way, for various architects, and now he is sent down on
an unimportant church-restoration job to an out-of-the-way little
place in Cornwall called St Juliot. The rector has a sister-in-law,
Emma Lavinia Gifford, living in his household, and she and Hardy
almost immediately fall in love. Emma is rather plain, but she has
a good figure, rides well, is vivacious, and has enough in the way
of literary interest to be excited when a blue paper sticking out of
Hardy's pocket proves to be not an architectural drawing but the
manuscript of a poem. Emma's own ambition as a writer (which is
to have embarrassing consequences long afterwards) percolates
into *A Pair of Blue Eyes*, as does much else from Hardy's courtship—although Emma, indeed, was the same age as Hardy, and
theirs was not in the least a boy-and-girl affair. The *Life* gives no
hint that the courtship was in any way impeded by what may be
called its Poor-Man-and-Lady aspect. Hardy goes out of his way,
indeed, to state that everybody approved of it. But this seems to be

untrue. Emma's father was an obscure provincial solicitor, but he had pretentions to being of good family, and is said to have denounced Hardy as a 'base churl'. Emma herself, though losing her heart or her head to the young architect, directed an ominous class-consciousness upon him from the first; her account of their initial meeting speaks of his 'homely appearance' (later changed to 'familiar appearance') and his 'slightly different accent'.

That Hardy, too, was class-conscious, but in a more complicated way than the naïvely and at times offensively snobbish Emma, is apparent in those early pages of the *Life* which introduce us to 'an old family of spent social energies'; a homestead which, although now 'reduced', had lately enjoyed the propinquity of 'two retired military officers' and 'one old navy lieutenant'; a father who occasionally employed 'from twelve to fifteen men'; and a grandmother who had 'thirty gowns'. Emma was to be unimpressed either by the small latterday village consequence of the Hardys or by what was conjectured of their lineage; she refused to let her husband's parents, who lived only three miles away, come to Max Gate; and she is recorded as having reminded Hardy in public that he had 'married a lady'. This is all very absurd—but also a grievous thing, and undoubtedly a factor in the division that was to come between them. It took them, we must notice, four years to get married, so precipitancy cannot be pointed to as the occasion of their misfortune. The *Life* speaks of the first few years of the marriage as comprehending 'their happiest days', and the implication carried by this can hardly be missed. I doubt whether Hardy's rusticity and Mrs Hardy's snobbery, even when reinforced by Hardy's agnosticism and Mrs Hardy's hysterically tinged piety, would in themselves have brought about so rapid a *débâcle* as we sense from the total record. Perhaps this love match—for it was very much that—ran sharply up against some unexpected sexual incompatibility: the sort of thing we are shown wrecking the marriage of Jude Fawley and Sue Bridehead. Anything of the kind would be another important factor, although not, perhaps, so overwhelmingly important as our modern sexual dogmas and orthodoxies insist. But I think myself that the nub of the matter was simply this: that Emma Lavinia Hardy was a desperately inept and foolish person, and that her husband's charity towards her failed.

Socially, it is clear, a curious irony overtook them: an irony or incongruity right up Hardy's street. For it so came about that the 'base churl' was received into a society in which the solicitor's daughter (even although, as she informs us, 'the original spelling of Gifford was Gui-de-Ford—a Norman knight's name') had no

particular claim to regard. The position of a celebrated writer's or
artist's wife is often difficult; that of Emma Hardy was, we can see,
complicated by the fact that there was something absurd about
her. A poem called 'You Were the Sort that Men Forget' is of
interest here:

> You were the sort that men forget;
>   Though I—not yet!—
> Perhaps not ever. Your slighted weakness
> Adds to the strength of my regret!
>
> You'd not the art—you never had
>   For good or bad—
> To make men see how sweet your meaning,
> Which, visible, had charmed them glad.
>
> You would, by words inept let fall,
>   Offend them all,
> Even if they saw your warm devotion
> Would hold your life's blood at their call.
>
> You lacked the eye to understand
>   Those friends offhand
> Whose mode was crude, though whose dim purport
> Outpriced the courtesies of the bland.
>
> I am now the only being who
>   Remembers you
> It may be. What a waste that Nature
> Grudged soul so dear the art its due!

Professor Carl J. Weber, a devoted if not invariably persuasive
student of Hardy, says that we have in this poem 'the most un-
pleasant example of back-biting in his poetic list'; that in it we see
Hardy 'retaliate on his wife . . . strike back'. It seems to me, on the
contrary, to embody a very generous interpretation of Emma's
character and comportment. Indeed, in none of the poems reflecting the relationship do I find any laying of blame upon the woman.
And this is only just and right. It is easy to exhibit Emma Hardy as
a rather dreadful person, and also—as we shall see—hard to deny
that she was at times a little mad. But she had a great deal to put
up with. I suspect that she had quite a bit to put up with from
fairly early on.

When Hardy declared that 'the highest flights of the pen are

mostly the excursions and revelations of souls unreconciled to life'
it was certainly not without reference to his own temperament and
ambition. In old age his sadness and disillusionment made his
second wife feel a failure (and even depressed the parlourmaid).
Melancholy lay deep in his nature, and it seems probable that he
would have imported it fairly rapidly into any intimate relationship. It is not unfair to say that he was given to taking a dark view
of things, including women and marriage, and that even during
those 'happiest days' with Emma which the *Life* calls their
'Sturminster Newton idyll' he was writing into *Far from the
Madding Crowd* much that would be painful to an affectionate and
unintellectual and orthodoxly pious wife. Emma did a great deal
of devoted transcribing of Hardy's manuscripts. *The Return of the
Native* went to the printer partly in her hand. One reads in this
novel about 'sinking into the mire of marriage'.

Some of Hardy's manuscripts are much corrected, cancelled,
overwritten by himself, so that in copying them Emma had to sort
out the sense as she went along. This may have been the origin of
her later persuasion that she had collaborated with her husband in
the Wessex novels, and herself contributed most of what is polite
and edifying in them. With the later books she was certainly wholly
out of sympathy, and there is a story that when *Jude the Obscure*
was about to be published she went up to London to call upon
Richard Garnett at the British Museum in the strange belief that
he had some power to prevent the appearance of so scandalous a
book. But anecdotes of this kind are to be received with reserve.
They circulate readily in literary society.

At St Juliot it may have been one of Emma's attractions for
Hardy that she had literary ambitions of her own—a fact reflected
in *A Pair of Blue Eyes* when Elfride Swancourt is represented as
publishing an ingenuous romance. And Emma, it seems, wrote a
novel during the first year of her marriage; it was called *The Maid
on the Shore*, had a setting and some elements of situation
reminiscent of *A Pair of Blue Eyes*, and was preserved in typescript
by Hardy among his wife's papers after her death. She also wrote
verse, and it is curious that Hardy's 'The Darkling Thrush', which
is dated 31st December 1900, may have been prompted by an
artless poem, 'Spring Song', which Mrs Hardy printed in the
Sphere in April of that year. 'Spring Song' begins:

> There's a song of a bird in a tree,—
> A song that is fresh, gay, and free,
> The voice of a last summer's thrush,
> Shaking out his trills—hush! hush!

Weber exhibits the mild absurdity of this. But if Hardy was embarrassed by his wife's ventures his sense of the bizarre was deserting him. Later on, Emma caused to be printed locally a little volume of poems which she called *Alleys*, and a similar volume of prose with the title *Spaces* and a statement that it contains an 'Exposition of Great Truths'. The first section of *Spaces* concerns 'The High Delights of Heaven', and among these we learn that there is to be numbered 'ease of locomotion—whether by wings or otherwise'. Here we are certainly in the presence of marked eccentricity. And Emma's conduct was occasionally odd. In the later 1890s, for example, she appears to have spent a period of obstinate seclusion in an attic. At Max Gate that must have been very uncomfortable indeed.

But Hardy was uncomfortable too. One literary gossip, T. P. O'Connor, declared that Mrs Hardy's 'whole bitter purpose was to belittle, irritate, and discourage her husband'; she had described him as 'Very vain and very selfish' and added: 'These women that he meets in London society only increase these things. They are the poison; I am the antidote.' Hardy's policy appears to have become that of avoiding the antidote as much as he decently could. Thus the Hardys lived together in disharmony perhaps for more than thirty years. Then Emma died. And at once the widower sat down and wrote to her memory a series of love-poems unexcelled in the language. Let us say, provisionally, that this is simply another instance of the sovereignty of the incongruous over Hardy.

3

But now we may consider the poem called 'At an Inn'. It begins with one of Hardy's most notable prosaicisms—but it is not a prosaic poem:

> When we as strangers sought
>   Their catering care,
> Veiled smiles bespoke their thought
>   Of what we were.
> They warmed as they opined
>   Us more than friends—
> That we had all resigned
>   For love's dear ends.
>
> And that swift sympathy
>   With living love
> Which quicks the world—maybe
>   The spheres above,

B

Made them our ministers,
    Movéd them to say,
'Ah, God, that bliss like theirs
    Would flush our day!'

And we were left alone
    As love's own pair;
Yet never the love-light shone
    Between us there!
But that which chilled the breath
    Of afternoon,
And palsied unto death
    The pane-fly's tune.

The kiss their zeal foretold,
    And now deemed come,
Came not: within his hold
    Love lingered numb.
Why cast he on our port
    A bloom not ours?
Why shaped us for his sport
    In after hours?

As we seemed we were not
    That day afar,
And now we seem not what
    We aching are.
O severing sea and land,
    O laws of men,
Ere death, once let us stand
    As we stood then!

And here is a shorter poem, 'The Division':

Rain on the windows, creaking doors,
    With blasts that besom the green,
And I am here, and you are there,
    And a hundred miles between!

O were it but the weather, Dear,
    O were it but the miles
That summed up all our severance,
    There might be room for smiles.

> But that thwart thing betwixt us twain,
>   Which nothing cleaves or clears,
> Is more than distance, Dear, or rain,
>   And longer than the years!

The first of these poems must be called extremely impressive and moving; the second shares with it, and with a number of others such as 'A Broken Appointment', 'In Death Divided', and 'Last Love-Word', the same intense note of frustration and sorrowful retrospection. Alike in burden and in quality, these stand close to Emma's poems, which Hardy called *Poems of 1912-13*. But it seems likely that they concern quite a different relationship, and one which we cannot but suppose altogether less significant in Hardy's life.

Florence Henniker was one of the women—judged by Emma to be 'poison'—whom Hardy met 'in London society'. A daughter of Richard Monckton Milnes, first Lord Houghton, she had married in 1882 a soldier who was presently to become Major the Hon. Arthur Henry Henniker-Major, and she had some years later begun writing a series of very mildly talented novels of high life. Hardy first saw her in 1893, when he and Emma paid a visit at her invitation to the Viceregal Lodge, Dublin, where she was acting as hostess for her younger brother (the second Lord Houghton, later Marquess of Crewe) who was at the time Lord Lieutenant of Ireland. In the *Life* Hardy takes the augustness of this occasion very much in his stride, and describes Mrs Henniker as 'a charming, *intuitive* woman apparently'. She was thirty-eight. He, like Emma, was fifty-two. The friendship developed rapidly. There was what Purdy calls a 'vigorous' correspondence. Hardy took various measures to further Mrs Henniker's literary career, including collaborating with her in a short story. (There is no record of his ever thus assisting the similar ambitions of his wife.) When Mrs Henniker was living at Southsea and Hardy at Max Gate they used to meet at Winchester or Salisbury as a half-way house. Hardy was to tell his friend Hermann Lea, the pedestrian topographer of *Thomas Hardy's Wessex*, that 'At an Inn' was written 'at the George Inn at Winchester'. It was through Mrs Henniker that, in 1904, there was introduced to the Hardys a young woman, also of some literary ambition, called Florence Dugdale, who was to assist in hunting up references for *The Dynasts*, and who became the second Mrs Thomas Hardy in 1914. She was to tell Professor Purdy that Sue Bridehead was in part drawn from Mrs Henniker. If this is true, chronology obliges us to believe that Hardy fell to making copy out of his middle-aged attachment with notable speed. He began *Jude the Obscure* in the year in which he and Mrs Henniker first met.

Is there anything of significance for us in all this? I think there is. The poem that comes after 'When I set out for Lyonnesse' in *Lyrics and Reveries* is called 'A Thunderstorm in Town'. After the title we read, in parenthesis, 'A Reminiscence: 1893'. This very definitely makes it a Henniker poem (as the second Mrs Hardy explicitly declared it to be), and we must feel a distinct perversity in its being placed as it is. And here it is, for what it is worth:

> She wore a new 'terra-cotta' dress,
> And we stayed, because of the pelting storm,
> Within the handsom's dry recess,
> Though the horse had stopped; yea, motionless
>   We sat on, snug and warm.
>
> Then the downpour ceased, to my sharp sad pain
> And the glass that had screened our forms before
> Flew up, and out she sprang to her door:
> I should have kissed her if the rain
>   Had lasted a minute more.

We don't know how Mrs Henniker would have responded to the kiss. But we do, I think, get a hint that Hardy is *imagining* things. (It is worth glancing at his doing decidedly this in the poem that immediately follows, called 'The Torn Letter'.) To me, at least, the Henniker affair suggests itself as being compounded out of middle-aged sentiment and a little sex-in-the-head. But set a poet brooding on such an episode, and then rhyming on it, and the result may be an opening up of subterraneous channels of communication between it and matters of far deeper emotional involvement. So the poetry comes.

We cannot, in fact, safely infer from the emotional intensity or urgency of a poem the degree of emotional intensity or urgency actually attending upon its immediate prompting occasion. The poet carries about with him habits of feeling, idiosyncrasies of response, taking their origin in hiding-places, it may be, much more than ten years deep.

3

Intellectual Background

THE YEAR 1906, WHICH SAW THE PUBLICATION OF THE MIDDLE volume of *The Dynasts*, also produced a book by G. M. Trevelyan called *The Poetry and Philosophy of George Meredith*. I doubt whether today anybody would publish a book called *The Poetry and Philosophy of W. B. Yeats* or *The Poetry and Philosophy of T. S. Eliot*. There is, of course, no lack of writing on Yeats as an esoteric poet or on the thought embodied in the *Quartets*. But criticism has become a litle shy of imposing upon a poet's 'message' quite the emphasis carried by Trevelyan's title.

The Victorian novelists, like the poets, had to stand somewhat stiff appraisal as sages. T. H. Green, an eminent Oxford philosopher, wrote a book with the suggestive title *An Estimate of the Value and Influence of Works of Fiction in Modern Times*. And there are a great many works of literary history which reflect a sense of the importance of a novelist's implication with the speculative problems of his age. The Cazamians' *Le roman social en Angleterre* and *Le roman et les idées en Angleterre: L'influence de la science* are still standard works, and books like J. E. Baker's *The Novel and the Oxford Movement* were well reputed in their time.

Hardy was in due season established as a sage. In 1910 F. A. Hedgcock published in Paris *Thomas Hardy: Penseur et Artiste*, a work in which Hardy took no pleasure at all. In the following year there arrived on him, with the compliments of the author, *Thomas Hardy, an Illustration of the Philosophy of Schopenhauer* by an American lady, Helen Garwood, who had collected with it a Ph.D. from the University of Pennsylvania. Thus established as something of a pioneer-sufferer from this sort of thing, Hardy wrote civilly to the lady: 'My pages show harmony of view with Darwin, Huxley, Spencer, Hume, Mill, and others, all of whom I used to read more than Schopenhauer'. This might incline us to suppose that Miss Garwood was herself a pioneer—a pioneer in the pursuit of what examiners of such dissertations have come to speak of as a 'non-subject'. But the facts would not quite justify us. Schopenhauer's own doctoral dissertation at Göttingen was published in English in 1889 with the title *On the Four-fold Root of the Principle of Sufficient Reason*, and Hardy owned a copy which he marked and annotated with care. But German pessimistic philosophy, whether Schopenhauer's or von Hartmann's, cannot have affected him at any radically formative stage of his career. It is clearly true that he was much more decisively influenced by the native English speculative tradition of the age, in the exploration of which he may have been assisted by his friend Horace Moule. His surviving notebooks show that he had the habit of following closely, and making excerpts from, the debates on intellectual topics which went on freely in the more serious journals of the period.

Questions of particular indebtedness to previous thinkers may be left to specialists. The general picture to emerge is of a Hardy who, although with no particular endowment or indeed bent for either philosophical or sociological study, accepted the Victorian view (which is also a very ancient view) of the poet as teacher— and even as prophet in the sense that he proclaims new truths to a generation unprepared to part with the old. It is even possible to view *The Dynasts* (which is, of course, the main point of reference in discussing Hardy's approach to something like a formal philosophy) as the consequence of a burdensome false conscience in this regard: the drama was to be an imaginative projection of a world-view which it was incumbent upon him to declare. When the first part was published he noted:

I suppose I have handicapped myself by expressing, both in this drama and previous verse, philosophies and feelings as yet not well established or formally adopted into the general teaching; and by thus over-stepping the standard boundary set up for the thought of the age by the proctors of opinion, I have thrown back my chance of acceptance in poetry by many years. The very fact of my having tried to spread over art the latest illumination of the time has darkened counsel in respect of me.

The Dynasts lies a long way ahead of us at this stage of our enquiry; nevertheless it may be useful to pause on it for a moment here. What does Hardy mean by saying that he has tried to spread over his drama 'the latest illumination of the time'? One of his earliest notes for it, written down in 1881, reads:

Mode for a historical Drama. Action mostly automatic; reflex movement, etc. Not the result of what is called *motive*, although always ostensibly so, even to the actors' own consciousness. Apply an enlargement of these theories to, say, 'The Hundred Days'!

A year later, there is another note, which begins, 'Write a history of human automatism . . . '. In this context, 'the latest illumination of the time' means simply that sort of modern scientific knowledge which lends inescapable cogency to a purely deterministic view of the universe. *The Dynasts* in its evolved form contains certain other, and modifying, ideas, and these appear glimmeringly quite early in notes connected with the drama. The one just quoted, for example, reads in full:

Write a history of human automatism, or impulsion—viz., an account of human action in spite of human knowledge, showing how very far conduct lags behind the knowledge that should really guide it.

The concatenation of ideas here is not at all clear, but the note is of interest when we are considering not merely *The Dynasts* but the novels as well. And it is with the novels that I am first to be concerned. What is really going on in the Wessex novels? What philosophical presuppositions underlie them? What are they designed to tell us about human destiny and human conduct?

These questions turn out not altogether easy to answer, but some preliminary points can be made with reasonable confidence. The first is that Hardy took his novel-writing seriously, although he often affected not to do so. When he records in the *Life* that the reviewer in the *Spectator* had suggested that *Far from the Madding Crowd* was perhaps by George Eliot, he adds that he himself regards her as a 'great thinker' but 'not a born storyteller by any means'—and the implication is that it is as a born storyteller and no more that he sees himself. One can say 'no more' because his expressed conception of the business of telling a story is a thoroughly unassuming one. Here is one of the bleak statements on the matter of which he was rather fond:

The real, if unavowed, purpose of fiction is to give pleasure by gratifying the love of the uncommon in human experience, mental or corporeal.
This is done all the more perfectly in proportion as the reader is illuded to believe the personages true and real like himself.

Solely to this latter end a work of fiction should be a precise transcript of ordinary life: but,

The uncommon would be absent and the interest lost. Hence, the writer's problem is, how to strike the balance between the uncommon and the ordinary so as on the one hand to give interest, on the other to give reality.

In working out this problem, human nature must never be made abnormal, which is introducing incredibility. The uncommonness must be in the events, not in the characters; and the writer's art lies in shaping that uncommonness while disguising its unlikelihood, if it be unlikely.

But we must not ourselves be 'illuded' by this sort of thing. High seriousness was as much a touch-stone of art with Hardy as it was with Matthew Arnold; his self-conscious disparagement of the Novel reflects the old-fashioned view of the kind as something no more than lightly recreative; in practice Hardy was temperamentally quite unable *not* to import high seriousness into his fiction, although he no doubt did his bit in importing the pleasurably uncommon and so forth as well.

This brings us to the first thing which we become pretty sure of after only a brief exposure to the Wessex novels. They have, as Keats said Wordsworth's poetry has, 'designs upon us'. Baldly put, we are to be taught sense as we read. '"Justice" was done, and the President of the Immortals, in Aeschylean phrase, had ended his sport with Tess.' There is no nonsense about this; we are being hit hard. Only, when we have finished our reading of Hardy, we are not quite sure *what* has hit us. What are we being asked to believe, or processed to subscribe to?

We can say at once—it is another certainty we may record before debate begins—that we are not being instructed to any very cheerful effect. We are presented to ourselves as inhabiting a universe which seems to specialize in misfortunes and calamities. Things can go wrong in it at an alarming rate. Hardy infers from his exhibited spectacle something he calls 'the general grimness of the human situation'. (The grimness is at play, indeed, upon all sentient creatures. If you are a snail, incomprehensible forces may be released upon you and crush you—incomprehensible forces known to a different order of beings as the Battle of Waterloo. If you are a goldfinch, you may be put in a cage, forgotten as the casual consequence of something called a human tragedy, and left to starve as a result.) Johnson's Imlac in *Rasselas*, we must feel, would have read Hardy's books with satisfaction. They enforce the view that 'human life is every where a state in which much is to be endured, and little to be enjoyed'.

Such a view must always be determined in part by temperament. Hardy, like many other depressives, was fond of company and perked up in it; in the last months of his life he could strike Edmund Gosse as 'full of spirit and gaiety'. But few dispute the sombre character of his vision. He was a man whose sensitiveness rendered him particularly vulnerable to whatever was disillusioning and discouraging in the circumstances of his age, and in particular to all that was bleak and alarming in the findings of contemporary science. We are still within the area of general critical agreement here, and his own view of the climate of opinion within which he lived is expressed frequently enough. 'What we gain by science', he wrote to a friend, 'is, after all, sadness. . . . The more we know of the laws and nature of the Universe, the more ghastly a business one perceives it all to be.' And it is among the uneducated 'that happiness will find her last refuge on earth, since it is among them that a perfect insight into the conditions of existence will be longest postponed'.

But what, more precisely, are those 'conditions of existence' which Darwin and Huxley reveal? What ought we to do in face of them? Is there anything we can do in face of them? On Hardy's answers to these questions his critics begin to disagree.

2

In the same year that Miss Garwood published her book explaining that Thomas Hardy was an illustration of the philosophy of Schopenhauer an English critic, Arthur Symons, contributed an article on him to the eleventh edition of the *Encyclopaedia Britannica*. 'He is a fatalist,' Symons wrote, 'perhaps rather a determinist, and he studies the workings of fate or law.' By 1911 this had already become a common enough way of interpreting Hardy's books. Alike in our largest destinies and our smallest motions we are the creatures of the inevitable sequences of natural law. Hopes and fears, desires and strivings may accompany us on our path. But they and the path alike are but the products of the strictest causality.

Many of Hardy's lyrics undoubtedly reflect this persuasion. *The Dynasts*, his most ambitious work, systematically presents us with a universe in which virtually all things take place of necessity—although an odd piece of home-made metaphysic allows for occasional incursions of something that may be thought of as free will. And it is possible to read the Wessex novels at large as being designed to cast emphasis upon the pervasive grip of mere fatality on human life; to insist, as Professor John Holloway expresses it, that 'a determined system of things ultimately controls human affairs without regard to human wishes'.

It is true that the books continually show us human wishes being set at naught, but not all readers will agree that a system of determinism, in its strict sense, is pervasive in them. Many will assert that they are made aware of the external universe not so much as *subject to rigid and undeviating law* as simply *neutral*. What science has *imported* into our thinking in the form of a sharpened awareness of physical causality is less an occasion of 'sadness' than is what it has *banished*: the notion of a cosmos ordered, equally with our own lives, by a divine providence. Beyond the unfathomably mysterious world of our own sentience lies nothing but a vast regardlessness. In so far, of course, as intelligence is conceived as something outside and controlling matter, its absence from the cosmos is much the same thing as the all-pervasiveness of brute casualty there. Or we may say that the notion that what is out there is regardlessness or indifference represents a doctrine of determinism with a kind of negative animism added to it. However that may be, it is human life seen against the background of a total mindlessness that seems to some the most poignant of Hardy's themes. It is the theme, certainly, of one of his earliest poems, 'Hap':

> If but some vengeful god would call to me
> From up the sky, and laugh: 'Thou suffering thing,
> Know that thy sorrow is my ecstasy,
> That thy love's loss is my hate's profiting!'
>
> Then would I bear it, clench myself, and die,
> Steeled by the sense of ire unmerited;
> Half-eased in that a Powerfuller than I
> Had willed and meted me the tears I shed.
>
> But not so. How arrives it joy lies slain,
> And why unblooms the best hope ever sown?
> —Crass Casualty obstructs the sun and rain,
> And dicing Time for gladness casts a moan. . . .
> These purblind Doomsters had as readily strown
> Blisses about my pilgrimage as pain.

'Hap' is not a very good poem, but it puts its idea across. We are not at the mercy of gods like wanton boys. But we are at the mercy of chance, and about this there is something intolerable which we must cry out against. Here many critics find the whole burden of the novels.

3

For others the problem of Hardy's attitude, or philosophy, only begins here. They are much troubled by the fact that his Chance seems sometimes very like a malign intelligence—or a wanton boy—after all. To a quite unnatural and unverisimilar degree, it deals out far more 'pain' than 'blisses'. The objective picture may be dark, but Hardy insists on darkening it further. He does this to an extent only to be accounted for on the score of some dreadful personal morbidity.

Something like this was the opinion expressed by T. S. Eliot in *After Strange Gods*. Eliot came to dislike the tone of that book, and was reluctant to reprint it; and about Hardy, in particular, he substantially changed his mind. Yet his strictures have real cogency and will always retain a place in Hardy criticism. So I will consider them briefly now.

Here is the onslaught with which Eliot begins:

The work of the late Thomas Hardy represents an interesting example of a powerful personality uncurbed by any institutional attachment or by submission to any objective beliefs; un-hampered by any ideas, or even by what sometimes acts as a partial restraint upon inferior writers, the desire to please a large public. He seems to me to have written as nearly for the sake of 'self-expression' as a man well can; and the self which he had to express does not strike me as a particularly wholesome or edifying matter of communication.

Strictly speaking, Eliot is not charging Hardy with expressing an unwholesome self, since he is holding him up as being probably a case of diabolic possession. But he also expresses his dislike by insisting that Hardy is a thoroughly morbid writer. I would not myself deny an element of the morbid in Hardy, although I am far from thinking it raged in him uncontrolled. Eliot, who did not really know his Hardy very well, relies much on a short story called 'Barbara of the House of Grebe', which is to be found in *A Group of Noble Dames*. It is certainly rather a revolting story—but harmlessly so, I should say, in a consciously Gothic mode. Much more indicative of morbidity, to my mind, is *A Pair of Blue Eyes*, that early and essentially poetic novel which was

to become a great favourite with Tennyson. We may pause
on it for a moment, for more immediately relevant reasons than
one.

First, it is a novel, like Lawrence's *Sons and Lovers*, written
from the middle of the personal experience upon which it is based.
It is about a young architect of peasant stock falling in love with
a lady, and it was written while Hardy, a young architect of
peasant stock, had fallen in love with a lady and was proposing
to marry her. The general situation, indeed, had already occurred
in *The Poor Man and the Lady*; and Hardy had apparently
thought out some sort of rehandling of the theme before he
met Miss Gifford. Still, the courtship in the novel is Hardy's
courtship. While he was writing about Elfride Swancourt Emma
must have been closely associated with her in his head. Now, the
most dreadful things befall Elfride in the story, so that she finally
dies of a broken heart. Is it not disconcerting that Hardy's
imagination is inflicting these upon the image of the woman he
is shortly to marry? He telescopes his own courtship, it may be
said, with a thorough-going version of the immemorial sadistic
tale of the Persecuted Maiden. Surely this is far more 'morbid'
than the nasty little story about Barbara.

Secondly, it is in the manner in which Elfride's mischances
crowd one upon another that we are first sharply aware of a
general tendency in the novels which has disturbed many critics,
Eliot among them. 'What again and again introduces a note of
falsity into Hardy's novels,' Eliot says, 'is that he will leave
nothing to nature, but will always be giving one last turn of the
screw himself, and of his motives for so doing I have the gravest
suspicion.' Eliot means that there is something of the professional
torturer in Hardy. Let me expand this a little. Hardy's characters
are designed, we have supposed, as having their being within
some vast system of determinism, and upon the unhappy accident
of their sentience the mere regardlessness of things bears heavily
enough. But Hardy must give that further turn to the screw—
or better, must constantly be giving further fractional turns to it.
Nature can be trusted to be sufficiently ruthless, yet the novelist
must be ever at her side, nudging her on and pointing to one or
another favouring chink in our armour discerned by that small
dark bilberry eye—the eye on account of which, Hardy said,
he used often to be taken for a detective. Of the already lowering
universe of modern materialism he gleefully inspissates the
gloom. Drawn to and skilled in the infliction of pain, he would
persuade us to a world dedicated to such a purpose—and such
a world is, as Eliot expresses it, one of 'pure Evil'.

I do not think that this argument is to be ignored. That Hardy 'will leave nothing to nature' is true from the start. Already there is emerging in his first published novel, *Desperate Remedies*, a world in which coincidence regularly operates to intensify the plight of the deserving, and in which decisive catastrophe follows, as if by a series of ingenious and patient tactical arrangements, from seemingly trivial events. An eye strays by chance to the wrong column of a time-table and a woman who is therefore not expected seeks admission to a house which is by chance empty for the moment; she therefore goes on to an inn which is by chance promptly burned to the ground; and upon these and other concatenated accidents disaster eventually hangs. Always in Hardy it is certain that the incidence of fatality within the general operation of chance will be higher than we are commonly prepared to accept of its being in nature. Why? Can the facts be interpreted other than in Eliot's psychopathological terms?

Nothing disturbed Hardy more than the suggestion that he did in effect deny the neutrality of nature and suppose human destiny subject to the control or intervention of a maleficent power. Where he could be read in such a sense—so he frequently maintained—it was merely as a consequence of his employing some figure of rhetoric. Thus of the celebrated statement about 'the President of the Immortals' he declared that:

> The forces opposed to the heroine were allegorized as a personality (a method not unusual in imaginative prose or poetry) by the use of a well-known trope, explained in that venerable work, Campbell's *Philosophy of Rhetoric*, as 'one in which life, perception, activity, design, passion, or any property of sentient beings, is attributed to things inanimate'.

And when the power behind his universe was declared by Alfred Noyes in a public lecture to be an imbecile jester Hardy wrote:

> My imagination may have often run away with me; but all the same, my sober opinion—so far as I have any definite one—of the Cause of Things, has been defined in a score of places, and is that of a great many ordinary thinkers: that the said Cause is neither moral nor immoral, but *un*moral. . . . This view . . . I am quite unable to see as 'leading logically to the conclusion that the Power behind the universe is malign'.

Thus Hardy did not feel called upon to explain away what many, with Eliot, have regarded as the artificially piled up agony in the novels. Nevertheless there is the basis of an explanation in certain of his critical pronouncements—an explanation turning upon his basic acceptance of a thoroughly serious view of prose fiction as instructive, corrective, and concerned to set significant aspects of the human situation in a clearer light than, for the generality of readers, they had stood before. I have cited his saying that the business of his art was 'to intensify the expression of things . . . so that the heart and inner meaning is made vividly visible'. He judged that each of us inclines to take an unwarrantably rosy view of his own individual destiny. As early as *Desperate Remedies* we are told that 'there is an unquenchable expectation, which in the gloomiest time persists in inferring that because we are *ourselves*, there must be a special future in store for us'; and in *Two on a Tower* somebody remarks that 'we generally think we shall be lucky ourselves, though all the world before us, in the same situation, have been otherwise'. Just because I am *I* it is my instinct to believe that things are likely to go not too badly with me; and from this proceeds a general tendency to minimize the extent to which nature's mere indifference falsifies our calculations and betrays our hopes. 'To intensify the expression of things', therefore, so as to make vividly visible 'the heart and inner meaning' of the human plight to us who will ignore or misinterpret the evidence if we can, the writer must sharply step up the incidence upon human destiny of the mere blind recalcitrance of the universe—all art being just such 'a changing of the actual proportions of things' as will bring out the artist's perception.

All this is valid enough, I think, at the level at which Hardy chooses to touch upon the matter, and consciously, no doubt, he was engaged upon no other enterprise than he here asserts. Nevertheless we should be rather easily satisfied were we to enquire no further, for the explanation does not quite cover a pressure of feeling of which we are regularly aware. And upon the evidence of the novels as a whole we shall probably conclude that within the mature Hardy there lurked, as there lurks in most of us, something of the child for whom every tumble is the work of a hostile power—or of the child who, having discerned injustice in his universe, would support his own sense of it in the face of others' indifference by multiplying the occasions upon which 'it isn't fair'. This unconscious factor in the fabricating of so unnaturally heavy an incidence of inimical chance upon his characters' destinies brings us, if it be accepted, within hail of Eliot's reading of Hardy. But it does not, I think, at all oblige us to accept the essence of that reading. The strain of personal morbidity in Hardy was not inordinate; at most we can say that it stands a little nearer to that which would be veritably disabling than to the minimum that the artist cannot very comfortably do without. For there is, after all, evidence that the pearl of art characteristically forms itself round the irritant grain of some psychic distress, and it was Eliot himself, indeed, who at a dramatic moment endorsed James Thomson's observation that 'lips only sing when they cannot kiss'.

We must not go witch-hunting after neurotic strains in great artists, for deprivation of one sort or another is at the roots of their achievement. Shelley said nothing else when he spoke of poets as learning in suffering what they teach in song; and we may acknowledge the fact without, like Scythrop's friend Mr Toobad, hastily assuming that the very Devil himself is come among them (which is the thesis of *After Strange Gods*). Hardy's temperamental pessimism, then, was not uncontrolled and disintegrative, as in the writers of a decadence. It was but one aspect of a personality by no means pervasively unhealthy or atonic; and that personality held open and fruitful commerce with a character of marked strength, responsibility, and probity.

4

I have been venturing to draw, in the last few pages, upon an attempted rescue-operation in the face of Eliot's indictment which I printed more than twenty years ago. Since then there has been a more thorough-going refutation of Hardy's supposed morbidity, and also of the view that an entirely pessimistic determinism is what he is concerned to enforce upon us, put forward by Mr Roy Morrell in his book *Thomas Hardy: the Will and the Way*. Its contention is that we ought to allow much more weight than we do to Hardy's claim that the idea of 'evolutionary meliorism' is at the basis of his thinking. Providence is not going to help us, since we now know that Providence simply isn't there. But we *can* help ourselves. If we are only sufficiently alert and adaptable (which science shows to be the prime evolutionary demand) we have a fair chance of mastering our environment. The novels show some people managing this: Gabriel Oak, for example, in *Far from the Madding Crowd*. They also show a greater number of people precisely failing to do so. But the failures, equally with the successes, show what Hardy thinks. 'Not the disaster, but the disaster's unnecessariness' is what strikes Hardy as tragic in the human spectacle.

Morrell shows, among other things, how much there was

in Hardy's reading of J. S. Mill to promote the view that nature can, and must, be *controlled*. When, in 1902, Hardy wrote that 'to model our conduct on Nature's apparent conduct, as Nietzsche would have taught, can only bring disaster to humanity', he was perhaps recalling Mill's assertion that man comports himself aright 'not by imitating but by perpetually striving to amend the course of nature', and that

> from [nature] he must wrest, by force and ingenuity, what little he can for his own use, and deserves to be applauded when that little is rather more than might be expected from his physical weakness in comparison to those gigantic powers.

Mill had argued, too, in his *System of Logic*, that no effect was inevitable, unless the causes tending to produce it were left uncontrolled. Hardy's determinism, according to Morrell, is much modified by thinking of this kind; Hardy is always on the look out for what he himself calls 'chinks of possibility', for those occasions upon which the iron pressures of 'crass Casualty' are momentarily suspended, and something—perhaps much—may be achieved by the individual will. Even in *The Dynasts* 'the value of discipline, co-operation, and carefully timed effort is recognized clearly'. Men are to be *blamed* for.

> Acting like puppets
> Under Time's buffets.

Even in his 'grimmest poems . . . Hardy is not protesting against man's helplessness in the hands of Fate, but against his putting himself, by foolish and irresponsible actions, into such a helpless position'; his complaint is 'that the game of life should be played without that modicum of vigilance that might turn the balance'; 'man makes life worse than it need be', he once told William Archer. And what Hardy has to say about pessimism—including the celebrated reflection that 'if way to the Better there be, it exacts a full look at the Worst'—has a context in evolutionary theory. Morrell puts this thus:

> Gradually, the 'optimistic' species—those that assume, or behave as if they assume, that no adaptation is necessary, that luck will go on favouring them, that their one good trick will work for ever whatever the change in conditions—will be eliminated. And the 'pessimists'—those that seem to imagine that even the best trick may be bettered, that enemies will increase in number and experience . . . will survive.

What finally emerges as Morrell's Hardy is an Existentialist, enforcing the ineluctability of Choice. Man is doomed to be free. 'Hardy is tireless in his exploration of choice and freedom in different contexts.' But it is not exactly *moral* choice that Morrell seems to be talking about. It is rather choice within the sphere of the prudential: choice as it may be conceived in a highly evolved and therefore, in a fashion, reasoning animal.

5

Morrell, we see, is turning the commonly received Hardy upside-down. He does not, I think, succeed in the sense of convincing us that we have all been inexplicably wrong. But he does persuade me, at least, that I have insufficiently attended to something that really is there in the Wessex novels; that I have known to be there, but have not properly paused upon. Again and again when disaster strikes we know that there was something that could have been done to prevent it. Again and again individuals do make an *ill* (rather than a *wrong*) choice—and although sometimes they could not have known better, quite often they could. Again and again individuals make no choice at all; they take up instead a fatalistic attitude as if concurring in their own puppetry. This last attitude—a kind of deterministic abnegation of responsibility—produces some of the worst messes of all. Yet at the same time chance and consequence *do* bear upon them—and often so heavily that we cease to believe they inhabit a universe in which any amount of wariness and adaptability would be of the slightest use to them. Hardy's reading of life, in fact, falls well short of philosophical consistency. He was not, indeed, quite justified in speaking of his views as 'mere impressions that frequently change'. He never really wavers in his conviction of life's 'grimness'. But he responded to, and reflected, more interpretations of human experience than one, and a certain emotional and intellectual volatility here is an element in the life and poignancy of his writing. Although he is sometimes dogmatic in the novels, and frequently so in general pronouncements scattered through the *Life*, he always had a very sufficient sense of the fluidity in attitude and opinion essential to the artist. In 1899 he replied as follows to some approach made to him by the Rationalist Press Association:

Though I am interested in the Society I feel it to be one which would naturally compose itself rather of writers on philosophy, science, and history, than of writers of imaginative works, whose effect depends largely on detachment. By belonging to a philosophic association imaginative writers place themselves in this difficulty, that they are misread as propagandist when they mean to be simply artistic and delineative.

This does not quite get away from the fact that Hardy *is* propagandist; that his writing does have designs upon us of a sort to give the Rationalist Press Association some reason to expect that he would be willing to sign on. But as well as 'the latest illumination of the time' Hardy was aware of other and older lights—and chief among them, I suppose, that shed by what he called the 'emotional morality and altruism that was taught by Jesus Christ'. Morrell praises Hardy for being 'more logical in his agnosticism' than George Eliot. George Eliot 'saw an order which mysteriously and arbitrarily survived the divine order in which she no longer believed', whereas Hardy—it is implied— saw a more limited but more realistic hope in man's ability, if he chooses, to play the evolutionary game and survive as an alert and wary and adaptable animal. But I doubt whether this sort of evolutionary meliorism greatly moved Hardy or quickened his imagination. There is much that is inconsistent in the philosophic hinterland of his Wessex. The territory might not live for us as it does if this were not so.

6

For Morrell, then, Hardy's chief concern is with success and failure (but mostly failure) in man's power of adaptation to changing circumstances. But there is another general view of the Wessex novels which deserves consideration. This one presents Hardy as chiefly taken up with chronicling the decay of an order: the old agricultural order in England. There is argument to such an effect in many studies of Hardy, notably in Lionel Johnson's early and admirable book, *The Art of Thomas Hardy*. But the case is most systematically stated by Mr Douglas Brown in his *Thomas Hardy*, a small volume first published in 1954, and so frequently reprinted that I imagine it to be a good deal in use in schools. Here is Brown's statement of his theme:

> The five great novels have a common pattern. Lionel Johnson
> first suggested it and illuminated it by commentary. Hardy
> presents his conception through the play of life in a tract of the
> countryside. His protagonists are strong-natured countrymen,
> disciplined by the necessities of agricultural life. He brings into

relation with them men and women from outside the rural world, better educated, superior in status, yet inferior in human worth. The contact occasions a sense of invasion, of disturbance. The story unfolds slowly, and the theme of urban invasion declares itself more clearly as the country, its labour, its people and its past consolidate their presence. Then the story assumes some form of dramatic conflict, strong and unsubtle, and the invasion wreaks its havoc. A period of ominous waiting may follow; what the situation means becomes more evident: it is a clash between agricultural and urban modes of life.

So much for the 'pattern'. And Brown is quite clear how Hardy feels about it:

This pattern records Hardy's dismay at the predicament of the agricultural community in the south of England during the last part of the nineteenth century and at the precarious hold of the agricultural way of life. It records a profound activity of the memory, a deep-seated allegiance of the writer's personality, a degree of dependence upon an identified and reliable past. This activity of the memory, and this dismay, directed and continually informed Hardy's imaginative fictions.

In all this there is, in my opinion, the basis of at least an entirely mistaken emphasis. Hardy was of course capable of a warm nostalgic regard for sundry rural simplicities passing out of mind. He could write about them beautifully. But that he was deeply troubled by the decline and fall of the older agricultural order seems to me quite untrue. He was much more troubled by what he supposed to have been the decline and fall of the Hardys. 'So we go down, down, down', he writes in a notebook when nearly fifty, as he recalls his mother pointing out to him some shambling peasant who 'represented what was once the leading branch of the family'. Nor did he ever envisage his literary career as to be devoted to a succession of *Dorfgeschichten*; 'he had not the slightest intention of writing for ever about sheepfarming', the *Life* tells us apropos the success of *Far from the Madding Crowd*. In the whole course of the *Life*, moreover, there is only one extended consideration of contemporary agricultural conditions. This is in a letter of 1902, answering enquiries he had received from Rider Haggard, famous as the author of *King Solomon's Mines* and other romances, but also a landowner with a serious interest in rural economy. In the second half of the nineteenth century, Hardy tells his correspondent, the condition of the agricultural labourers has vastly improved. 'Their present life is almost without exception one of comfort, if the most ordinary thrift be observed.' There are bicycles by the doorways of their cottages, and brass-rods on the staircases. 'But changes at which we must all rejoice have brought other changes which are not so attractive.' And Hardy enumerates these. 'The labourers have become more and more migratory', and as a consequence 'village tradition—a vast mass of unwritten folk-lore, local chronicle, local topography, and nomenclature—is absolutely sinking, has nearly sunk, into eternal oblivion'. Hardy gives much more space to this antiquarian's lament than to underlying economic problems. Nineteen years earlier, indeed, in an article entitled 'The Dorsetshire Labourer' contributed to *Longman's Magazine*, he had written an informed and balanced account of the life of field workers. It has passages suggesting a vivid enough sympathy with its subject—he even found it possible to incorporate one or two of them to poignant effect in later novels—but the tone, on the whole, is cool and consciously literary:

A pure atmosphere and a pastoral environment are a very appreciable portion of the sustenance which tends to produce the sound mind and body, and thus much sustenance is, at least, the labourer's birthright.

The labourer who drifts to the town is moving from an environment in which drudgery induces no more than 'painless passivity' to one in which its consequence is likely to be 'a mood of despondency which is well-nigh permanent'. Such a move, on the other hand, does reflect adaptability and enterprise. Moreover (as Hardy was to be able to point out to Haggard in his letter, although it wouldn't have done for *Longman's*):

If in a town-lodgings an honest man's daughter should have an illegitimate child, or his wife should take to drinking, he is not compelled by any squire to pack up his furniture and get his living elsewhere, as is, or was lately, too often the case in the country.

Old orders change, and give place to new—and some sort of balance of advantages and disadvantages results. This, on the whole, seems to me how Hardy views things. If anything, he inclined towards change. It was as an advanced man and progressive thinker, after all, that throughout his life he consistently viewed himself.

4
Early Writing

WHEN HARDY FIRST THOUGHT TO WRITE A NOVEL IT WAS CLEAR
to him that, for its setting, the country in itself would not do.
One of the things he states most definitely about the lost *The
Poor Man and the Lady* is that 'the most important scenes were
laid in London—the city to which his own enterprise had transferred him from a rural background at the age of twenty-one'.
'He considered', the *Life* says, 'that he knew fairly well both
West-country life in its less explored recesses and the life of an
isolated student cast upon the billows of London with no protection but his brains. . . . The two contrasting experiences seemed
to afford him abundant materials out of which to evolve a striking
socialistic novel. . . .' It is of some curiosity that Hardy began
his novel-writing career as he was to end it: with a fierce attack
upon privilege. The theme of social disparity between lovers he
returned to in the interim frequently enough, but he never
returned, until *Jude the Obscure*, to more than a muted social
satire.

We possess a good deal of information about *The Poor Man
and the Lady*. Immediately after Hardy's death Edmund Gosse
communicated to *The Times* an account of the story which he
had gleaned from Hardy in conversation seven years earlier, when
Hardy was already eighty-one. This may well be unreliable. But
there is an outline of the story in the *Life*, and there also exists a
letter—and it is a model of its kind—which Alexander Macmillan
sent Hardy in 1868 when he declined to publish it. From these
and from a number of more fragmentary references something
can be built up.

The hero of the story is called Will Strong, from which we may
infer he was not conceived of as the passive character that many
of Hardy's later men are sometimes charged with being. He is of
humble and rustic birth, and he falls in love with the squire's
daughter, Miss Allamont, as she does with him. The arrogant
parents of Miss Allamont forbid the lovers to meet. Will goes

off to London in the hope of making himself a more eligible
suitor, and becomes with some rapidity a successful architect.
But he also becomes horrified by the heartlessness of the nobility
and gentry, the vulgarity of the middle class, the hypocrisy of the
Church, and the state of public and domestic morals in general.
This leads him into political activity of a proletarian and revolu-
tionary order. (Writing in the later 1860s, Hardy would calculate
that this must command considerable topical interest). The
Allamonts come to town. Miss Allamont, driving through
Trafalgar Square, is much shocked to see Will haranguing the
populace. Nevertheless the love-affair is renewed. At this point
one would suppose all to be going fairly well, despite such continued opposition as Miss Allamont's parents may be proposing to
put up, since Will Strong has attained an independent position,
and he can scarcely have done this without the passing of a
sufficient number of years for his mistress to have come of age.
But, in fact, the story ends in disaster, since Miss Allamont's
constitution fails to stand up to the strains of the situation, and
she dies.

Here, as later in *A Pair of Blue Eyes*, Hardy's imagination can
see only a fatal ending to a love-affair in which the lover is a
very obvious projection of himself into a fictional situation. But
it was not the inconsequence of the tragedy that worried Alexander
Macmillan. It was what he conceived to be the extravagance and
crudity of the book's satirical element. He put this point to Hardy
with kindness and address. He acknowledged in Hardy a writer
'at least potentially, of considerable mark, of power and purpose'.
And he brought Thackeray into comparison with this unknown
young correspondent:

> Thackeray was in many respects a really good man, but he
> wrote in a mocking tone that has culminated in the *Saturday
> Review* tone, paralysing noble effort and generous emotion.
> You seem in grim earnest, and, as I said, 'mean mischief', and
> I like your tone infinitely better.

But the difference between Thackeray and Hardy, Macmillan
says in effect, is that Thackeray knew what he was talking about.
Whereas Hardy's 'black wash' will be received only as 'ignorant
misrepresentation'. He is writing, it is implied, quite outside
his social experience. And 'Nothing could justify such a wholesale
blackening of a class but large and intimate knowledge of it'.
Macmillan commended various features of the book. 'The
scene in Rotten Row', he wrote, 'is full of power and insight.'

Hardy seems to have made a note of this, and resolved not to let a passage in which he had attained these qualities perish, for the satirical scene in question is almost certainly being drawn upon in Chapter XIV of *A Pair of Blue Eyes*. It is so embarrassingly bad (despite Macmillan's perhaps rather random commendation) that we can only feel relieved that the work from which it is excerpted has for the most part perished.

It cannot be said to have perished wholly. Along with his own opinion Macmillan had transmitted to Hardy some remarks made by his reader, John Morley, including one to the effect that 'the opening pictures of the Christmas-eve in the tranter's house are really of good quality'. It seems certain that these 'pictures' were in Hardy's mind when he began the opening chapters of *Under the Greenwood Tree*—a book described on its title-page as 'A Rural Painting of the Dutch School'—and it may even be that these opening chapters actually reproduce substantial stretches of the earlier novel.

There is another, and rather odd, derivative of *The Poor Man and the Lady*. This is the longest of Hardy's short stories, 'An Indiscretion in the Life of an Heiress', which appeared in the *New Quarterly Magazine* in 1878, was never reprinted during Hardy's lifetime, and receives no mention in the *Life*. It appears to be a dehydrated, or otherwise debilitated, version of the novel, concentrating entirely on the love-story, and with the element of social protest reduced virtually to zero. Will Strong has become Egbert Mayne, and although he is a young village schoolmaster living with a maternal grandfather who is a tenant farmer in a small way we are told that his father had been 'a painter of good family, but unfortunate and improvident'. Egbert becomes not a successful architect but a successful writer. Miss Allamont becomes Miss Allenville; she is saved by Egbert from being reduced to a 'mangled carcase' in a threshing machine. The story-line of *The Poor Man and the Lady* is then pursued. The hero and heroine contrive a runaway marriage and have two or three nights together as husband and wife. After this, the young bride goes off to face her enraged father alone, and fatally bursts a blood-vessel under the strain of this encounter. The whole story is insipid, and the lovemaking almost comically inept:

> Suddenly rushing towards her, he seized her hand before she comprehended his intention, kissed it tenderly, and clasped her in his arms. Her soft body yielded like wool under his embrace. As suddenly releasing her he turned, and went back to the other end of the room.

If 'An Indiscretion in the Life of an Heiress' reasonably preserves the merits and qualities of *The Poor Man and the Lady* in its aspect as a love-story, then we must conclude that, even if the myth of the poor man and the lady was already vividly with Hardy, he was still quite without the ability to give it any convincing embodiment. But I suspect that he was chiefly thinking of other things, and in particular of how bitter it was to be intelligent, sensitive, and recognizably not a gentleman in Victorian England.

2

The Poor Man and the Lady did not end its career on Macmillan's desk, but went on to that of Chapman and Hall. Frederick Chapman agreed to publish it if Hardy would put up twenty pounds, but later hedged a little, and brought Hardy up to London to be talked to by his reader, who was nobody less than George Meredith. Meredith urged Hardy to take away the manuscript and tone things down, or better still, simply to put it aside for a time and write a new novel. It would be imprudent for Hardy to 'nail his colours to the mast' so definitely in a first book, and when he wrote another he would do well to give it 'a more complicated plot'. Meredith's advice was no doubt sound in a general way, and was based on a responsible wish to guard the reputation of a young writer. But something slightly perfunctory sounds in it, and Hardy must have felt that he was being told to lower his sights. He took the manuscript away, and later offered it to a publisher of inferior status, William Tinsley, who rejected it out of hand. Thereupon Hardy took Meredith's advice in full, put *The Poor Man and the Lady* in the drawer, and began to write *Desperate Remedies*.

This very complicated mystery story (as it turned out to be) was produced fairly rapidly, being begun in the autumn of 1869 and in a state to offer to a publisher by the beginning of March 1870. Hardy sent it to Macmillan, who took a month to reply that it was 'of far too sensational an order for us to think of publishing'. The refusal was fair enough; it had not been Macmillan who had recommended Hardy to go after something with an emphatic plot; it had been Chapman and Hall's Mr Meredith. But now Hardy by-passed Chapman and Hall—which suggests, perhaps, that he had found Meredith unsympathetic. Instead, he tried Tinsley again. Tinsley eventually agreed to publish the book if Hardy would put seventy-five pounds into the venture. Upon a young architect's assistant, with nobody behind him except a father in a small way of business as a stone-mason, this was a stiff demand. Hardy, however, found the money, and the novel was published. It was not much of a success. The *Spectator* printed a savage review, condemning the book as viciously immoral. Hardy was stunned, and 'wished he were dead'. He was always to be sensitive to what reviewers wrote of him. And that, for a writer, is a dreadful fate.

It is likely that Hardy believed he had put a great deal of such passion and art as was in him into *The Poor Man and the Lady*, and into *Desperate Remedies* only such melodramatic contrivance as any clever man could produce in the hope of making money. This was not the actual state of the case. It is evident that *The Poor Man and the Lady* laboured at a kind of satire which Hardy lacked sufficient knowledge to render convincing, and that a large effect of 'ignorant misrepresentation' was indeed the result. In *Desperate Remedies*, on the other hand, the often absurd complexities of plot native to a sensation novel were, to a considerable extent, native to Hardy's authentic imagination too. Nevertheless, he obviously felt something demeaning in writing a thriller. The *Life* refers to '*Desperate Remedies*, the melodramatic novel, quite below the level of *The Poor Man and the Lady*, which was the unfortunate consequence of Meredith's advice to "write a story with a plot"'. His later settled disparagement of novels and novel-writing, which sometimes approached the comical, may have had its origin in this period.

Let us now consider what Hardy supposed to be meant by 'writing a story with a plot'.

> Diseases desperate grown,
> By desperate appliances are reliev'd
> Or not at all . . .

The 'appliances' employed by the novel's villain, Charles Manston, are quite as desperate as those of Shakespeare's Claudius. Manston grows tired of his wife and hits her; unfortunately his hand comes 'edgewise exactly in the nape of the neck—as men strike a hare to kill it', and she dies instantly. He immures her body in a brew-house; secures 'three or four fragments of leg and back-bones' from a churchyard; and so disposes of these that it is concluded she has perished in a fire. He is thus free to marry Cytherea Graye, the *protégée* of a wealthy woman, Miss Aldclyffe, who is eventually going to turn out to be Manston's mother. But a false suspicion is aroused that the first Mrs Manston is still alive, and Cytherea is carried off by her brother and her true lover from the hotel in which what is thus possibly a bigamous marriage is on the brink of being consummated. In order to avert the darkest speculations, Manston persuades another woman to impersonate his first wife and appear to return to live with him. He performs a number of laboured feats of duplicity, involving much eavesdropping, tampering with mails, substituting of photographs, and the like. But somebody finds a poem in which he has described his wife's eyes as azure, and it is remarked that the woman now claiming the role has eyes of deepest black. Eventually Manston feels it necessary to recover the body of his authentic wife and bury it more securely. 'Intentness pervaded everything; Night herself seemed to have become a watcher.' Certainly three other characters are watchers, each independently of the others. Manston flees, and his trail is followed by various ingenious means: the pattern of what is somehow known to be his watch-chain is discovered in mud; a shepherd points out that 'wherever a clear space three or four yards wide ran in a line through a flock of sheep lying about a ewe-lease, it was a proof that somebody had passed there not more than half-an-hour earlier'. This rural detection is not so efficient as to come up with the fugitive before he has had a chance to burst in upon Cytherea in her lonely dwelling and brutally attempt to possess himself of her:

> The panting and maddened desperado—blind to everything but the capture of his wife—went with a rush under the table: she went over it like a bird. He went heavily over it: she flew under it, and was out at the other side.

> 'One on her youth and pliant limbs relies,
> One on his sinews and his giant size.'

> But his superior strength was sure to tire her down in the long-run. . . .

But all in fact is well. Cytherea's devoted suitor (who is a young architect) again bursts in, and this time apprehends the villain. Detained in the County Gaol, Manston writes a full confession and hangs himself.

It has been customary, in such short discussions as *Desperate Remedies* has received, to concentrate upon dissecting out from the abundant melodrama such prelusive hints of Hardy's characteristic powers as can be shown to be present. There is a good deal of interest in the exercise. But it is equally pertinent to observe that this first novel is notably good in its kind. A modern reader may well

judge it too long-winded, and in places too conscientiously
'literary', for a successful mystery story. But a certain amplitude
was required of the thriller or sensation novel in the Victorian
period. The two most successful examples in the decade preceding
Hardy's book are *The Woman in White* and *The Moonstone* by
Wilkie Collins; both ingeniously combine sustained suspense
(tautening and slackening, indeed, as the long narrative proceeds)
with a full deployment of social observation, humour, descriptive
writing, and a confident if conventional 'love interest'. Hardy is
not far behind the practised Collins in the mere logistics of his
plot; he husbands his big surprises and strings out his little ones
expertly; and if the narrative is in danger of dragging he is
resourceful in producing a fresh cloud over some past life, a
shadow on a blind, a misread timetable, an unanswered knock
(which is to turn up much more tremendously in *The Return of
the Native*), a peep through a shutter, a concealed drawer, a man's
revealing manner of leaving his bank, an ambiguous letter,
riddling talk: precisely enough to keep boiling the modest but
exciting sort of brew on hand.

It is also notable that such more significant literary endowments
as he already shows himself possessed of are exhibited only to a
very limited extent *aside* from the progress of the fable; rather
they fortify it and give it edge, so that we lose the effect of them if
we simply study their quality in isolation. This holds particularly
in the field of visual effects. These are regularly so sharp that they
actualize scenes and situations which, psychologically, carry no
great conviction; and they frequently remain operative despite
marked clumsiness of style. Thus, near the beginning of the
novel, the heroine, while listening to a 'much talked-of reading
from Shakespeare' in a Town Hall, looks through a window and
sees her father (yet another architect) perched high on a church
spire. He slips and reels off into the air, 'immediately disappearing
downwards'. When we have finished being amused by the heavy
tautology of the last three words, we realize that we have been in
the presence of an incident so vividly evoked as to put us in mind
of the catastrophe of Ibsen's *The Master Builder*.

Yet more striking is the command of the natural scene. Hardy
was interested in painting, and the text carries references to
Greuze, Crivelli, Correggio which we may consider to be only a
cultural showing-off. But sheep under shade in the distance
are a pale blue, and the light of the westering sun over heather
'so intensified the colours that they seemed to stand above the
surface of the earth and float in mid-air like an exhalation of red'.
So too with people. Cytherea first sees Miss Aldclyffe silhouetted

in a doorway against the direct blaze of the afternoon sun, 'like a tall black figure standing in the midst of fire'. A moment later, 'she could for the first time see Miss Aldclyffe's face in addition to her outline, lit up by the secondary and softer light that was reflected from the varnished panels of the door'. The capturing of such effects ('like those of the modern French painters', Hardy in one place obligingly pauses to point out) is something beyond the scope of a Wilkie Collins. And the power to see and record does again and again credibilize scenes and episodes not wholly persuasive in themselves. Children dutifully singing in church, for example, 'their heads inclined to one side, their eyes listlessly tracing some crack in the old walls, or following the movement of a distant bough or bird with features petrified almost to painfulness',[1] lend authority, after the odd fashion of artistic creation, to the tricky scene in which Cytherea has to be represented as accepting Manston's hand—a scene which begins on the same page.

Hardy's ear is perhaps even more remarkable than his eye. Sometimes it alerts us fleetingly in passing, as when we are told of a pleasure cruise that 'the sea was so calm, that the soft hiss produced by the bursting of the innumerable bubbles of foam behind the paddles could be distinctly heard'. Sometimes it enforces effects of mystification and the macabre, for example when a long sequence of night sounds heard by Cytherea culminates in 'a very soft gurgle or rattle—of a strange and abnormal kind' which later turns out to have been an old man's death agony. And sometimes it is used in a subtle interaction with muted visual effects, most notably in a long passage in which the varying crops traversed in a nocturnal walk are conjured up in terms of the sound of the rain on their several surfaces.

This vigilance and delicacy of the senses, which is to be an increasing strength throughout Hardy's work, is not matched in *Desperate Remedies* by any sustained command of human character and relationships. His people as much as his plot derive for the most part from the stereotypes of popular fiction. Manston is wholly absurd. He has committed homicide and concealed his crime; he employs evil means to subdue and marry Cytherea because of 'the hot voluptuous nature of his passion for her'; yet he is able to declare in his final confession that 'never did a bridegroom leave the church with a heart more full of love and happiness, and a brain more fixed on good intentions'.

[1] This image reappears, with only slight verbal changes, in the opening paragraph of 'An Indiscretion in the Life of an Heiress'. It may thus be presumed to have first appeared in *The Poor Man and the Lady*.

The women, if only in odd flashes, have rather more of nature than the men. Miss Aldclyffe's feelings for her unacknowledged son are competently if conventionally portrayed. But her relationship with Cytherea (before the demands of the plot restrict it) is another matter. Proposing first to engage the penniless young girl as a maid, she imagines her own 'luxurious indolent body' under her hands; and later this surprising current of feeling is given free play: 'The instant they were in bed Miss Aldclyffe freed herself from the last remnant of restraint'. It was to be fifteen years before Henry James, in *The Bostonians*, treated a Lesbian theme in his own ponderous and circumspect manner. It cannot be claimed that Hardy makes anything significant out of this brief episode of sexual morbidity. But we are made aware that he was (as he claims in a poem) a man who noticed things.

Victorian novelists were expected to pause every now and then in their narration in order to edify the reader with general observations of a moral or reflective character. Hardy fulfils this obligation conscientiously from the first, and usually with a careful observance of what he takes to be an appropriately gnomic or aphoristic manner. The result is commonplace for the most part, but if we are hunting for the thought of the mature writer we shall come upon it frequently enough:

> Reasoning worldliness, especially when allied with sensuousness, cannot repress on some extreme occasions the human instinct to pour out the soul to some Being or Personality, who in frigid moments is dismissed with the title of Chance, or at most Law.

This has the form in which Hardy liked jotting down reflections in his notebooks. There are other places in which such musings are dramatized—and often in the persons of the simple or uncultivated, so that there is an implication that we are receiving a kind of folk-wisdom. Thus Miss Aldclyffe's coachman, remarking that his mistress 'has had seven lady's-maids this last twelve-month', concludes that 'the Lord must be a neglectful party at heart, or he'd never permit such overbearen goings on'. Or again, in the final chapter, two farmers are moved by the sight of Manston's coffin to this dialogue:

> 'Ah, Baker, we say sudden death, don't we? But there's no difference in their nature between sudden death and death of any other sort. There's no such thing as a random snapping off of what was laid down to last longer. We only suddenly light

upon an end—thoughtfully formed as any other—which has
been existing at that very same point from the beginning,
though unseen by us to be so soon.'

'It is just a discovery to your own mind, and not an alteration in the Lord's.'

'That's it. Unexpected is not as to the thing, but as to our
sight.'

'Now you'll hardly believe me, neighbour, but this little
scene in front of us makes me feel less anxious about pushing
on wi' that threshing and winnowing next week, that I was
speaking about. Why should we not stand still, says I to myself,
and fling a quiet eye upon the Whys and Wherefores, before
the end o' it all, and we go down into the mouldering-place,
and are forgotten?'

"'Tis a feeling that will come. But 'twont bear looking into.
There's a back'ard current in the world, and we must do our
utmost to advance in order just to bide where we be.'

Such passages look forward in one aspect to the stiff determinism
of which Hardy's developed thought was to take so much account;
the second contains, for example, the central thought of his
grim poem on the loss of the 'Titanic', 'The Convergence of the
Twain': nature was fashioning the iceberg at the same time that
man was fashioning the liner, and their convergence can be
called unexpected 'but as to our sight'. But in another aspect we
have in such exchanges early examples of the convention of
quaint rustic talk of which Hardy was to display such a command
in the immediately succeeding novel.

3

Desperate Remedies displays a young writer, discouraged by the
rejection of a first novel written passionately if naïvely from his
own experience, abruptly lowering his sights and studying a
market. But he must have been well aware of standards other
than those of the successful Sensation Novel such as George
Meredith had recommended to him. Meredith himself published
The Adventures of Harry Richmond within a few months of
Desperate Remedies, and George Eliot's *Middlemarch* appeared
in the same year. Although some of the melodramatic elements
in Hardy's novel came naturally to him and were to remain a
staple of his fiction, and although he was going to cling obstinately
to the notion of that fiction as an unassuming bread-and-butter,
he cannot but have been aware that he had put much labour into

a radically unambitious book. In particular it must have shown up as artificial and insignificant when set beside George Eliot's work—and yet the basis of her achievement was a knowledge of English provincial life close to that which he himself possessed. *Adam Bede* (which had been published when he was nineteen) would have seemed especially impressive, since it is a novel of great power moving preponderantly among people of humble station.

There is a passage, indeed, at the beginning of the second part of *Adam Bede* in which George Eliot expatiates on this deliberate circumscription:

> So I am content to tell my simple story, without trying to make things seem better than they were; dreading nothing, indeed, but falsity, which, in spite of one's best efforts, there is reason to dread. Falsehood is so easy, truth so difficult. . . . It is for this rare, precious quality of truthfulness that I delight in many Dutch paintings, which lofty-minded people despise. I find a source of delicious sympathy in these faithful pictures of a monotonous homely existence, which has been the fate of so many more among my fellow-mortals than a life of pomp or of absolute indigence, of tragic suffering or of world-stirring actions. I turn, without shrinking, from cloud-borne angels, from prophets, sibyls, and heroic warriors, to an old woman bending over her flower-pot, or eating her solitary dinner, while the noonday light, softened perhaps by a screen of leaves, falls on her mob-cap, and just touches the rim of her spinning-wheel, and her stone jug, and all those cheap common things which are the precious necessaries of life to her;—or I turn to that village wedding, kept between four brown walls, where an awkward bridegroom opens the dance with a high-shouldered, broad-faced bride, while elderly and middle-aged friends look on, with very irregular noses and lips, and probably with quart-pots in their hands, but with an expression of unmistakable contentment and goodwill.

Here was a pointer to what Hardy himself could do from first-hand knowledge and with lively sympathy. It is not perhaps coincidental that he described *Under the Greenwood Tree* on its title-page as *A Rural Painting of the Dutch School*.

4

As a first contrast with *Desperate Remedies*, the new book tells only the very simplest story. Dick Dewy is the son of the

Mellstock tranter (meaning a carrier in a small way of business) and he falls in love at first sight with the new schoolmistress, Fancy Day, whose father, being Lord Wessex's gamekeeper, is of some consequence in the peasant world in which the tale is set. Dick has two rivals, of whom one is the young vicar of the parish. At the prospect of marrying a gentleman Fancy's fidelity falters. But the cloud is quickly dispelled, and she and Dick are happily united in the end.

It is, however, only some way on in the book that this theme predominates. The earlier chapters, which reflect or perhaps incorporate the parts of *The Poor Man and the Lady* approved by John Morley, exhibit the rural society of Mellstock at large, but with a chief emphasis upon the amateur instrumentalists who constitute the church choir. The fiddles of these worthies are about to be superseded by an organ, and the two strands of the book are loosely interwoven by making the new organist Fancy Day. It has to be noted that Hardy is here writing about an already bygone state of affairs. His grandfather had played the bass-viol for thirty-five years in Stinsford Church, and his father had played the violin for twenty; but this form of church music had passed into desuetude before Hardy himself could have formed any impression of it. The events in *Under the Greenwood Tree* are described in the second paragraph of the novel as having taken place 'within living memory'. Perhaps the best 'historical' novels—certainly the best of Sir Walter Scott's—are just on or a shade over this border. Hardy was constantly to frequent it. But except in his dealing with the age of Napoleon (and that is scarcely an exception) there is very little that is obtrusively 'period' in his writing. Yet by far the greater part of his most significant fiction is in fact distanced by two or three generations from the period of its production. There is, in fact, a certain historical legerdemain about it. Things passed away are given the air of things passing away. It is a powerful imaginative instrument that is thus released.

The Mellstock Quire (who, under this older spelling, were originally to have provided the novel with its title) represent the first appearance of that rustic chorus who are to travel with Hardy far along the road of his maturing fiction. He is distinguishably not yet quite confident about them. Nor, occasionally, are we. We are inclined to feel, at the start, that we are in the presence of a literary convention—one running back through George Eliot to Shakespeare. The elder Mr Dewy, together with his wife, father, father-in-law, and cronies, seem a little too hard at work sustaining their own quaintness, their unfailing command of eccentric modes of thought, of homely wisdom gnomically expressed. Yet the rustic sages gain on us as we read on. "A can keep a very clever silence—very clever truly,' the village wittol, Thomas Leaf, says of Fancy's father. "A do look at me as if 'a could see my thoughts running round like the works of a clock.' 'The man's well enough,' Fancy's father has just said of the vicar; "tis what's in his head that spoils him.' "A was a right sensible pa'son,' Michael Mail says of the previous incumbent. 'He never entered our door but once in his life. . . . There's virtue in a man's not putting a parish to spiritual trouble.' 'All true stories,' the tranter declares, 'have a coarseness or a bad moral, depend upon't. If the story-tellers could ha' got decency and good morals from true stories, who'd ha' troubled to invent parables?' Aphorisms of this sort range from the profound through the idiosyncratic to the absurd. Dick Dewy is a little late for his wedding, after all, since he has had a small crisis as an apiarist. 'Well, bees can't be put off,' his grandfather says. 'Marrying a woman is a thing you can do at any moment; but a swarm o' bees won't come for the asking.' 'Good, but not religious-good,' is the temperate epitaph upon a deceased Mellstock man. The choir, faced with dismissal, meditate upon degeneracy and decay in their avocation:

'Times have changed from the times they used to be,' said Mail. . . . 'People don't care much about us now! I've been thinking we must be almost the last left in the county of the old string players? Barrel-organs, and they things next door to 'em that you blow wi' your foot, have come in terribly of late years.'

'Ay!' said Bowman, shaking his head; and old William, on seeing him, did the same thing.

'More's the pity,' replied another. 'Time was—long and merry ago now—when not one of the varmits was to be heard of; but it served some of the choirs right. They should have stuck to strings as we did, and keep out clar'nets, and done away with serpents. If you'd thrive in musical religion, stick to strings, says I.'

'Strings be safe soul-lifters, as fur as that do go,' said Mr Spinks.

'Yet there's worse things than serpents,' said Mr Penny. 'Old things pass away, 'tis true; but a serpent was a good old note: a deep rich note was the serpent.'

'Clar'nets, however, be bad at all times,' said Michael Mail. . . .

C

'I can well bring back to my mind,' said Mr Penny, 'what I said to poor Joseph Ryme (who took the tribble part in Chalk-Newton Church for two-and-forty year) when they thought of having clar'nets there. "Joseph," I said, says I, "depend upon't, if so be you have them tooting clar'nets you'll spoil the whole set-out. Clar'nets were not made for the service of the Lard; you can see it by looking at 'em," I said. And what cam o't? Why, souls, the parson's set up a barrel-organ on his own account within two years o' the time I spoke, and the old choir went to nothing.'

This surely represents something near to perfection in its kind, but Hardy nevertheless obeys a sound artistic instinct in withdrawing the chorus through much of the latter part of the book. The scene in which the choir present themselves before the vicar to protest against their impending dismissal has become justly famous. But it holds a shade too much of the freakish, and the elder Mr Dewy in particular—a perfectly sensible man—is constrained to too clownish a role. A similar hazard appears when the authorial voice in the book seeks too pertinaciously for a whimsical note—as when we learn that Mr Haylock the butcher has 'a little office consisting only of a door and a window' and an account-book 'possessing length but no breadth'. The fact is that Hardy has on hand, in other aspects of his novel, persons and things so sensitively observed as to be congruous with only the most refined comedy.

This holds of the Mellstock folk at large. Their gentleness and mutual consideration as displayed in all the common traffic of the parish are quite as genuine as is the occasional outspokenness of their speech. Their party manners (as when those who 'loved eating and drinking put on a look to signify that till that moment they had quite forgotten that it was customary to expect suppers on these occasions') evince an outward absurdity and an inward delicacy of feeling which comes to us as something deeply civilized. Their mingled stoicism and innocent conviviality within a world in which Thomas Leaf's mother can lose eleven of her twelve children by miscarriage or in early infancy evoke our compassion and respect. Hardy withdraws them a little from our gaze at just the point where a balance between all this and their sheerly comic quality might become hard to maintain. The foreground is then occupied by the rustic hero and heroine. Here again we may be conscious that Hardy is in some difficulty between conflicting modes of perception and representation. Is this simple love-story an idyll, in the words of the book's first publisher 'as pure and sweet as new-mown hay'? Or is it far from being without intimations of that disenchantment before the ways of men and women which was to be so abundantly Hardy's later?

Dick Dewy is an attractive creation: a lover at once forthright and delicate, with a large ingenuousness which yet leaves him far from being a fool. If his character is too much without shade it is nevertheless presented with so keen a perception of a young lovers' hopes and fears, fond assumptions and awkwardnesses that it always remains within the range of our sympathy; plenty of gentle fun is made of Dick, and this preserves him from the depressing role of a rural paragon. A first impression may suggest that in all this Fancy Day is a match for him, but we are later likely to conclude that she is rather far from being the idealized farmhouse maiden of romance. That she is not so nice a person as Dick becomes clearer as the book proceeds—according to one or two critics, indeed, emerges with some abruptness, as if Hardy had decided to dislike her. This is scarcely so, but she is certainly the more closely observed of the two, and therefore the more interesting if the less estimable. Like Cytherea before her and many of Hardy's women later, she can be indecisive, inconstant, 'gery' (in Chaucer's word). She is undeviatingly concerned with her own attractions; too much of her nature is summed up by Dick's grandfather James for the benefit of Dick's grandfather William when he says, 'Remember the words of the prophet Jeremiah: "Can a maid forget her ornaments, or a bride her attire?"'; and Dick himself comes to a perception of this:

> 'What she loves best in the world,' he thought, with an incipient spice of his father's grimness, 'is her hair and complexion. What she loves next best, her gowns and hats; what she loves next best, myself, perhaps!'

This is no doubt reprehensible in Fancy Day, but it is only men of notably serious and elevated mind who would austerely rule out a girl on such an account. Fancy's 'coquettishness', we are told, 'was never so decided as to banish honesty', and her swift response to real devotion—her vulnerability, in fact, before the masculine principle to which, conversely, she is potentially so dangerous—is something which makes us reluctant to turn down any sort of thumb on her. Yet Fancy is decidedly not all curds and cream—and what brings this home to us is, paradoxically, her own unconscious assumption that it is precisely this that she is. When for example, she has been caught out by Dick in dressing

up with particular splendour for an occasion upon which it was
known that he could not be present, we have this:

> 'I must go,' she said with sudden gaiety, and skipped back-
> wards into the porch. 'Come here, sir;—say you forgive me,
> and then you shall kiss me;—you never have yet when I have
> worn curls, you know. Yes, in the very middle of my mouth,
> where you want to so much,—yes, you may!'
> Dick followed her into the inner corner, where he was not
> slow in availing himself of the privilege offered.
> 'Now that's a treat for you, isn't it?' she continued. 'Good-
> bye, or I shall be late.'

If we pause on this, we shall dislike it. Yet Fancy is doing no
more than accept, for the moment, a shallow notion of courtship
and passion; and we are learning no more than does the vicar
when he discovers that this girl who has impulsively uttered three
words of acceptance to him, is in fact much more suitably
affianced to one of his unassuming parishioners: that Fancy Day
'was less an angel than a woman'. She is, in fact, so much a
woman that she a little threatens to crack the surface of the tranquil 'painting of the Dutch school'. And, like almost everybody
else in the book, she is of too fine a facture to cohere with any
breadth of comedy. When her father forbids her to marry Dick
because Farmer Shiner is a more affluent suitor, Fancy consults
an old woman with the reputation of a witch, and on her advice
puts up a show of being so love-lorn that she cannot eat and is
pining away. It is an index of the level of Hardy's writing in
Under the Greenwood Tree that this strikes a false note, as of
something belonging to farce upon a stage. It lets Fancy down.
And our consciousness of this tells us that substantial human
nature is coming increasingly within Hardy's grasp.

5

A Pair of Blue Eyes

WHEREAS *DESPERATE REMEDIES* IS AN EXTREMELY INTRICATE STORY, *A Pair of Blue Eyes* is in outline simple enough.[1] It appears otherwise only because of the amount of subsidiary and inessential complication, much of it exploiting grotesque situations and striking coincidences, which Hardy has worked into the fabric of his novel for the purpose of amusing the readers of *Tinsley's Magazine* —and (we are bound to feel) himself as well.

It is true that there is not much probability about either the opening or the close of the main action. We cannot believe that Mr Swancourt, even although a comparative newcomer at

[1] Stephen Smith is a young architect who comes to Endelstow in North Cornwall in connection with church restoration. He is received into the household of the vicar, Mr Swancourt, who is a widower with one child, Elfride. Smith and Elfride fall in love in a somewhat childish fashion, but Mr Swancourt discovers that Smith is the son of humble people in his own parish, and in effect turns him away. The two young people attempt an elopement, and find they have to travel all the way to London to get married. This discourages and frightens them, so that they simply go from one platform to another at Paddington, and return to Cornwall overnight.

Elfride manages to conceal this compromising exploit, and Smith departs for India, whence he hopes to return with a competence and claim her. Mr Swancourt meanwhile has married again, and this brings into his household as a visitor Henry Knight, a reviewer and essayist, whose maturer personality enables him to supplant Smith (whose patron and mentor he turns out coincidentally to have been) in Elfride's heart. Unfortunately Knight has never kissed a woman, and his ideal is a woman who has never kissed a man. The discovery that Elfride has had previous admirers disturbs him profoundly, and eventually—having got wind of the London escapade but not of the identity of the lover on that occasion—he renounces Elfride and departs on an extensive tour of the Continent. Smith, on a different motive, has renounced her already: returning prosperous to England and discovering her relationship with Knight, he had quietly resigned his suit and gone back to India.

An indefinite period of time elapses; both men are again in England; they meet and talk in a London hotel. Much remains unexpressed or not understood between them; neither divulges to the other his intention of renewing his courtship; but the next day they find themselves travelling to Cornwall on the same train. At the end of their journey Elfride turns out to have been on the train too, but in her coffin. At an inn called the Welcome Home the rivals (if they can be so termed) learn the full truth. Some five months before, Elfride had married Lord Luxellian, a widower whose children she had mothered; and she had then fallen into a decline and died.

Endelstow, should be unaware that his parishioners the Smiths (and he addresses Mrs Smith familiarly and condescendingly by her Christian name) have a clever son who has gone to be an architect in London. This is a flaw which any countryman will spot at once, and may conceivably be taken as an index of the extent to which Hardy's eye was already on an urban public. Again, Knight is represented as moving in good society; and even amid his continental wanderings he could not have failed to hear of Elfride's marriage to the fifteenth Baron Luxellian. Unlikely states of ignorance are a great stand-by of the popular novelist which Hardy was never going to disdain and it cannot be said that here they much impair the imaginative effect of the book. This holds, too, of his frequent manœuvring of the action in the interest of some *coup de théâtre* in an equally unassuming tradition. That the church tower should tumble to the ground within seconds of Elfride's invoking it as a symbol of stability; that Knight, scrambling among the debris a little later, should feel his hand 'lighted plump upon a substance differing in the greatest possible degree from what he had expected to seize—hard stone', and that this should prove not even what he guesses it to be—'a tressy species of moss or lichen'—but a dead woman's hair; that he, Smith, and Elfride, with their fated triangular relationship, should first come together, all three, in a tomb which has been fairly lavishly equipped with resonances from *Romeo and Juliet* and *Hamlet*: such *tableaux*, detached from their context, appear melodramatic enough. But much of Hardy's art is to consist in extracting a kind of poetry out of such goings-on. They heighten the strangeness (or at least the perfectly real oddity) of life without falsifying anything more prizeable than its prosaic probabilities.

But we are in contact with something different when we come to reckon with Elfride's sustained bad luck throughout the story. Indeed, this conducts us, as we have seen, straight to a central problem in Hardy. For a kind of loving ingenuity is lavished upon her reduplicated and cumulative small disasters. Disconcerting effects of comedy, moreover, are sometimes extracted from them.

Elfride is unlucky in her father, for a start—both in a general way on account of his blindness and snobbishness, and in the specific circumstance that each of them is contemplating a clandestine marriage simultaneously: if Mr Swancourt had not been preoccupied with intercepting the postman on his own account, he might have become aware that his daughter was doing so on hers.

She is unlucky in Smith. 'A youth in appearance and barely a man in years' and 'a very blooming boy' whose 'mouth was a triumph of its class', he possesses an emotional spontaneity deceptively suggestive of an effective lover; whereas in the end we shall be inclined to judge him a little too like William Worm, a leading member of the novel's rustic chorus, who so regularly announces himself 'a poor wambling man'. Smith's hero-worship of Knight (his face is 'glowing with his fervour' when he speaks of his mentor as the noblest man in the world) is an index of his immaturity, if also of something attractively generous in him as well. A small hitch about a marriage licence defeats him. 'The journey from Plymouth to Paddington,' we are told, 'by even the most headlong express, allows quite enough leisure for passion of any sort to cool.' Whatever we may think of this as a sombre generalization, it certainly fits Smith—for Elfride falters, and home he brings her. Such intensity as her love for him had achieved had been, after all, chiefly the consequence of 'a fanning from her father's opposition'. And now Smith's is really a lost cause. 'That last experience with Stephen had done anything but make him shine in her eyes. His very kindness in letting her return was his offence.' And Elfride begins 'to sigh for somebody further on in manhood. Stephen was hardly enough of a man.'

She is unlucky in Knight. One of the earliest things she learns from the enthusiastic Smith about his patron is that he has described as 'an excellent fault in woman' an inability to 'kiss nicely'. Knight appears to brood obsessively upon 'the art of tendering the lips for these amatory salutes'. 'The sweetheart,' he says, 'who is graceful under the initial kiss must be supposed to have had some practice in the trade.' Knight finds it hard to bear the thought that any sweetheart of his should have granted 'privileges', meaning kisses, to anybody else. He himself has never kissed anybody except his mother, and 'the older I have grown,' he tells Elfride, 'the more distinctly have I perceived that it was absolutely preventing me from liking any woman who was not as unpractised as I.' And he adds: 'I had a right to please my taste, and that was for untried lips.' There is nothing very morbid in the wish to be, as he says, 'the first comer in a woman's heart', or in having found that a girl's 'inexperienced state had a great charm'. But when he speaks to Elfride (to whom he is engaged) of all except 'untried lips' being 'second-hand', this vulgarity of utterance on the metropolitan reviewer and essayist's part highlights for us, at least, the pathological character of his chilly obsession. And it is not unnatural that it should unnerve Elfride and constrain her to an injudicious reticence. Nevertheless, she has been singularly unfortunate with two lovers. It seems a little excessive that she should have been equally unfortunate with an earlier one as well.

She has had a rustic admirer in 'Felix Jethway, a widow's only

son', and had thoughtlessly given some very slight encouragement to his advances. Jethway unluckily dies; and his widowed
mother, yet more unluckily, not merely concludes that Elfride's
heartlessness and levity have been responsible, but also goes more
or less off her head in the interest of becoming a kind of avenging
presence, perpetually bobbing up on Elfride in her most awkward
moments. By the time we are halfway through the novel we have
had quite enough of 'the bleak barren countenance of the widow
Jethway', who is inclined to say things like 'What I am, may she
be!' and are not displeased when the tower falls on her. But her
malignity is posthumously effective, since she has left behind her
a letter which finally alienates Knight from Elfride.

As with people, so with places and circumstances Elfride has
no luck. She and Smith are in the churchyard together when Felix
Jethway's existence first comes up between them. Here is how the
dialogue runs:

> 'Now, Elfride . . . had you really never any sweetheart at all?'
> 'None that was ever recognized by me as such.'
> 'But did nobody ever love you?'
> 'Yes—a man did once; very much, he said.'
> 'How long ago?'
> 'Oh, a long time.'
> 'How long, dearest?'
> 'A twelvemonth.'
> 'That's not *very* long' (rather disappointedly).
> 'I said long, not very long.'
> 'And did he want to marry you?'
> 'I believe he did. But I didn't see anything in him. He was not
> good enough, even if I had loved him.'
> 'May I ask what he was?'
> 'A farmer.'
> 'A farmer not good enough—how much better than my
> family!' Stephen murmured.
> 'Where is he now?' he continued to Elfride.
> '*Here.*'
> 'Here! what do you mean by that?'
> 'I mean that he is here.'
> 'Where here?'
> 'Under us. He is under this tomb. He is dead, and we are
> sitting on his grave.'
> 'Elfie,' said the young man, standing up and looking at the
> tomb, 'how odd and sad that revelation seems! It quite depresses
> me for the moment.'

And Jethway's tomb is to depress Knight too. In a subsequent scene it is he who is in the churchyard with Elfride. It is a cloudy night, but the tomb is suddenly brilliantly irradiated by a shaft of moonlight. Knight knows by this time that Elfride has had a sweetheart, who had once kissed her while sitting on a tombstone outside her father's church. He asks if *that* was the tomb, and she says it was. He presses her vehemently for the man's name, and speaks of the awkwardness of a possible future meeting with him.

'It cannot be,' she said.
'Why not?' he asked sharply.
Elfride was distressed to find him in so stern a mood, and she trembled. In a confusion of ideas, probably not intending a wilful prevarication, she answered hurriedly—
'If he's dead, how can you meet him?'
'Is he dead? Oh, that's different altogether!' said Knight, immensely relieved. 'But, let me see—what did you say about that tomb and him?'
'That's his tomb,' she continued faintly.
'What! was he who lies buried there the man who was your lover?' Knight asked in a distinct voice. . . . 'And I have been fancying you said—I am almost sure you did—that you were sitting *on* that tomb.'

Knight presses his questions remorselessly. How can a man sit upon his own tomb? This is an impossibility. But 'a lover in the tomb and a lover on it' if not impossible is wholly scandalous; and it is of according 'amatory salutes' to one while perched above the mortal remains of another that poor Elfride is thus indicted. Knight is later going to reflect gloomily (like some right-thinking person in Jane Austen) on Elfride's 'indifference to decorum'. This business of Jethway's tomb is certainly unfortunate evidence of behaviour which could be so described. It is clear that Hardy is not unconscious of its comic, indeed its farcical, overtones.

If Elfride is luckless in mortuary surroundings—her very most awkward moment is in the Luxellian family vault—she is no less unfortunate when she goes to the seaside. On an expedition with Smith early in the story, the two find a tempting alcove and seat on the brow of a cliff. There is a little mild kissing, and Elfride— although unaware of it until some time later—loses an ear-ring. She sends Smith back to look for it, but he has no success. Later, she happens to tell Knight that she had once carelessly lost an ear-ring. Later still, Knight gives her a pair; she puts them on;

and he kisses her. Then he proposes to kiss her again, and this is apparently regarded by Elfride as a little excessive:

> Elfride objected to a second, and flung away her face, the movement causing a slight disarrangement of hat and hair. Hardly thinking what she said in the trepidation of the moment, she exclaimed, clapping her hand to her ear—
> 'Ah, we must be careful! I lost the other ear-ring doing like this.'
> No sooner did she recognize the significant words than a troubled look passed across her face, and she shut her lips as if to keep them back.
> 'Doing like what?' said Knight, perplexed.
> 'Oh, sitting down out of doors,' she replied hastily.

Finally (rather as with Jethway's tomb) the scene associated with the first lover is revisited with the second. Knight and Elfride are in the little rocky recess above the cliff:

> Not a word had been uttered by either since sitting down, when Knight said musingly, looking still afar—
> 'I wonder if any lovers in past years ever sat here with arms locked, as we do now. Probably they have, for the place seems formed for a seat.'
> Her recollection of a well-known pair who had, and the much-talked-of loss which had ensued therefrom, and how the young man had been sent back to look for the missing article, led Elfride to glance down to her side, and behind her back. Many people who lose a trinket involuntarily give a momentary look for it in passing the spot ever so long afterwards. They do not often find it. Elfride, in turning her head, saw something shine weakly from a crevice in the rocky sedile. Only for a few minutes during the day did the sun light the alcove to its innermost rifts and slits, but these were the minutes now, and its level rays did Elfride the good or evil turn of revealing the lost ornament.

Knight becomes aware of Elfride's awareness, retrieves the ear-ring, puts two and two together, and begins one of his awkward catechisms—with his usual emphasis upon kisses. The whole episode seems redundant and inartistic. Yet if we seek the mainspring of the entire novel, what we do best to pause upon is the statement: 'but these were the minutes now'. It is as if we are to be prompted to feel that not only the sun, but also all the other stars in their courses, must be charged with some complicity in Elfride Swancourt's tragedy.

Elfride's final piece of bad luck is simply that she dies for no particular reason. Her affections have been wavering but not light; she has married a man of honour and position, younger than Knight, and we are told that he can express his devotion in ways that please her; moreover, step-children who are fond of her are under her protection. It is not extravagant to say that her death is the final grim joke in the book. Certainly the railway journey, during which Knight and Smith exemplify 'the selfishness of love and the cruelty of jealousy' even while unknowingly glimpsing every now and then the 'dark and curious-looking van . . . quite new, and of modern design' which contains Elfride's body, is a conclusion very much in the key of *comédie noire*.

Yet Hardy's purpose in exhibiting Elfride as so singularly hapless throughout her history is essentially serious, and is based on his conviction that each of us is inclined absurdly to over-estimate the likely degree of his control over his individual destiny—as Smith is doing when he says to Elfride, in planning their runaway marriage: 'All we want is to render it absolutely impossible for any future circumstance to upset our future inten-tion of being happy together'. So Hardy, once more, is 'changing the actual proportions of things' in order to drive home the naïvety of such assumptions. And at the close of the novel Elfride's fate is explained to Smith by the intellectual Knight in terms which Hardy clearly accepts as consonant with objective fact: 'Circum-stance has, as usual, overpowered her purposes—fragile and delicate as she—liable to be overthrown in a moment by the coarse elements of accident. I know that's it,—don't you?' But in fact, and in order 'to intensify the expression of things', Hardy has substituted for 'the coarse elements of accident' something very like a malign virtuosity—as in the matter, for example, of the sunlight and the ear-ring. When he can write of a character, as he can at one point of Smith, 'A strange concomitant of his misery was the singularity of its form', or of things in general, 'Strange conjunctions of circumstances, particularly those of a trivial every-day kind, are so frequent in an ordinary life, that we grow used to their unaccountableness, and forget the question whether the very long odds against such juxtaposition is not almost a disproof of it being a matter of chance at all', or merely, 'A strange concurrence of phenomena now confronts us', we are perhaps justified in feeling that he has a kind of stealthy design upon his readers. Nor are we wholly clear that it is by way of redressing a balance, as it were, and rendering us clear-eyed before a neutral and regardless uni-verse. When Knight's life is in peril on the Cliff without a Name—the most powerfully rendered single episode in the book—and we are told of 'Nature's treacherous attempt to put an end to him', Hardy, if questioned, would probably have asserted, as he did about that more famous place in *Tess of the d'Urbervilles*, that here is merely a trope of rhetoric, natural to a kindled imagination, whereby something inanimate is represented as 'a powerful being endowed with the baser human passions'. But whatever the intention in such places, the effect is to set stirring in our minds certain ways of taking experience remote from the world of nineteenth-century scientific determinism. Indeed, Knight himself, as he feels 'Death really stretching out his hand', is visited by just such thoughts:

> However, Knight still clung to the cliff.
> To those musing weather-beaten West-country folk who pass the greater part of their days and nights out of doors, Nature seems to have moods in other than a poetical sense: predilections for certain deeds at certain times, without any apparent law to govern or season to account for them. She is read as a person with a curious temper; as one who does not scatter kindnesses and cruelties alternately, impartially, and in order, but heartless severities or overwhelming generosities in lawless caprice. Man's case is always that of the prodigal's favourite or the miser's pensioner. In her unfriendly moments there seems a feline fun in her tricks, begotten by a foretaste of her pleasure in swallowing the victim.
> Such a way of thinking had been absurd to Knight, but he began to adopt it now.

Hardy is well aware that, under sufficient stress, the most 'modern' mind will fall back upon primitive interpretations of the cosmos. To Jude Fawley and Sue Bridehead in his last novel 'affliction makes opposing forces loom anthropomorphous'.

2

It is not, however, as adumbrating philosophical persuasions which are to be more fully developed later that *A Pair of Blue Eyes* is most interesting. Some readers, indeed, find little merit in it at all. Lascelles Abercrombie describes it as 'a well-ordered system of charming, pathetic, but unimportant occurrences'. Mr Edmund Blunden, although speaking of it as 'sketchily beautiful and daringly contrivanced', judges it 'probably lapsed into the registers of literary history'. Mr Irving Howe calls it 'singularly unimpressive', but adds 'in fairness' that it has been praised 'by such English literary men as Tennyson and Coventry Patmore'. Tennyson in fact preferred it to any other of Hardy's novels; and Patmore—who felt it to be more akin to poetry than prose—was in the habit of having it read aloud to him over a period of more than twenty years. If, as somebody has declared, *A Pair of Blue Eyes* is the most 'Victorian' of the novels, it has possibly dated since being so highly praised. Yet some readers, at least, find it perennially pleasing and moving, although not in a manner at all easy to define.

With the exception of the Cliff without a Name, which is vividly evoked alike in its most massive features and in the minute particulars of the fossil bodies embedded in it, the natural setting is not remarkable. There are a few of Hardy's familiar colour-notes ('dark-blue fragments of cloud upon an orange-yellow sky') and delicate evocations of sound (the snakes hissing 'like little engines', 'the crackle of a dead leaf which a worm was endeavouring to pull into the earth'). There are several of those sharply evoked nocturnal scenes—some in a harsh Caravaggesque chiaroscuro, others gently mysterious in their lighting, as if in the manner of La Tour or the Le Nains, at which Hardy is always to excel. The *genre* scenes of peasant gatherings are unequal. One, tediously elaborated, is redeemed in part by the appearance of Robert Lickpan, the pig-killer ('But 'a fatted well, and I never seed a pig open better when 'a was killed'). Another, in the Luxellian vault, is so Shakespearian as almost to be disconcerting:

'Ay, 'tis a thought to look at, too, that I can say "Hullo!" close to fiery Lord George, and 'a can't hear me.'

'And that I be eating my onion close to dainty Lady Jane's nose, and she can't smell me.'

'What do 'em put all their heads one way for?' inquired a young man.

'Because 'tis churchyard law, you simple. The law of the living is, that a man shall be upright and downright; and the law of the dead is, that a man shall be east and west. Every state of society have its laws.'

But it is none of these things that carries the novel far into the sympathies of at least a few readers. It is rather something in the balance of sympathy within the book itself.

Hardy's heroines, Abercrombie remarks, commonly prove decidedly disastrous to their lovers. This is true; indeed, a marked sexual pessimism is present in his novels from the start, and deepens throughout his career. It finds regular expression not merely in the actions he devises, but also in that sort of detached observation, aphoristic or moralising in tone, a generous measure of which was judged by most Victorian novelists to conduce to the dignity of their fiction. We have seen that *Desperate Remedies* already provides instances of this, for example:

> Perhaps, indeed, the only bliss in the course of love which can truly be called Eden-like is that which prevails immediately after doubt has ended and before reflection has set in—at the dawn of the emotion, when it is not recognized by name, and before the consideration of what this love is, has given birth to the consideration of what difficulties it tends to create.

In *A Pair of Blue Eyes* a certain misogyny begins to appear in such passages:

> Directly domineering ceases in the man, snubbing begins in the woman; the trite but no less unfortunate fact being that the gentler creature rarely has the capacity to appreciate fair treatment from her natural complement. . . .
> When women are secret they are secret indeed; and more often than not they only begin to be secret with the advent of a second lover.

Already in *Under the Greenwood Tree* Fancy Day's behaviour can be seen as affected by this sort of disenchantment in her creator. She is engaged to Dick Dewy and in love with him; her quick acceptance of Mr Maybold may be argued—as it is by Mr Albert J. Guerard—simply not credible. The entire little episode, indeed, is ephemeral and delicately handled; yet for a moment or two Fancy is constrained to exemplify a thesis about women. In *A Pair of Blue Eyes* Knight is to Smith a little as Maybold is to Dewy: the maturer man, and the man more impressively in possession of intellectual pretension and social position. And Elfride is a Fancy who definitively forsakes a first love for a second; from the moment that (in the tomb which is eventually to receive her) she dissimulates even her acquaintance with Smith in his supplanter's presence, she is behaving to Smith very badly indeed—and to Knight at least with a sad absence of candour. From this point on, Elfride appears booked for our severe disapprobation.

But it fails to work out that way. With Hardy we are in a masculine universe extremely susceptible to the attraction of women, and therefore extremely aware of their fatality. But he no more turns down his thumb on Elfride than Chaucer does on Criseyde.

Progressively through her charm and the ineptitude of her comical concealments we are afforded a view of her helplessness and pathos; and in the end it is upon Knight that certain sufficiently grim words are spoken. 'The moral rightness of this man's life was worthy of all praise.' Yet:

> It is a melancholy thought, that men who at first will not allow the verdict of perfection they pronounce upon their sweethearts or wives to be disturbed by God's own testimony to the contrary, will, once suspecting their purity, morally hang them upon evidence they would be ashamed to admit in judging a dog.

This is not altogether fair to Knight. Under considerable provocation, he has reasonably represented to Elfride that 'a secret of no importance at all may be made the basis of some fatal misunderstanding only because it is discovered, and not confessed'; and he has received only weak prevarication in reply. But if eventually he is seen as no better than Othello, and if both he and Smith on their final train-journey are reduced to slightly ludicrous figures sketched in the margin of a girl's heartbreak and death, these adjustments of vision or emphasis are greatly to the advantage of the art of the book. We are not required to feel that we have simply assisted at an arraignment of feminine inconstancy. Rather our sympathies have been called now here and now there, as must be so before any actual spectacle of intervolved human fates.

6

Far from the Madding Crowd

IN DECEMBER 1872, THREE MONTHS AFTER *A PAIR OF BLUE EYES* HAD begun to appear in *Tinsley's Magazine*, Leslie Stephen invited Hardy to provide a serial story for the *Cornhill*. He had been reading *Under the Greenwood Tree*; had found its 'descriptions admirable'; and was sure his subscribers would find equal satisfaction in similar work.

The standing of the *Cornhill*—of which Thackeray had been editor in the previous decade—made this a kind of promotion which Hardy was always quick to understand. He accepted the commission and took the hint; there was already in his mind, he declared, a 'pastoral' tale of which the title should be *Far from the Madding Crowd*. We may suppose that he saw the book as developing in setting and tone from *Under the Greenwood Tree*; as relying substantially upon a detailed and vivid evocation of typical rural occasions; and as exhibiting at the same time a variety of unusual and surprising incidents, and a lively interplay of at least the prescriptively permitted passions between characters broadly and vigorously drawn, such as were likely to give satisfaction in a magazine serial spreading over many months. The achieved novel compasses these modest aims admirably; and as its conclusion—which is the weakest part—is carefully accommodated to popular moral sentiment there is nothing surprising in its having been a great success.[1] But this acclaim, the *Life* records,

---

[1] Bathsheba Everdene, the vain and lively daughter of a bankrupt tailor in Casterbridge, comes to live in modest circumstances with an aunt at rural Norcombe. Her arrival is observed by Gabriel Oak, a young shepherd whose industry has lately enabled him to set up with a small flock of his own. She rejects his addresses and soon moves to Weatherbury, succeeding—in circumstances which are never made clear—a deceased uncle as tenant of a flourishing farm and owner of his stock. As she rises in the world, Oak sinks. Having lost his sheep through an accident, he sets out to seek employment, sees a rick on fire, takes the lead in saving it from destruction, finds that it is Bathsheba's, and accepts employment as her shepherd. It is an eventful night at Weatherbury Upper Farm: the bailiff, Pennyways, is found to be dishonest

produced 'quizzing personal gossip'; the novel was even rumoured
to be the work of a house-decorator; and this prompted Hardy to
put aside 'a woodland story he had thought of [which later took
shape in *The Woodlanders*] and make a plunge in a new and
untried direction'. The result was one of his least successful books,
The Hand of Ethelberta.

In a cordial notice in the *Spectator* following the appearance of
the first instalment of *Far from the Madding Crowd* there
occurred a turn of phrase which might be taken as suggesting that
the novel was the anonymous work of George Eliot. Hardy was to
profess himself perplexed by this, since it seemed to him that
George Eliot 'had never touched the life of the fields'. Her country-
people were 'more like small townsfolk than rustics . . . evidencing
a woman's wit cast in country dialogue rather than real country

and is dismissed; one of Bathsheba's servants, Fanny Robin, is reported as
having disappeared.

Bathsheba has a neighbour, William Boldwood of Little Weatherbury
Farm. His character is grave and reserved; alone of the men who frequent
Casterbridge Corn Exchange he appears uninterested in the young woman
who has so surprisingly appeared among them. Bathsheba in a fit of folly
sends him a valentine with the message 'Marry me', and this precipitates in
him a lasting and mounting passion to which in fact she has no impulse to
respond, and before which she can only temporize and equivocate. She is
rebuked by Oak, who is dismissed and then reinstated because his veterinary
skill is invaluable. Bathsheba encounters Sergeant Troy from a neighbouring
garrison: a fallen gentleman and libertine who carries her heart by storm.
He has in fact been the seducer of the missing Fanny Robin.

Boldwood is goaded to fury by his rival's success, and Bathsheba persuades
herself that she must visit Troy at Bath in order to prevent his returning to
Weatherbury with some dangerous consequence. Troy persuades her to
immediate marriage. He mocks and humiliates Boldwood, and neglects
Bathsheba's farm; at harvest-home he ignores a menacing storm and persuades the labourers to drink themselves into a stupor. Oak and Bathsheba
together save the stacks.

News comes to Weatherbury that Fanny Robin has died in the Union
workhouse at Casterbridge. Her coffin is brought to Bathsheba's farm to
await burial. Troy is absent. Alerted and alarmed, Bathsheba unscrews the
coffin, and discovers along with Fanny's body that of the child to whom
she had died giving birth. Troy enters the room. He declares Fanny to have
been his wife in the sight of heaven; brutally rejects Bathsheba; arranges for
the immediate erection of an elaborate tombstone; and soon afterwards
leaves the district. He goes swimming and gets into difficulty; in fact he is
rescued by a vessel standing nearby; but at Weatherbury it is believed that he
has been drowned.

Boldwood's infatuation continues and deepens, and eventually Bathsheba
gives him a doubtful promise of marriage in six years' time. Thus encouraged,
Boldwood holds a Christmas party. But Troy has returned to the district as a
circus performer, and at the circus he has seen Bathsheba once more. (The
disgraced bailiff Pennyways makes a reappearance in some subsidiary intrigue
at this point.) Troy turns up at the party and orders Bathsheba to leave with
him. Boldwood, in an agony, at first calls out to her to obey. But when
Troy grasps her roughly she screams, and at this Boldwood seizes a gun and
discharges it point-blank at Troy, who falls dead.

Boldwood is confined as insane, and Bathsheba eventually marries Oak.

humour, which he regarded as rather of the Shakespeare and
Fielding sort'. Whatever be the truth of these remarks, Hardy
was certainly justified in asserting the independent excellence of
his own creation. He was always to maintain that there did
veritably exist such a peasant humour as he endowed these characters with, and it is perhaps rash to call them 'literary' or to
assert that their voices come to us by way of Shakespeare's
Bankside rather than direct from Puddletown and Bockhampton.
'Nater requires her swearing at regular times, or she's not herself,'
the maltster says, 'and unholy exclamations is a necessity of life.'
'He liked to copy comforting verses from the tombstones,'
Joseph Poorgrass recalls of Bathsheba's father at the end of a
long discussion, '. . . and he would box the charity-boys' ears,
if they laughed in church, till they could hardly stand upright,
and do other deeds of piety natural to the saintly inclined.' 'A
stammering man,' Henry Fray reports of Andrew Randle, 'and
they turned him away because the only time he ever did speak
plain he said his soul was his own, and other such iniquities, to
the squire.' To assert that such speech can simply be invented, and
projected upon a class of persons who do not so speak at all, is
merely to minister to the vanity of authors.

It is characteristic of Hardy that, having undertaken to furnish
Stephen with a 'pastoral' tale, he should have refreshed himself,
before beginning to write, from the well-springs of the kind.
Jacob Smallbury's ballad is 'as inclusive and interminable as that
with which the worthy toper old Silenus amused on a similar
occasion the swains Chromis and Mnasylus, and other jolly dogs
of his day'. Gabriel Oak is a little like Spenser's Colin Clout:
English-made, but given the correct antique associations. When we
hear him calling his vanished sheep, it is as if we were present
'when the sailors invoked the lost Hylas on the Mysian shore'.
And among the other sounds we distinguish early on—the
different notes with which the grasses, the trees, the hedges respond
to the wind in their several situations; the sheep-bell which now
has more mellowness than clearness, 'owing to an increasing
growth of surrounding wool'—is that of Gabriel's flute. We have
had a comical description of his watch, which tolerably fixes him
within the stream of time. But with his flute he joins timeless
beings. It is an oaten stop, a rural reed, the very pipe of Pan.
'Oak could pipe with Arcadian sweetness.'

Moreover—as one of Hardy's earlier critics, Joseph Beach, has
pointed out—another 'pastoral' tradition colours the novel. It
comes from Holy Scripture, and its idiom is very different from
that of Poorgrass and his friends. Here is Boldwood:

Your dear love, Bathsheba, is such a vast thing beside your pity, that the loss of your pity as well as your love is no great addition to my sorrow, nor does the gain of your pity make it sensibly less. Oh sweet—how dearly you spoke to me behind the spearbed at the washing-pool, and in the barn at the shearing, and that dearest last time in the evening at your home! Where are your pleasant words all gone—your earnest hope to be able to love me? Where is your firm conviction that you would get to care for me very much?

This heightened but grave and measured language is recurrent in the novel. Yet Hardy is seldom long in command of a congruous style, and there are places in which deep or at least lively emotion generates only awkward locutions or unpersuasive rhetoric. When Bathsheba's temper rises we are told that her face 'coloured with the angry crimson of a Danby sunset'; on a later occasion we learn that 'the ducts to her eyes were painfully full' and hear her say: 'Yes! the independent and spirited Bathsheba is come to this!'

2

Hardy's art, in the substantial sense, is so plainly maturing and deepening in *Far from the Madding Crowd* that the obstinately primitive character of much of his craft stands out the more clearly. 'He said this to himself, and they all distinctly heard it', we read of Boldwood on one page—and on the very next it is Boldwood who is overhearing something in his turn. At times these simple devices for propelling the narrative forward are susceptible of interpretation which would appear to be alien to the writer's conscious intention. The novel opens upon a scene in which Bathsheba, perched on top of her possessions on a waggon, takes advantage of the waggoner's short absence to unpack a mirror and admire herself. She believes that she is unobserved, but Gabriel Oak is watching. In the next scene, a nocturnal one, Oak sees an unaccustomed light in a shed:

Oak stepped up behind, where, leaning down upon the roof and putting his eye close to a hole, he could see into the interior clearly.

The place contained two women and two cows. . . . One of the women was past middle age. Her companion was apparently young and graceful; he could form no decided opinion upon her looks, her position being almost beneath his eye, so that he saw her in a bird's-eye view, as Milton's Satan first saw Paradise.

Paradise here is, of course, Bathsheba once more. And Oak's next glimpse of her, a couple of pages on, is in similar circumstances. This time, he is peeping through a loophole in his own lambing-hut, watching Bathsheba's approach on horseback:

> The boughs spread horizontally at a height not greater than seven feet above the ground, which made it impossible to ride erect beneath them. The girl, who wore no riding-habit, looked around for a moment, as if to assure herself that all humanity was out of view, then dexterously dropped backwards flat upon the pony's back, her head over its tail, her feet against its shoulder, and her eyes to the sky. . . . Thus she passed under the level boughs. . . . She had no side-saddle, and it was very apparent that a firm seat upon the smooth leather beneath her was unattainable sideways. Springing to her accustomed perpendicular like a bowed sapling, and satisfying herself that nobody was in sight, she seated herself in the manner demanded by the saddle, though hardly expected of the woman, and trotted off in the direction of Tewnell Mill.

These passages are doing a great deal of work. The mirror and the saddle stand for two sides of Bathsheba's nature, and there is a further touch of homely definition in the intervening activity with the cows. Moreover, her first relationship to Oak is established when, in their immediately succeeding interview, she realizes that she has been observed:

> A perception caused him to withdraw his own eyes from hers as suddenly as if he had been caught in a theft. Recollection of the strange antics she had indulged in when passing through the trees, was succeeded in the girl by a nettled palpitation, and that by a hot face. It was a time to see a woman redden who was not given to reddening as a rule; not a point in the milkmaid but was of the deepest rose-colour. From the Maiden's Blush, through all varieties of the Provence down to the Crimson Tuscany, the countenance of Oak's acquaintance quickly graduated; whereupon he, in considerateness, turned his head away.

The point of this passage (with its characteristically odd dip into a rose-grower's catalogue) is at the beginning and end: 'A perception caused him to withdraw his own eyes . . . he, in considerateness, turned his head away'. Oak, like Diggory Venn in *The Return of the Native* after him, is very much a character who waits and watches. 'His special power . . . was static.' But we shall be going quite astray if, noting all the peeping, we suppose Hardy to be debiting these honourable characters with any touch of the *voyeur*. Oak's 'considerateness', indeed, fails to make him change his courses. 'He continued to watch through the hedge at her regular coming.' To find anything morbid in this is to import quite an alien world of ideas. What we ourselves are being invited to watch is nothing but the simple *mores* of the folk.

It has become a critical commonplace that much incident and feeling in Hardy can be paralleled in the traditional ballads. In one brought up as he had been, it would be strange if it were not so. Popular balladry and song had been around him in childhood, and he himself frequently points out the affinity explicitly:

> For his bride a soldier sought her,
>   And a winning tongue had he:
> On the banks of Allan Water
>   None was gay as she!

So Bathsheba sings at the shearing-supper. 'Subsequent events', Hardy tells us with the heavy authorial prolepsis in which he sometimes indulges, 'caused . . . the verses to be remembered for many months, and even years, by more than one of those who were gathered there.' It is fair enough. On the same night, at a touch from an invisible hand upon Bathsheba's dark lantern, Sergeant Troy springs into being before her, brilliant in his brass and scarlet. 'His sudden appearance was to darkness what the sound of a trumpet is to silence.' And at once the 'winning tongue' is at work.

3

But if the ballads influence Hardy's art here, so do stage melodrama, the derivatives of that melodrama in popular prose romance, and—more significantly—that melodrama's great hinterland in the theatre of the Elizabethan age. The scene—again it is nocturnal —in which Boldwood is tricked and tricked again by Troy is a striking example. Troy has returned to Weatherbury after his absence in Bath. Boldwood, frantic to keep him from Bathsheba, offers him fifty pounds down, with five hundred more to follow, if he will agree to marry Fanny Robin. Troy assents and takes the money, but when Bathsheba joins them for a few moments he at once speaks to her in a way that makes it clear he is going to spend the night with her—and this she seems to take for granted. Boldwood, horrified at what he supposes to be her fall, now implores Troy to marry her, hands over what cash he has left, and promises that the five hundred pounds shall be for Bathsheba and not Fanny. Troy, who has casually agreed to this change of matrimonial plan, then produces a newspaper which shows that he has married Bathsheba already, tosses Boldwood's money contemptuously at his feet, and goes off laughing.

It is like some savage gulling scene in an Elizabethan drama, and it is arrived at by what critics of that drama have called the technique of episodic intensification. The writer has spotted the possibility of a scene or episode strikingly effective in itself, and has brought it within the scope of his action at the expense of some passing distortion of character, or at least of accenting certain traits to the subordinating of others. Boldwood, despite what is said from time to time of his lurking insanity, is the one figure in the book who rises towards tragic stature. This grotesquely conceived scene is out of key with anything of the sort. And Bathsheba's part, too, will be found to creak in the interest of what is essentially a stage deception.

Elsewhere in the framework of the story there is a good deal that is threadbare enough. An example is the chapter, inserted as an afterthought and seemingly with an eye to Mrs Grundy, in which Troy actually gets himself into church to marry Fanny— and Fanny goes to the wrong church: this suffers, as we read, from our memories, whether detailed or merely vague, of too many similar places in Hardy. The same consideration holds of the 'presumed dead' theme as it applies to Bathsheba's husband, with its perfunctory 'Unfortunately for Troy a current unknown to him existed outside'; to the whole business of Troy, disguised and necessarily dumb (but 'a young man whom we instantly recognize'), enacting the part of Dick Turpin before a Bathsheba somewhat improbably brought to see the circus; to the subsequent intrigue with 'the knavish bailiff Pennyways, his wife's sworn enemy'; to the long-drawn-out, if powerful, pathos of Fanny's dying crawl into Casterbridge; to the routine working-up of suspense over Boldwood's final fate.

There are other places in which we find ourselves doubtfully suspended between the crudity and the strength of the imagination at work for us. This holds of some of the more violent projections upon external nature of one or another mood, commonly a dismal one:

> The general aspect of the swamp was malignant. From its moist and poisonous coat seemed to be exhaled the essences of evil things in the earth, and in the waters under the earth. The

fungi grew in all manner of positions from rotting leaves and tree stumps, some exhibiting to her listless gaze their clammy tops, others their oozing gills. Some were marked with great splotches, red as arterial blood. . . . The hollow seemed a nursery of pestilences small and great.

Effective though this is, and as many similar places are, we yet grow tired of a face of nature across which appropriate expressions pass thus pat. There is too aggressive a design upon us. And something of the same sort applies to the schematic rigidity of sub-structure which is frequently apparent beneath the Gothic exuberance and extremity of the narrative. When Lascelles Abercrombie tells us of the fabric of the major novels that 'its finely fitted joinery may well have been suggested by Hardy's loving study of Sophocles', he is at least putting upon one of their prominent features a construction which would have been highly approved at Max Gate. In this novel, as in *The Return of the Native* and *The Woodlanders*, 'the groups as they first definitely arrange themselves' can, according to Abercrombie, be algebraically expressed. This, too, Hardy might well have approved, for he likes establishing symmetries and antitheses as much as any writer of exemplary tales. Sometimes, as if he feels that we are not being sufficiently attentive to this grace of art, he presents us with an instance in brisk summary:

And Troy's deformities lay deep down from a woman's vision, while his embellishments were upon the very surface; thus contrasting with homely Oak, whose defects were patent to the blindest, and whose virtues were as metals in a mine.

This may be called the technique of the nudge, and it is pervasive in the novels. What it too often suggests is that the writer is working from a blue-print.

4

Other strictures might be directed against *Far from the Madding Crowd*, but they would only further document the fact that Hardy is an uneven writer. And to balance them there are at least merits sufficiently numerous to make it difficult to know where to begin. We may say first that it is a very good serial story, which is what it was designed to be. That George Eliot is 'not a born story-teller by any means' is an opinion that Hardy could at least offer without

impertinence. For he is. Indeed, it is one of the strangest facts
about this major English poet who got involved in the main
entertainment business of his time that he excels even Dickens,
the greatest of the English novelists, as a master of the long
popular story. Nobody else except in isolated achievements
—Charlotte Brontë, say, in *Jane Eyre*—comes anywhere near
him.

Yet when we come, fresh from reading *Far from the Madding
Crowd*, to ask why this should be so, our first critical impulse
may be to say that it ought not to be so. The novel—as we now
rapidly turn over its pages, recalling this and that—reveals itself
as indeed uneven to a disturbing extent, and its most evident
virtues are of the sort that bob up here and there. Joseph Conrad
in a famous place declared his wish to make us *see*; and it is
something in which he succeeds, yet not as Hardy does. Hardy's
love of the plastic arts makes itself felt again and again in his
writing, and in ways that sometimes amuse us, as when Bathsheba's
blush becomes, as we have seen, a Danby sunset, or when the
coat of one of Oak's dogs can be determined only by reference to
the unstable chemistry known to disturb Turner's pigments. But
Hardy's painter's eye is a real painter's eye—far beyond, for
example, the painter's eye so agreeably cultivated by Henry James.
The heavy water-drops upon some creeping plants have 'upon
objects behind them the effect of minute lenses of high magnifying
power'. Elsewhere 'the rusty-red leaves of the beeches' are 'hung
with similar drops, like diamonds on auburn hair'. Visual similes
like this last can turn strange and even bizarre without losing
their authenticity. Oak, with the disaster to his flock before him,
sees that 'the pool glittered like a dead man's eye'. Or the bizarre
is authenticated by the minutely observed. Of the sheep-washing
pool it is said, in a manner prelusive of the aerial photography of
The Dynasts, that 'to birds on the wing its glassy surface, reflecting
the light sky, must have been visible for miles around as a glistening Cyclops' eye in a green face'. But a moment later we are simply
looking at Boldwood's boots, 'which the yellow pollen from the
buttercups had bronzed in artistic gradations'.

There is something not fully accountable in this power of
Hardy's to make us see—and feel as we do so. Why, for example,
is that 'stately progress through the stars' evoked in Chapter II
so unforgettable? 'The sensation may be caused by the panoramic
glide of the stars past earthly objects. . . . The poetry of motion
is a phrase much in use. . . . After such a nocturnal reconnoitre
it is hard to get back to earth.' The language seems inadequate
to what it is about. But of the vividness of our impression there

can be no doubt at all. This by itself places the opening of *Far from the Madding Crowd* as a true Hardy opening: of its kind, superb.

Yet such effects seem to have little directly to do with actual story-telling—except indeed that they do plant us, again and again, with absolute fidelity before the enacted scene. Consider the following passage from the climactic Chapter XLVI, '*The Gurgoyle: its Doings*':

> He remembered his position, arose, shivered, took the spade, and again went out.
> The rain had quite ceased, and the sun was shining through the green, brown, and yellow leaves, now sparkling and varnished by the raindrops to the brightness of similar effects in the landscapes of Ruysdael and Hobbema, and full of all those infinite beauties that arise from the union of water and colour with high lights. The air was rendered so transparent by the heavy fall of rain that the autumn hues of the middle distance were as rich as those near at hand, and the remote fields intersected by the angle of the tower appeared in the same plane as the tower itself.
> He entered the gravel path which would take him behind the tower.

There is no reason to suppose that Troy owns a painter's eye, or would at this moment be under any prompting to exercise it, if he did. But it is offered to us in the concluding observation on the tower with a precision which serves to spread the sense of closely observed fact over the extravagant 'doings' which are the subject of this strange chapter. And it is so with all the crucial places— the major 'enactments', as Hardy would say—in the story. We are *there* because our eye is there.

Sometimes (as with the Cyclops' eye) the evoked image involves an 'image' in the technical sense. Thus in the first of these key scenes, that of the disaster to Oak's flock, the dog responsible for the senseless slaughter of an innocent population is seen 'standing against the sky—dark and motionless as Napoleon at St Helena'. In the second, when Oak is approaching Bathsheba's burning rick, there is straight description:

> The blaze, enlarging in a double ratio by his approach and its own increase, showed him as he drew nearer the outlines of ricks beside it, lighted up to great distinctness. A rick-yard was the source of the fire.

So far, we are seeing *with* Oak. Then:

> His weary face now began to be painted over with a rich orange
> glow, and the whole front of his smock-frock and gaiters was
> covered with a dancing shadow pattern of thorn-twigs—the
> light reaching him through a leafless intervening hedge—and the
> metallic curve of his sheep-crook shone silver-bright in the same
> abounding rays.

The effect is again, in a sense, superior to the language in which
it is conveyed, and the change of focus is perhaps the chief reason
for this.

There is another big stack-yard scene in the novel: that in which
Oak fights the storm. It is a point of considerable curiosity that
Hardy lifted a good deal of this from Ainsworth's *Rookwood*, a
romance to which he had been attached as a boy. What is not in
Ainsworth—and it is another and related power in Hardy—is the
bringing of tactile and auditory feeling into close association with
the visual. In the darkness Oak kicks something 'which felt and
sounded soft, leathery, and distended, like a boxing-glove'. It is a
toad, 'humbly travelling across the path'. A hot breeze fans him
from the south, 'while directly opposite in the north rose a grim
misshapen body of cloud, in the very teeth of the wind. So unnaturally did it rise that one could fancy it to be lifted by machinery
from below.' As the storm gathers the darkness becomes intense.
'Gabriel worked entirely by feeling with his hands.' There is a
shift to something bordering on symbolic statement in this last
sentence.

There are three scenes—one with a sequel—more compelling
than any of these. They all centre on Bathsheba and Troy, and
suggest the extent to which these characters constitute the central
focus of the book. (There is some evidence that Oak was at least in
Hardy's mind from the beginning, but that Boldwood was an
afterthought.) The first is the encounter by the light of Bathsheba's
lantern, when Bathsheba's dress catches in Troy's spur. Troy deftly
makes the tangle worse, and she wonders whether by 'a bold and
desperate rush she could free herself at the risk of leaving her
skirt bodily behind her' (as Grace Melbury in *The Woodlanders* is
in fact to do when she escapes from a man-trap). We are here at
length definitely in the presence of one of Hardy's basic endowments as story-teller, and it is one in close alliance with the
visualizing power we have been considering. It may be called a
command of the symbolic *tableau vivant*, in which the characters
act out in brief an episode which catches and reflects their larger

destiny. The second scene of this order is the most famous in the book.

This is the episode in which, in a 'hollow amid the ferns', Troy begins to show Bathsheba the various cuts and thrusts of sword-exercise, and goes on to direct these upon her person. It is a highly sexual affair, and of quite startling imaginative resonance. Like other things of the kind in Hardy, it trembles on the verge of the absurd:

> Never since the broadsword became the national weapon had there been more dexterity shown in its management than by the hands of Sergeant Troy. . . . It may safely be asserted with respect to the closeness of his cuts, that had it been possible for the edge of the sword to leave in the air a permanent substance wherever it flew past, the space left untouched would have been almost a mould of Bathsheba's figure.

'That outer loose lock of hair wants tidying,' he says, and in a moment a lock drops to the ground. Finally he sees a caterpillar on her bosom, and thrusts with such precision that he splits it on the point of his weapon. His skill, in fact, is overdone, and so perhaps is Bathsheba's intrepidity. ('Stand your ground, and be cut to pieces', is her advice to her maid Liddy long afterwards, apropos of marriage.) But again, for a start, the scene is inescapably before us, and never more so than when we are seeing it—sheerly as an ocular experience—from Bathsheba's point of view. The clumsy prose of the 'Never since the broadsword' passage has this before it:

> 'Is the sword very sharp?'
> 'Oh no—only stand as still as a statue. Now!'
> In an instant the atmosphere was transformed to Bathsheba's eyes. Beams of light caught from the low sun's rays, above, around, in front of her, well-nigh shut out earth and heaven— all emitted in the marvellous evolutions of Troy's reflecting blade, which seemed everywhere at once, and yet nowhere specially. These circling gleams were accompanied by a keen rush that was almost a whistling—also springing from all sides of her at once. In short, she was enclosed in a firmament of light, and of sharp hisses, resembling a sky-full of meteors close at hand.

And after it there is this:

> Behind the luminous stream of this *aurora militaris*, she could see the hue of Troy's sword arm, spread in a scarlet haze over

the space covered by its motions, like a twanged harpstring, and behind all Troy himself.

We are not here called upon to think of those old stand-bys of Hardy's, Ruysdael and Hobbema, or even of the Impressionists of whom he was soon to be aware. We may find ourselves thinking instead of Duchamp's *Nude descending a Staircase*, or of Balla's *Dog on a Leash* and the Futurist assertion that 'motion and light destroy the materiality of bodies'.

5

The crisis of the action, after which the momentum of the novel has to be regained and maintained by increasingly mechanical expedients, comes in the set scene before Fanny Robin's open coffin, and in its equally macabre pendant in the churchyard. Hardy must be said to have had a hazardously keen relish of such occasions, and to be apt to assume with satisfaction the role of a First Grave-digger who piles it on a bit thick. But at least there is again much that is visually compelling:

> He, still holding her, came up the room, and thus, hand in hand, Troy and Bathsheba approached the coffin's side.
>
> The candle was standing on a bureau close by them, and the light slanted down, distinctly enkindling the cold features of both mother and babe. Troy looked in, dropped his wife's hand, knowledge of it all came over him in a lurid sheen, and he stood still.

As in a great La Tour, the candle-light is present at once as a physical illuminant and as expressing a fact of mind. And visually this whole scene is subdued, or at least set in a kind of Caravaggesque chiaroscuro. It is preluded by a scene in which Bathsheba, from the darkness outside Oak's cottage, sees him through a lighted window saying his prayers before he goes to bed. Later, having discovered the truth, she is conscious of hating the dead woman:

> Bathsheba became at this moment so terrified at her own state of mind that she looked around for some sort of refuge from herself. The vision of Oak kneeling down that night recurred to her, and with the imitative instinct which animates women she seized upon the idea, resolved to kneel, and, if possible, pray. Gabriel had prayed; so would she.

Presently Troy kneels as well, 'with an indefinable union of remorse and reverence upon his face'. But it is not to pray. He kisses the dead woman, and so elicits Bathsheba's climactic, '*Frank, kiss me too!*' But Troy addresses the dead woman as his wife:

At these words there arose from Bathsheba's lips a long, low cry of measureless despair and indignation, such a wail of anguish as had never before been heard within those old-inhabited walls. It was the τετέλεσται of her union with Troy.

We may feel that the elevation has been achieved on melodramatic stilts, but the associations of the Greek word tell us again by what standard Hardy is thinking to measure himself. That he has indeed achieved something of pure tragic intensity is best realized when we go on to the contrasting impression made by the final one among these major tableaux. With the doings in the churchyard—first Troy's and then the gurgoyle's—there is a return to highly graphic portrayal. But we have a sense that Troy's inner travail is no longer being successfully followed through. The 'horrible stone entity' whose vomit desecrates Fanny's grave really commands more of Hardy's eye than does Troy down below—and when that eye does shift it is to travel, as it were, farther aloft. Troy sees a 'pitiless anathema' written in the 'spoliated effort of his new-born solicitousness'. And we are told:

To turn about would have been hard enough under the greatest providential encouragement; but to find that Providence, far from helping him into a new course, or showing any wish that he might adopt one, actually jeered his first trembling and critical attempt in that kind, was more than nature could bear.

This is almost the only place in the novel in which Hardy explicitly shakes his fist at his creator, or can at least be felt as rather hoping a character may be prompted to do so. The tragic action which has chiefly moved him is now over, and he is facing the long slog of another hundred pages before he can ring down the curtain. It is possible to sense the influence of fatigue in this ritual imprecation.

Several of what are supposed to be qualities pervasive in Hardy are scarcely present at all in *Far from the Madding Crowd*. As Morrell insists, there is far more emphasis upon the possibility of responsible human action, and the misfortune attending its neglect, than there is upon the mocking fatality passingly represented in the gurgoyle or again in the fleeting reference to Troy as 'the impersonator of Heaven's persistent irony' towards Boldwood. Any expression of agnosticism is concentrated in one superbly effective place, the description of the great barn which 'on groundplan resembled a church with transepts':

> One could say about this barn, what could hardly be said of either the church or the castle, akin to it in age and style, that the purpose which had dictated its original erection was the same with that to which it was still applied. Unlike and superior to either of those two typical remnants of mediaevalism, the old barn embodied practices which had suffered no mutilation at the hands of time. . . . The fact that four centuries had neither proved it to be founded on a mistake, inspired any hatred of its purpose, nor given rise to any reaction that had battered it down, invested this simple grey effort of old minds with a repose, if not a grandeur, which a too curious reflection was apt to disturb in its ecclesiastical and military compeers. For once mediaevalism and modernism had a common stand-point. The lanceolate windows, the time-eaten arch-stones and chamfers, the orientation of the axis, the misty chestnut work of the rafters, referred to no exploded fortifying art or out-worn religious creed. The defence and salvation of the body by daily bread is still a study, a religion, and a desire.

At the end of the chapter in which this comes, Joseph Poorgrass has his own way of saying much the same thing. 'Yes; victuals and drink is a cheerful thing, and gives nerves to the nerveless, if the form of words may be used. 'Tis the gospel of the body, without which we perish, so to speak it.'

Another theme which we have seen represented as compulsive with Hardy, that of the destructive percolation of urban standards into rural life, cannot be established as present in *Far from the Madding Crowd* except in the most fugitive manner. Thus when Brown sees as 'the pivotal tragedy of the tale' the fact that Bathsheba 'chooses the invading lover, and with him flies from the country' to the city (or, as the wondering Cainy Ball calls it, the kingdom) of Bath, he is producing a significance which we can scarcely feel to have been in Hardy's head. Nor does the rapid worsening of the agricultural economy which marked the seventies really seem to cast a shadow over the book. Guerard declares that in *Far from the Madding Crowd* as compared with *Under the Greenwood Tree* 'the laborer is already less secure', and adds that 'the hiring-fair is a sinister annual event'. But the latter statement, at least, is not remotely supported by the text, where the passage in question opens upon 'two to three hundred blithe and hearty labourers waiting upon Chance—all men of the stamp to whom labour suggests nothing worse than a wrestle with gravitation, and pleasure nothing better than a renunciation of the same'. It was not until ten years later that Hardy, in his essay 'The Dorsetshire Labourer', records that 'to see the Dorset labourer at his worst and saddest time, he should be viewed when attending a wet hiring-fair at Candlemas'. But he was already concerned about that popular picture of 'Hodge' at which he tilts in his essay. When he heard that the serial publication of the novel in *Cornhill* was to be illustrated, he expressed 'a hope that the rustics, although *quaint*, may be made to appear intelligent, and not boorish at all'.

6

If Hardy does shake a slightly obsessed fist in *Far from the Madding Crowd* it is neither at Crass Casualty nor at the decay of the times but at Woman. There is a certain biographical curiosity about this. 'The fact was,' he records of himself in the *Life*, 'that at this date he was bent on carrying out later in the year an intention beside which a high repute as an artistic novelist loomed even less importantly than in ordinary. . . . Back again in Dorsetshire he continued his application to the story, and by July had written it all, the last few chapters having been done at a gallop, for a reason to be told directly.' The 'reason' was of course his marriage. It cannot be said that his sexual pessimism and inclination to misogyny are mitigated by this approaching event; indeed, the disillusion and animus distinguishable in *Desperate Remedies*, *A Pair of Blue Eyes*, and even *Under the Greenwood Tree* seem, if anything, to be sharpening:

> It appears that ordinary men take wives because possession is not possible without marriage, and that ordinary women accept husbands because marriage is not possible without possession; with totally differing aims the method is the same on both sides.

This, it is true, slaps out at either sex indifferently, but most of these acrid aphorisms have only one quarry:

> The facility with which even the most timid women sometimes acquire a relish for the dreadful when that is amalgamated with a little triumph, is marvellous.

Women are never tired of bewailing man's fickleness in love, but they only seem to snub his constancy.

These and similar generalizations all take their origin in some specific aspect of Bathsheba's behaviour. In the matter of the valentine her 'insensibility to the possibly great issues of little beginnings' brings her within a judgement of women which Hardy expresses more than once elsewhere. Or again:

Bathsheba, though she had too much understanding to be entirely governed by her womanliness, had too much womanliness to use her understanding to the best advantage. Perhaps in no minor point does woman astonish her helpmate more than in the strange power she possesses of believing cajoleries that she knows to be false—except, indeed, in that of being utterly sceptical on strictures that she knows to be true.

And near the end of the chronicle Boldwood asks Oak, 'Does a woman keep her promise, Gabriel?' and gets the answer, 'If it is not inconvenient to her she may'. It is with 'faint bitterness' that Oak speaks at this point. We certainly end by feeling that this bitterness haunts Oak's creator too. Yet we can seldom, if ever, say that Hardy is talking gloomy nonsense in this sphere, or that the colouring from his temperament impairs the sensitiveness with which, within certain limits of psychological perception, Bathsheba is observed. We become aware that it is less the original foolish freak of the immature girl than the ineradicable indecisiveness of the maturing woman that destroys Boldwood. The exhibition of this is made integral with her acts. But it is an exhibition which, for the purposes of a developed fiction, is at least not much assisted by the element of generalized reflection to which the action prompts the writer. In this regard Hardy's art does not yet compare favourably with that of his greatest predecessor, George Eliot.

7

The Return of the Native

THE RETURN OF THE NATIVE WAS BEGUN IN 1876, SHORTLY AFTER
Hardy's thirty-sixth birthday. It is the first of his novels with a
claim to stand among the major works of English fiction, and it is
consequently the first before which we are likely to be made fully
aware of certain problems posed for him by the literary conventions and assumptions of the age.[1]

A case can be advanced, indeed, for his having faced no
significant problem at all, since as a novelist he was without any
sustained seriousness of intention. Critics who take this view and

[1] Eustacia Vye, a nineteen-year-old girl of romantic inclination living with
a neglectful grandfather on lonely Egdon Heath, has engaged in a clandestine
love-affair with Damon Wildeve, a young man of indifferent morals who has
abandoned an unsuccessful career as an engineer and is keeping an inn.
But Wildeve has transferred his affections, or at least his desires, to a simpler
girl, Thomasin, who lives with her aunt, Mrs Yeobright, and he has agreed to
marry her. There is an obscure hitch about the ceremony, and Thomasin
has to return home a virgin indeed, but embarrassed and humiliated. She is
chivalrously aided by Diggory Venn, the reddleman, who has taken to his
lowly occupation as a result of Thomasin's having formerly rejected him as a
suitor. The uncertain resulting situation is for a time exploited by Eustacia,
who although largely disenchanted with Wildeve is unwilling to relinquish
him to another woman.

Clym Yeobright, Mrs Yeobright's son, returns to his native heath from
Paris. There he has been making his way in the employment of a diamond-
merchant, but he has come to regard this as an unworthy manner of life
and is determined to remain on Egdon and promote a scheme for the educa-
tional advancement of its rural populace. When he falls in love with Eustacia
it is in the hope that she will assist and support him in this dedicated work. She
in turn is attracted by him essentially because of the glamour of his Parisian
background, and she comes to dream of herself as escaping from the heath, which
she hates, to a brilliant life as Clym's wife in the French capital. Being afraid that
Clym may be attracted by his cousin Thomasin, she does what she can to
promote the previously impeded marriage to Wildeve; when it takes place—
and by way of taunting Wildeve—she contrives to be present as a witness.

Mrs Yeobright disapproves of her son's lowering himself to become a
teacher, and still more of his growing infatuation with Eustacia. The result is a
complete breach between mother and son; Clym leaves home, takes a small
house some miles away, makes Eustacia his bride, and at once embarks upon
an absorbed course of study. Eustacia's marriage rekindles or intensifies
Wildeve's feeling for her; he treats his wife Thomasin unkindly; when Mrs
Yeobright sends gifts of money to Thomasin and Clym respectively, he

D

call Hardy 'cynical' may point not merely to the celebrated place in which he tells Leslie Stephen that he simply wishes to be accounted 'a good hand at a serial' and to the equally celebrated bowdlerising of *Tess of the d'Urbervilles*, but also to the curious note which, in 1912, he caused to be appended to page 473 of the definitive (Wessex) edition of *The Return of the Native* itself:

> The writer may state here that the original conception of the story did not design a marriage between Thomasin and Venn. He was to have retained his isolated and weird character to the last, and to have disappeared mysteriously from the heath, nobody knowing whither—Thomasin remaining a widow. But certain circumstances of serial publication led to a change of intent. Readers can therefore choose between the endings, and those with an austere artistic code can assume the more consistent conclusion to be the true one.

We need not have advanced upon the novel itself, nor have any information about Thomasin and Venn, to find a good deal of

intervenes with a malicious prank which an odd combination of circumstances makes the occasion of a yet more serious estrangement between Mrs Yeobright and her daughter-in-law. Venn has again been helpful, but this time has unwittingly made matters worse.

Clym continues to study, and Eustacia to dream of Paris. Clym's eyesight is impaired; his 'culture scheme' becomes impracticable; he adopts the calling of a furze-cutter, which is the humblest of Egdon rural employments. Eustacia, bitterly disillusioned, begins to see Wildeve again. One very hot day Clym comes home exhausted by his labour, lies down on the hearthrug, and goes to sleep. Wildeve arrives to visit Eustacia, and suddenly they become aware that Mrs Yeobright is at the door. She has come on a visit of reconciliation. Eustacia delays to admit her, and then supposes that Clym has awakened and done so. When Eustacia at length opens the door, Mrs Yeobright, who has seen her at a window and also knows that Clym is at home, has gone away. Mrs Yeobright dies of exhaustion and the bite of an adder on the heath, but not before she has told a small boy that she is a broken-hearted woman cast off by her son.

Eustacia conceals the truth of what has happened, but Clym eventually pieces it together. There is a scene of bitter recrimination, and Eustacia returns to her grandfather. A servant-lad who is devoted to her lights a bonfire to cheer her up, and this is taken by Wildeve to be a signal from her such as he had formerly been used to receive. He appears. She talks wildly of going to Paris, and does not know whether she is proposing to make use of Wildeve as a friend or close with him anew as a lover. Clym, upon his cousin Thomasin's insistence, has written a letter to Eustacia proposing forgiveness and reunion. But he is just too late; Eustacia has sent a signal to Wildeve and fled to join him on a stormy night. She falls into a pool below a weir; Wildeve jumps in to rescue her; despite the efforts of Clym and Venn, both are drowned.

In a final section of the novel, called 'Aftercourses' and not part of Hardy's original design, Clym recovers sufficiently from his tragedy to have some thought of marrying Thomasin. But Thomasin marries the faithful Diggory Venn, and Clym becomes 'an itinerant open-air preacher and lecturer on morally unimpeachable themes'.

oddity in this. The readers 'with an austere artistic code' are
scarcely being treated with much respect, since the writer has let
some thirty-four years go by without any attempt to produce 'the
more consistent conclusion' which might satisfy them, and is now
doing no more than grant them permission to ignore the novel's
existing ending if they please.

There can be no doubt that Hardy came to look back on his
own career in prose fiction with discomfort. But most of the
novelists of the age, and some of their publishers, were in one
degree or another uneasy about the concessions they felt constrained to make to the novel-reading public. Thackeray com-
plained about it, and so later did Henry James—although neither,
in fact, would have been precisely happy if suddenly bidden to
luxuriate in the exhibition of libidinous passion. Stephen, a
devotee of the robust fiction of the eighteenth century, made,
when editor of the *Cornhill*, an uncomfortable joke of the whole
thing. At the same time he was, as it were, quite resolutely timid.
He would have nothing to do with *The Return of the Native* as soon
as he sensed that it might admit adulterous or even merely extra-
marital relationships.

But the 'circumstances of serial publication' which persuaded
Hardy to conclude his novel as he did had nothing to do with
Victorian sexual tabus in the narrow sense. What he added
against his artistic conscience was simply the conventional concluding upon a satisfactory marriage. Publishers and editors, who
were concerned to make money for themselves, and if possible for
their authors as well, took it for granted that their customers
would identify as they read with the more virtuous characters in a
novel, and be displeased if they failed to find these rewarded in the
end. So Venn gains Thomasin, as Oak has gained Bathsheba.
From Hardy's point of view as serious artist—and it is silly to see
him as, basically, anything else—there was not really a great deal
to complain of here. His bent, indeed, was towards tragedy. But
there are a great many effective tragedies, whether written for the
theatre or as novels, which close upon calm after tempest, or
promise harmony and tranquillity for such of the characters as
remain alive to enjoy it.

Hardy, however, tended to equate tragedy with the plays of
Aeschylus and Sophocles; and the 'good hand at a serial' was in
fact seldom without consciousness as he worked of what he took
to be their canons. In *The Return of the Native* there are a number
of pointers to this, some of them comparatively superficial. By
confining the action to Egdon Heath he achieved, he said, a 'unity
of place . . . seldom preserved in novels', and he resolved to draw

attention to this by providing his readers with a map. He planned
for the book a curious unity of time: the action (in five parts) was
to occupy a year and a day. Throughout the novel, moreover, he
scattered various reminders of the Greek drama. Indeed, none of
his succeeding works of importance is to refrain from hinting the
shadowy presence of this formidable Attic yardstick. So here
Hardy really had a problem. It is not easy to become the Sophocles
of the magazine-serial and the circulating library.

And so too with the matter of sexual conduct. Hardy might well
feel himself progressively hemmed in as the scope of his art
enlarged itself here. In a panoramic novel of manners and society
such as *Vanity Fair* it was quite possible, by the exercise of some
discretion and ingenuity, to make an important phase of the action
turn upon marital infidelity. But in an action of Hardy's sort,
designed to transact itself upon the stage of the primary passions,
both technique and tact were abundantly required.

Already while working on *Far from the Madding Crowd* Hardy
had alarmed Stephen over Sergeant Troy's seduction of Fanny
Robin. The theme must be treated, Stephen insisted, in 'a gingerly
fashion'. Hardy was not particularly resourceful or versatile
before this sort of exigency. One obvious manœuvre was to have
the woman believe herself married before yielding herself. A
simple girl could be the victim of crude imposture (necessitating a
perhaps arbitrary darkening of the character of the man); the case
of an educated woman (like Lady Constantine in *Two on a Tower*)
was likely to require some more tortuous ingenuity on the author's
part. In *The Return of the Native* Hardy appears first to have
envisaged Thomasin as duped by a false marriage ceremony, and
as having lived with Wildeve for a week before discovering the
truth—which is approximately what happens to the heroine in the
serial version of *Tess of the d'Urbervilles*. In abandoning this
element in his plot in favour of a muddle over the marriage licence,
Hardy is virtually rehearsing Fanny Robin's muddle over churches,
as well as echoing Elfride Swancourt's misadventure with Stephen
Smith. Like most of the changes he can be shown to have made
during the writing of *The Return of the Native*, this—however
threadbare the actual resource—is in fact an improvement, if only
because it relieves Wildeve of a purely melodramatic villainy.[1] We
are made to feel that although Wildeve's subconscious mind may
have been at work in the circumstances rendering the wedding
abortive, he has nevertheless been the victim of a certain element of

---

[1] Hardy appears also to have considered the desperate expedient of a
marriage ceremony the invalidity of which neither Thomasin nor Wildeve
realized.

bad luck—not least in the censorious and alienating attitude which Thomasin's aunt, Mrs Yeobright, at once takes up; in this, indeed, and in the instant ruthlessness with which Eustacia Vye exploits her rapidly gained knowledge of what has happened.

But there was a more formidable difficulty of this sort confronting Hardy. What were the relations of Wildeve and Eustacia at the start of the action? Was Eustacia Wildeve's mistress, or had nothing but flirtation been going on? Most early readers of the novel would have been alienated by a heroine who had taken a lover—and particularly so by a heroine who had done this while an unmarried girl. But against this propriety had to be set an urgent imaginative propriety. If Eustacia's character were to exhibit anything of the largeness proposed for it, there could hardly be a worse start than to credit her with making a great to-do over having accorded Wildeve only the more innocent favours. Hardy's first response to this dilemma is precisely Thackeray's in *Vanity Fair*: we are left to work it out for ourselves. But in 1895 (the year of *Jude the Obscure*, when he was in an aggressive mood) he revised the text so as to leave no doubt that Wildeve and Eustacia had been lovers. Yet later, he bowdlerized this alteration, thus putting his public back where it had started. Most modern readers will agree with Beach, speaking out boldly in 1922: 'Already Eustacia has experienced the passion of love, yielding herself to the wooing of Mr Wildeve, the gentlemanly innkeeper, whom she has met in the lonely places of the heath beneath Rainbarrow'. But in 1968 *A Hardy Companion*, that most admirable of compendia, supposes that Hardy recognized that it had been an error 'to suggest illicit relations between Eustacia and Wildeve at the opening' since anything of the sort must 'weaken respect for a Promethean heroine'.

There was a further area, having little to do with sex, in which concession to popular taste might have seemed likely to conflict with the growing gravity of Hardy's art. A large fondness for surprising events and unusual situations, and in particular for serial stories keyed number by number to these, would appear to be an undesirable proclivity in a serious novelist's public. Paradoxically, however, the ready admissability of the melodramatic and bizarre in Victorian fiction was something all in Hardy's favour as a writer of the most potent sort. His imagination seldom remains for long enkindled when operating upon a level of sober realism. It is a poetic and symbolic imagination, and many of its triumphs are a consequence of the transmutation of the common grotesque into instruments for the expression of a kind of vision which would not by any other means have been readily compassable within the bounds of prose fiction in his age. Diggory Venn, whose marriage with Thomasin the note tells us Hardy did *not* 'design', is a case in point.

Venn, like Troy in *Far from the Madding Crowd*, is created for us by a single stroke of the visual imagination. The story opens upon Egdon Heath, 'embrowned' at twilight; and then, as darkness deepens, bonfires are lit one by one over the whole vast region: 'Some were large and near, glowing scarlet-red from the shade, like wounds in a black hide. Some were Maenades, with windy faces and blown hair.' What is ostensibly being celebrated is the happy deliverance of England from the Gunpowder Plot. But the commemoration is in fact immemorial, and when the rustics of Egdon dance round their blaze on Rainbarrow they are doing as their remotest ancestors did as the days shortened and the iron reign of the *Winterkönig* began. It is into this 'whirling of dark shapes amid a boiling confusion of sparks' that there steps 'a young man in tight raiment, and red from top to toe'. It is Diggory Venn the reddleman. We have already glimpsed him in his mundane character; now we are instantaneously aware of him as a kind of tutelary spirit of Egdon. And it is no doubt true that tutelary spirits ought not to be married off to hardly used widows of rural station. Venn does arguably get a raw deal when he eventually loses his 'isolated and weird character' in such a way. In other words, one of Hardy's percurrent problems was that of finding an accommodation between the picturesquely out-of-the-way (here Venn as 'a curious, interesting, and nearly perished link' with an obsolete rural economy) and the imaginatively resonant (here Venn as an emanation). The strangest and perhaps most memorable scene in the novel, the gambling-match by the light of glow-worms, often excepted against as wildly improbable, has—significantly enough—Diggory Venn at its centre. Yet when we have followed through the entire course of the action we must recognize that Venn's quasi-preternatural aspect is far from predominant. His main role is not very different from Gabriel Oak's, and his 'isolated and weird character' is essentially something that came to glimmer on the horizon of Hardy's imagination as he worked.

That this is true, indeed, of a good deal that now seems to us of greater depth and larger implication in the novel becomes apparent when we study the phases of its development. Mr John Paterson has shown that the record here begins not merely with the preserved manuscript of the whole from which the serial version was printed, but with an 'Ur-novel' or stage anterior to this, well-founded conjectures about which a close study of the existing manuscript makes possible. What may have been in the first place no more than attempts to assuage the anxieties of editors on the score of moral propriety would appear to have led Hardy into a basic, and fruitful, reorganization of his story after he had completed perhaps as many as sixteen chapters.

It seems probable that Hardy began by proposing to himself something having very much the compass of *Far from the Madding Crowd*, and even that the social range intended was to be much that found in *Under the Greenwood Tree*. Matter illustrating this last point turns out to have a possible significance greater than might be supposed. Briefly, Hardy found himself as he worked giving his principal characters something between a step and a half-step up the social ladder. Diggory Venn is elevated in this way; he becomes a man of substance, taking a kind of sentimental holiday from dairy-farming; and moreover he is relieved of a certain amount of rustic dialect. Even so, the later Venn addresses Captain Vye respectfully as 'Sir' where the earlier Venn addresses him as 'neighbour', and from this and other indications we may conclude that the Vyes were first conceived as simple Egdon folk, without the rather nebulous upper-class background later hinted for them. And so with the Yeobrights, declared (on the strength of Mrs Yeobright's being the daughter of a curate) to be the only other 'genteel' people on the heath. Mrs Yeobright too has been relieved of dialect, as has her son Clym. Paterson speaks of their promotion a shade extravagantly, perhaps, when he calls it 'elevation to a kind of local nobility'. But that Hardy made many changes with this sort of class-shift in mind is incontestable.

There seems nothing very remarkable in this. Hardy's intimate knowledge was of that stratum of rural society which was neither a labouring class on the one hand nor a gentry on the other; writing about it was what came most naturally to him; when his purposes as a novelist took him outside it, there was always likely to be something uncertain and experimental in his manner of making the move. Similar transpositions are to be found in D. H. Lawrence. But this does not quite end the matter. Indeed, according to the persuasive argument of Paterson, it is scarcely a beginning. For Hardy, we are told, was led 'to reverse the fundamental values of the novel' as he worked on it, and the changes of social status are only a function of this. Initially here, as wholly in *Far from the Madding Crowd*, his basic stance was anti-romantic. Passion, excess, egocentric concern lead us astray; reason, conscience, common sense, simple loyalties, domestic affections: it is these that we approve and hope to see triumph. In the interest of this it was his instinct to contrive fables, Paterson suggests, which 'grew out of the stock characters and situations that early and late captivated his essentially unsophisticated and traditional imagination'. In *The Return of the Native* as first conceived, Thomasin Yeobright was to be more important than she eventually became, and Eustacia Vye was to be altogether more sinister: a 'Satanic antagonist' whose essential 'diabolism' was to be conveyed in part by attaching to her those associations with witchcraft which still cling to her in the completed novel. But when Eustacia progressively captured Hardy's imagination as he worked, it was not on the strength of this 'demonism' or 'Byronism of her character'. He came, indeed, to see her as something totally different, 'a romantic protagonist' of tragic stature. And he came so to see her against the background of Greek tragedy. She becomes a Promethean heroine in the end. It is in pursuit of 'Sophoclean grandeur', according to Paterson, that Hardy made those changes that serve to elevate his principal characters above 'the rank and file of Egdon Heath'. Hardy, in other words, is accepting the old doctrine of decorum, which forbids us to expect or accept from clowns behaviour and sentiments not proper to their class. Paterson notes too that 'by a virtually systematic accumulation of classical allusions, he evoked the atmosphere or background of Greek tragedy'. He also worked over his text, substituting words of Latin derivation for Saxon—'for the purposes of archaic effect and . . . tragic elevation'.

We may perhaps doubt this last contention. To the end of his days Hardy was very much an autodidact, and he appears to have felt that, in a quite general way, a Latinate vocabulary toned up a literary style. And similarly, more often than not, with classical allusions. They are frequently inapposite and a mere showing off. Yet in this novel as in others, a hard core of these embellishments certainly has the kind of significance Paterson discerns. Hardy *did* want to challenge comparison with what are prescriptively regarded as the supreme heights of tragic expression achieved at Athens in the age of Pericles. And the theory of a changing conception of his fable and a heightening sense of its scope proves to be a plausible way of accounting for the inequalities and incongruities in the completed novel of which every critical reader must be aware.

Yet intensely interesting as Paterson's genetic study is, too much must not be founded on it. Eustacia Vye unchallengeably gains in stature as her destiny closes in upon her, and if we do not quite feel with Lord David Cecil that she assumes 'the impersonal majesty of a representative of all mankind' we are likely to agree with him that she 'stands for all passionate imprisoned spirits' in the end. Yet we cannot be certain that, here or elsewhere, Hardy's basic conception, and in particular the designed pitch and height of his argument, was much modified as he worked. It is rather, perhaps, that he fails to pursue any one predominant type of interest consistently. The famous evocation of Egdon Heath in the first chapter is not merely of 'a lonely face, suggesting tragical possibilities'. It is also of a region represented as likely to be profoundly congruous with some state of the human soul which is coming ineluctably into being under the impress of vast historical forces. Clym Yeobright loves the heath because he has caught a glimpse of this congruity; what one of the rustics calls his 'high doctrine' is a matter of having come to see clearly 'the grimness of the general human situation'; and this 'recently learnt emotion' is expatiated upon in the set examination of Clym's disposition which opens Book Third:

> In Clym Yeobright's face could be dimly seen the typical countenance of the future. . . . The truth seems to be that a long line of disillusive centuries has permanently displaced the Hellenic idea of life, or whatever it may be called. What the Greeks only suspected we know well; what their Aeschylus imagined our nursery children feel. That old-fashioned revelling in the general situation grows less and less possible as we uncover the defects of natural laws, and see the quandary that man is in by their operation.

This vision is to become habitual to Hardy. Little Father Time in *Jude the Obscure* is precisely one of these 'nursery children', and Clym is in a sense his progenitor. But such reality as Clym possesses for us is not a consequence of Hardy's successfully projecting upon him that pressure of speculative thought which is plainly at work upon Hardy himself. Clym's unlikely sojourn in Paris is contrived, we must feel, in order that he may be conceived of as having picked up an adequately modern *Weltanschauung* there, and this is to inform his natural 'wearing habit of meditation' when he returns home. His story has been compared with that of Lydgate in *Middlemarch*, as that of a man of advanced ideas and some sense of dedication to them, whose good intentions are thwarted in part by provincial prejudice and in part through marriage to a woman who totally fails to sympathize with or comprehend him. But in these relations Clym is far less adequately realized than Lydgate. For one thing, the resolve which he forms upon returning to Egdon is damagingly nebulous. He invites Eustacia to benefit their neighbours by joining him in 'high class teaching'; he will have a school in Budmouth and make visits to the heath in order to run evening classes; eventually, under pressure from his mother who sees even this proposal as both unrealistic and demeaning, he declares that he hopes ultimately to 'be at the head of one of the best schools in the country'. To these confused ends Clym embarks upon a course of study which again is nebulous and unparticularized, but which brings about that failure of eyesight his response to which finally precipitates the wreck of his marriage. Nothing in all this has much to do with Aeschylus.

Clym Yeobright is not up to his job—if by his job we may mean that of protagonist in a novel of advanced ideas. This appears nowhere more clearly than in his reaction to his cousin Thomasin's predicament. Here he follows his mother, whose attitude is one which a Victorian curate's daughter would no doubt share with a respectable peasantry.[1] 'Marry him you must after this', Mrs Yeobright says to the unfortunate girl when she has returned a maid a few hours after leaving home to become Wildeve's wife. When Clym begins to hear of the story his attitude is that 'it is too ridiculous that such a girl as Thomasin could so mortify us as to get jilted on the wedding-day', and he is disturbed on suspecting that 'there is a scandal of some sort'. Clym does, indeed, have misgivings about the marriage when it actually takes place. But his attitude to the whole affair is decidedly not that of a philosopher. It is a folk-attitude in all essentials.

Clym's reality for us depends, in fact, very much upon his relationship with his mother, and the whole novel is basically a tragedy of family relationships. We may reflect that it need not be the less Aeschylean on account of that. Indeed, Hardy's instinct for the stuff of tragedy does not betray him in *The Return of the Native*. Paterson's investigation makes a crucial point here. The central action of Book Fifth develops directly from Mrs Yeobright's belief that Clym has been implicated in her being turned away from his door, and from Clym's learning from Susan Nunsuch's boy that she had in consequence described herself as 'a broken-hearted woman and cast off by her son'. But the manuscript shows that Book Fourth was completed in its entirety before Hardy had envisaged this intensification of the fatal conflict between his three principal personages.

2

If Clym gains little from the attempt to represent him as a figure of high representative significance for his time, neither does Eustacia

---

[1] In considering the Yeobrights' attitude to Thomasin's predicament we must recall the more serious manner in which the girl was to have been compromised in the episode as first envisaged by Hardy.

from a corresponding inflationary pressure to which she is subjected. She is an idle girl of nineteen, by nature luxurious rather
than sensual (although she has advanced, we are told, 'to the
secret recesses of sensuousness'), and she possesses beauty such as
gives her a long start in playing the romantic heroine. Eventually
the role commands her, so that she can proclaim its faith with
entire sincerity:

> Do I desire unreasonably much in wanting what is called
> life—music, poetry, passion, war, and all the beating and pulsing
> that is going on in the great arteries of the world? That was the
> shape of my youthful dream; but I did not get it. Yet I thought I
> saw the way to it in my Clym.

So she can cry out to Wildeve when her husband—the failure of
his eyesight having offered 'a justification of homely courses to an
unambitious man'—has settled down as a furze-cutter who sings
French songs as he works. She has seen Clym, in fact, largely as an
instrument, and what, in less exalted moods, she looks forward to
that instrument's bringing her is really something less grand than
poetry and passion and war:

> She was hoping for the time when, as the mistress of some
> pretty establishment, however small, near a Parisian Boulevard,
> she would be passing her days on the skirts at least of the gay
> world, and catching stray wafts from those town pleasures she
> was so well fitted to enjoy.

Idleness and near-solitude have been enforced upon her, and she
is justified in her feeling that all that she has lacked has been an
object to live for. In this vacancy she has longed 'for the abstraction
called passionate love more than for any particular lover', and it
has been Damon Wildeve's luck, or fate, to be idealized 'for want
of a better object'. Quite early, she can be brutal with herself about
this. 'I should have cared nothing for him'—she says to Venn—
'had there been a better person near.'
   There is folly in her marriage too, no doubt. Clym's almost
mystical attachment to the heath she hates should have been clear
to her better reason from the first. Before she has so much as met
him, and in the course of one of those eavesdropping episodes to
which Hardy has so constant a primitive recourse, she has received
a hint of it, and it is implicit in his attitude throughout. The total
disparity of their minds is equally apparent. 'He's an enthusiast
about ideas', she is to tell Wildeve despairingly. It is a despair

which, ironically, aligns her with her opponent, Clym's mother. 'It was bitterly plain to Eustacia that he did not care much about social failure.'

But for the purposes of a balance of sympathy within the novel, Eustacia's folly is very adequately matched by Clym's. Even during his courtship he is not blind to his position:

> He could not but perceive at moments that she loved him rather as a visitant from a gay world to which she rightly belonged than as a man with a purpose opposed to that recent past of his which so interested her.

Clym's regardlessness here belongs, no doubt, to the common way of love. But he is also one of those prigs, or insensitive sensitives, whom Hardy can draw so well—a gentle, self-lacerating, obstinate, and extremely tiresome man.

The first person to see Eustacia as a Promethean figure—at least the first person apart from her creator—is her husband himself. It is as a daughter of the rebellious Titan that Clym somewhat intolerably lectures the wife his infatuation has landed him with:

> Yeobright placed his hand upon her arm, 'Now, don't you suppose, my inexperienced girl, that I cannot rebel, in high Promethean fashion,[1] against the gods and fate as well as you. I have felt more steam and smoke of that sort than you have ever heard of. But the more I see of life the more do I perceive that there is nothing particularly great in its greatest walks, and therefore nothing particularly small in mine of furze-cutting. If I feel that the greatest blessings vouchsafed to us are not very valuable, how can I feel it to be any great hardship when they are taken away? So I sing to pass the time. Have you indeed lost all tenderness for me, that you begrudge me a few cheerful moments?'

We are bound to feel that Eustacia is due a few cheerful moments too. And if we are puzzled it is because we are not quite sure what Hardy feels—or designs us to feel. What we can first get clear, perhaps, is an element in his presentation of Eustacia which is not very helpful in coming to a just appreciation of the quality of the novel. This is the attempt—balancing the attempt to create a Clym Yeobright of the highest representational significance for an

[1] The denizens of Egdon, we have been told, evince 'Promethean rebelliousness' with their bonfires at the onset of winter.

entire world-view—to give her inches, or a stature, which she has not, as it were, the hard bone to carry. When she is first half-revealed to us in the darkness on Rainbarrow it is 'as though side shadows from the features of Sappho and Mrs Siddons had converged upwards from the tomb to form an image like neither but suggesting both'. This is the note elaborated in the extravagant, queerly superb, and sufficiently notorious chapter called 'Queen of Night'. 'A true Tartarean dignity sat upon her brow.' The single quotation gives the tone, and one other is enough to establish its uncomfortable falsity: 'Viewed sideways, the closing-line of her lips formed, with almost geometric precision, the curve so well known in the arts of design as the cyma-recta, or ogee.... It was felt at once that that mouth did not come over from Sleswig with a band of Saxon pirates whose lips met like the two halves of a muffin.' This, mixed up with Bourbon roses, rubies, tropical midnights, the march in 'Athalie', and much else, achieves an absurdity such as would sink most heroines for good. Nothing of the sort happens with Eustacia Vye. She is only an ignorant and wayward girl who plays at high passion, sees her fantasies fade in the bleak air of Egdon, and is rescued from insignificance by a capacity for suffering.

3

Neither Mrs Yeobright nor Damon Wildeve, who are the other principal personages in the novel, is obliged to sustain any burden of extraneous significance. Of Wildeve, indeed, we learn that 'he might have been called the Rousseau of Egdon'—this as carrying 'the true mark of the man of sentiment'. But in the main he is presented in the concrete, and with a success remarkable in view of the handicap under which he starts. In the Ur-novel he was clearly the stereotype of the unscrupulous seducer. But his practice against Thomasin is watered down to an obscure muddle, about which the other characters can simply take a dark view if they please, and in the serial any reference to his specific amatory success with Eustacia has to be so vague that even the mention of a kiss was deleted from the text. As we have seen, it is not until an edition of 1895 that he is absolved (and that with a good deal of caution) from singular ineffectiveness as a lover. Even when the novel reaches its definitive form in 1912 the ghost of Mrs Grundy hovers over him during its catastrophe. In general, Hardy would seem from an early stage to seek to exhibit Wildeve in not too unsympathetic a light. Thus in the serial he is 'about thirty-five', which would perhaps carry the suggestion of a settled libertine. In

the revision for book-publication his age is omitted; he becomes
'quite a young man'; and the fact of this is drawn attention to
more than once. But traces of the earlier conception remain, as
when we are told that 'the grace of his movement' was 'the
pantomimic expression of a lady-killing career'.

Eustacia, like Ophelia, dies by drowning, and like Ophelia's her
end is doubtful. In a way, indeed, it is doubly so.

The last words we hear from her are in the form of an agonized
soliloquy when, on her blind and desperate flight to Wildeve's inn
through the darkness, she realizes that 'the wings of her soul were
broken by the cruel obstructiveness of all about her':

> 'Can I go, can I go?' she moaned. 'He's not *great* enough for
> me to give myself to—he does not suffice for my desire! . . . If he
> had been a Saul or a Bonaparte—ah! But to break my marriage
> vow for him—it is too poor a luxury! . . . And I have no money
> to go alone! And if I could, what comfort to me? I must drag on
> next year, as I have dragged on this year, and the year after that
> as before. How I have tried and tried to be a splendid woman,
> and how destiny has been against me! . . . I do not deserve my
> lot!' she cried in a frenzy of bitter revolt. 'O, the cruelty of
> putting me into this ill-conceived world! I was capable of much;
> but I have been injured and blighted and crushed by things
> beyond my control! O, how hard it is of Heaven to devise such
> tortures for me, who have done no harm to Heaven at all.'

This broken utterance—as soon as we have discarded an inapposite demand for the canons of realistic fiction—must carry great
authority with us. It is spoken by a woman who has thought and
spoken of suicide, and of whom suicide has been feared. And the
next we hear of her is the fall of her body into the stream. Her
husband believes that she has destroyed herself ('It is I who ought
to have drowned myself,' he cries), and most readers and critics
have accepted this interpretation of the facts. Yet buried in the
text ('buried', because none of those characteristic nudges of
Hardy's accompanies it) there is another possibility. Eustacia has
been thinking to join Wildeve at the Silent Woman. And a light
which it is natural to suppose emanates from the inn (Thomasin,
also out in the storm, takes it for this) is in fact shining from
Wildeve's gig (as Thomasin's companion, Venn, discerns). Wildeve
has chosen to wait with the vehicle two or three hundred yards
from the building. This unconscious deception, but for Venn's
acuteness, would have disoriented Thomasin and taken her into a
'quag'. Equally, it could have disoriented Eustacia and taken her

into the stream unawares. There are thus two possibilities. Eustacia may have despaired and drowned herself. Or, still hurrying forward and with her problem unresolved, she may have perished by an accident.

Why are we left in doubt? Perhaps it is because we are again being invited to 'choose between the endings'. If Eustacia has committed suicide, she may be said to have preferred death to dishonour. Whatever her previous relations with Wildeve, she has indeed not broken her marriage vow, and has more than once expressed horror at the thought of doing so. 'As a wife, at least, I've been straight,' she has said to her husband. Here, perhaps, is the more conventional ending. But that blind chance should have caught her while still fleeing to whatever her appointment with Wildeve may bring is a conclusion possibly better matching her creator's cast of mind. Indeed, here is almost a habit of the President of the Immortals in Hardy's universe. He bides his time until passion or folly has rendered his victim vulnerable, and then he strikes. But yet again, we must not, in any given case, be in a hurry to declare his will malign. 'Neither the man nor the woman,' we read finally of Eustacia and Wildeve, 'lost dignity by sudden death.'

Howe rather surprisingly declares *The Return of the Native* to be the first book in which the novelist 'announces those grim preoccupations with fatality that will become associated with his name'. I think it would be more true to say that it is the first in which this disposition comes under rigid artistic control. For sheer incidence of bad luck, at least, *A Pair of Blue Eyes* heads it by a long way. In that novel it is difficult not to feel the presence of a power playing against Elfride Swancourt with loaded dice. Close consideration shows that we are seldom constrained to such a conclusion in *The Return of the Native*. Perhaps there is something arbitrary about the adder that adds to the horror of Mrs Yeobright's end. On the other hand, the failure of Clym's eyesight, a much more vital link in the tragedy's forging, does not come to us as the mere random misfortune that its surface appearance might suggest. It is Howe who says that Hardy is trying to say through the working of chance what later writers will try to say through the vocabulary of the unconscious. This is a penetrating observation, and it is applicable here. 'High class teaching' is not a goal to which Clym is at all likely to attain, and his sudden disability, which relieves him, for a time at least, from the attempt, has an obvious etiology in a neurotic constitution. And regularly when something goes wrong—when, for example, a letter or a sum of money miscarries in unreliable hands—some unreadiness or tardiness or unacknowledged motive lies in the background. Character and fatality are displayed in so close an interdigitation that the inevitability of the tragedy seems to assert itself again and again as we read.

This effect is closely dependent upon the skill of the story-teller —which is that aspect of Hardy as novelist which we can least afford to neglect for long. Despite all its inequalities—its lapses into mere statement and summary, its over-leisured and therefore languid-seeming exploitation of rural occasions and quaintnesses, its almost excruciating grabbing, again and again, at the first clumsy or inept locutions that come to hand—the organization of the novel as a dramatic spectacle is very notable indeed. This holds both of its larger dimensions and of the detailed fabrication of its crucial episodes. The entire action hinges, we may say, upon an unopened door. As it happens, we have met this door before, in *Desperate Remedies*.[1] And it is the long artistic discipline taking its origin amid that novel's sensations which here produces a rapid sequence of events positioned, timed, motivated and credibilized with an expertness leading us to accept each succeeding mischance as the necessary issue of the last.

And so with 'The Discovery' from which the compulsively absorbing Book Fifth takes its title—that anagnorisis upon which Aristotle knows that an effective drama must turn. The fatal truth advances upon Clym remorselessly step by step. Johnny Nunsuch, entering the shed in the instant of Mrs Yeobright's death, cries out 'in a shrill tone' that she had declared herself 'a broken-hearted woman and cast off by her son'. It is seven weeks later that Clym learns from Christian Cantle why, on the day of her death, Mrs Yeobright had wanted no vegetables brought in for dinner: she was intending to visit Clym and his wife. So one mystery is explained. 'And I have been wondering,' Clym cries, 'why she should have walked in the heath on that hot day!' On the following morning Clym seeks out Diggory Venn, who has been absent from Egdon, and tells him of the death. Venn thinks to have comforting news, since he knows that on the eve of the fatality Mrs Yeobright had spoken forgivingly of her son. But here, ironically, is a new mystery—a sinister enigma, indeed. For how, then, within hours of this, had she come to speak to Johnny as she did? On the following day again, Johnny's second revelation brings out the dire ultimate fact. Mrs Yeobright had collapsed not while making her way to Clym's house but while returning from it. Here, once more, we are back in the world of *Desperate Remedies*:

[1] *The Return of the Native* contains at least one verbatim borrowing from *Desperate Remedies*.

a world of melodramatic situation in which observers are observed. Johnny is watching Mrs Yeobright as Mrs Yeobright watches 'a gentleman' come up and enter the house—enter it by the door upon which Mrs Yeobright presently knocks in vain. Only, this time, we hear the authentic reverberation of tragedy in the unanswered knock.

8

The Mayor of Casterbridge

HARDY WROTE MOST OF *THE MAYOR OF CASTERBRIDGE* IN HIS FORTY-fifth year, when he had already pursued through seven novels his ambition to be judged 'a good hand at a serial'. But all this experience had been of publication in monthly parts, whereas the new novel was to appear weekly. He was thus meeting for the first time conditions that set a high premium upon a brisk narrative pace, a rapid succession of striking incidents, and an avoidance of expatiation whether of a descriptive, psychological, or philosophical order. In some regards the book benefits from these necessities. The life of a small country town—the pervasive background to the story—is conveyed all the more effectively because succinctly; the humbler and seedier citizens of Casterbridge who provide the familiar Hardy chorus are nowhere too much given their head; the past history and present social and commercial structure of the borough are not dwelt upon to any effect of the prosaically informative. Above all, the quick manipulation of event and character required by his crowded fable keeps Hardy's hands fully occupied, so that he has leisure for but few of those large cosmic gestures which have threatened to become routine with him. The action is its own commentary, and the characters are made real for us through what they do and suffer rather than through an attempted analysis in depth such as Hardy seldom shows much command of.

But we have only to try to summarize the story to realize that there was a debit side to writing a novel for twenty successive numbers of the *Graphic* and *Harper's Weekly*.[1] A complex plot

---

1 Michael Henchard, a young hay-trusser, is travelling in search of work with his wife Susan, of whom he is weary, and his infant daughter Elizabeth-Jane. During a drinking-bout he puts his wife up to auction and sells her for five guineas to a wandering seaman called Newson who at once departs with both wife and child, leaving no trace of his destination. Sober again, Henchard repents his brutal action and takes a vow not to touch strong liquor for twenty years. Having failed in some effort to trace his lost family, he settles in the Wessex town of Casterbridge, prospers as a hay and seed merchant, and eventually becomes Mayor.

goes bitty under such conditions, and a succession of vicissitudes, surprises, reversals, and discoveries which may please when received in small, spaced-out doses are likely to prove indigestible when we attempt to assimilate them over a week-end. It is undeniable that too much happens in *The Mayor of Casterbridge*, and equally undeniable that the developments of disposition and sentiment in the characters from which the kaleidoscopic action is to receive its dynamic come to us, occasionally at least, only in perfunctory summary and without adequate dramatic embodiment. This is a regular weakness in Hardy's novels, and one of the occasions of the striking inequality of his achievement within almost any one of them. We may be reading on, conscious only of the pressure of the intensely felt life presented to us. Suddenly the

Many years later—the term of his vow, indeed, is approaching—his wife turns up on him, since Newson is believed drowned and she seeks support for her daughter and herself. He sets her up as a 'genteel widow' in Casterbridge, and then goes through the form of courting and marrying her. This he does in expiation rather than affection, since it is only Elizabeth-Jane to whom his feelings are drawn. He resolves that the story of the auction, and with it his own paternity of the girl, shall be withheld from her. But his wife is withholding a secret of her own. This Elizabeth-Jane is veritably what she believes herself to be, Newson's child, Henchard's own child having died in infancy. There is a further looming complication. During a business visit to Jersey, Henchard has formed a compromising intimacy with an impoverished young woman, Lucetta Le Sueur, the orphan daughter of an army officer. It has been his intention to marry Lucetta, and he now has to write and tell her that this is impossible.

The same day that brings his wife to Casterbridge sees the arrival there, *en route* for America, of a young Scot, Donald Farfrae, who has a knowledge of modern agricultural methods still unknown in Wessex, and who casually communicates to Henchard a method of doctoring some bad corn which has become an embarrassment to him. Henchard takes a great fancy to Farfrae, persuades him to remain as his manager, and in a rough and domineering fashion makes the young man his friend and confidant. Farfrae tentatively pays court to Elizabeth-Jane, but Henchard soon becomes jealous of his success and popularit·· in the town, and dismisses him. Farfrae sets up as a grain merchant on his own account, and thenceforward everything goes well with him and badly with Henchard.

Mrs Henchard dies; Henchard tells Elizabeth Jane that he is her father, and then immediately makes the discovery that he is not; while she is trying to feel towards him as a dutiful daughter he takes to treating her unkindly because of this concealed knowledge that she is no child of his.

Lucetta inherits money and appears unheralded in Casterbridge, where she rents one of the most substantial houses in the town—this as preparation for marrying Henchard and thus guarding her imperilled reputation. But she prosecutes her intention in a wayward manner, her first action being to engage the unsuspecting Elizabeth-Jane (who is now anxious to leave Henchard's household) as her companion. Henchard finds himself once more strongly attracted by her, but she is a fickle woman and soon transfers her designs to the younger and more personable Farfrae. Farfrae succumbs at once, and no longer pays attention to Elizabeth-Jane. Henchard's jealousy drives him to threaten Lucetta with the exposure of their former relations unless she agrees to marry him, and under this infamous blackmail she is forced to promise submission.

The following day sees Henchard's ruin. Sitting as magistrate in judgement atmosphere we breathe is evacuated as it were through the page, and we are left existing as we can upon thin synopsis. It is as if a mere working jotting, a first rudimentary outline of a character or guess at a motive, had tumbled out of the author's notebook and into our text.

There was another liability. Hardy had facility—gained perhaps through unassuming early reading unknown to us—in the stage-carpentry of melodrama. At a certain level of contrivance, he is very good indeed at fabricating a plot. There is much in *The Mayor of Casterbridge* that is like the stuff of *Desperate Remedies*, better done. A signal example is the handling of the paternity of his heroine. The first chapter opens upon Michael Henchard, his wife Susan, and their infant daughter Elizabeth-Jane. The third opens, nearly twenty years later, upon Susan and her grown daughter Elizabeth-Jane, thus:

The highroad into the village of Weydon-Priors was again carpeted with dust. The trees had put on as of yore their aspect

upon an aged female vagrant (who is charged with committing a nuisance against the church wall), he suddenly hears himself denounced by the prisoner as a man who, twenty years before, had sold his wife for five guineas in a booth at Weydon Fair. Henchard acknowledges the truth of the story, and leaves the court. When Lucetta hears of this she realizes that she has nothing to fear from anything that the disgraced and humiliated man may say, and she at once marries Farfrae.

Misfortunes, some of them perversely courted, now crowd upon Henchard. His efforts to defeat Farfrae in the grain trade hopelessly miscarry; he himself goes bankrupt; soon he is only a labourer in the employ of his former protégé, who now lives in Henchard's former house and is to become the new mayor. The period of his vow having expired, Henchard takes grimly to drink. He makes a foolish exhibition of himself upon the occasion of a royal visit to Casterbridge, so that Farfrae has to haul him away by the collar beneath the gaze of the assembled citizens. He plans a fight to the death with his rival, having already drawn back from sheer murder only in the nick of time. He thinks to betray Lucetta's past as effectively as he can, but his innate generosity returns to him and he sends her back her compromising letters. Unfortunately he blindly chooses a malignant messenger, who opens the letters and reads them aloud in a low public house. The rabble organize a 'skimmington-ride', in which Henchard's effigy and that of Lucetta are paraded through the streets. Under the shock of this, Lucetta, who is pregnant, suffers a miscarriage and dies.

On the day following the skimmington-ride Elizabeth-Jane's true father, the supposedly drowned Newson, appears. He knows that Susan Henchard is dead, but asks for his daughter. Henchard tells him that she is dead too, and he goes away. Henchard and Elizabeth-Jane (who still supposes herself to be his daughter) come together again, and she cares for him. But Farfrae, being a widower, shows signs of courting the girl once more. This, together with a further appearance of Newson now in possession of the truth, puts Henchard to flight. He returns to Weydon-Priors, the scene of his first sin, to work as a hay-trusser. When later, and in desperation, he revisits Caster-bridge for Elizabeth-Jane's wedding, it is to find that she cannot forgive him his deceit. He departs with a promise never to trouble her again, and dies in despair and misery shortly afterwards.

of dingy green, and where the Henchard family of three had
once walked along, two persons not unconnected with that
family walked now. . . . One of the two . . . was she who had
figured as the young wife of Henchard on the previous occasion. . . . Her companion . . . appeared as a well-formed young
woman of eighteen. . . . A glance was sufficient to inform the eye
that this was Susan Henchard's grown-up daughter.

The obfuscation is—as the reader of a detective story might say—
'fair'. And it is nearly a hundred pages before we are allowed to
suspect that the girl we have been getting to know is not Henchard's
daughter, now grown up, but the daughter of Henchard's wife's
purchaser, the sailor Newson. And not only do the characters
regularly practise upon one another the kind of sleight here
practised upon us. They seem resigned to parting or coming together, to dying or bobbing up from the dead, with a precision and
punctuality in terms of the proposed exhibition suggestive of a
factory in which an advanced stage of automation has been
achieved. All this unresisting performance of routine duties of
sensation and surprise, particularly as now speeded up to the needs
of a sequence of 6,000-word instalments, is devitalizing, and it is
only Michael Henchard himself who is virtually unscathed by it.
The Mayor of Casterbridge is the most intricately and, for that
matter, successfully plotted of Hardy's major books. But there is
none of them before which we are more prone to ask ourselves
whether he has given adequate critical thought to the function of
plot in a developed prose fiction.

2

It is not improbable that the author of *Titus Andronicus* assured
his first employers that his prime aim was to be accounted a good
hand at a Tragedy of Blood. Established as the most successful
dramatist of his time, he may similarly have informed his col-
leagues that he was brushing up a revenge play which had enjoyed
some success not long before—and brought them *Hamlet* as a
result. And that to the end of his career he more or less successfully
catered for naïve and cultivated tastes at one and the same time
has been the contention of some persuasive critics.
   There is only a limited comparison to be drawn between
Shakespeare's circumstances and Hardy's, and it is a still more
limited equation that can be established between their arts. Yet
there is no doubt that Shakespeare ranked with the Greek
dramatists among Hardy's yardsticks. Hardy prepared himself for

a new novel by a little appropriate reading of Aeschylus, and he
would certainly have appealed to the *Oedipus Rex* if rallied on the
score of his recourse to tall stories. But in the preface to *The Return
of the Native* he judged it 'pleasant to dream' that Egdon might be
'the heath of that traditionary King of Wessex—Lear'. And when
in *The Mayor of Casterbridge* Henchard, rejected by one whom he
would fain think of as a daughter, finds refuge in a hovel (which is
in fact on Egdon), he is attended only by a humble and faithful
former employee called Whittle. The name is phonetically indistinguishable from an archaic English word for a fool. We shall
make no sense of Hardy's fiction if we deny its ambition.

It might be argued that he tried to wrest the effects of Shakespearian tragedy out of the materials of Shakespearian romance.
Ingenious intrigues, unsuspected relationships, timely resus-
citations, mutations of character and shifts of motive at the beck
of a fable or call of a suddenly glimpsed sensational effect: out of
these Shakespeare finally conjured moments of mysterious emotion, enchanting beauty. Hardy equips himself with the same
immemorial story-spinning resources when going in quest of pity
and terror.

But *is* this his quest? Is there not an element of self-deception,
or at least of muddle, in those evocations of the names of Shakespeare and Aeschylus? Perhaps the real purpose to which he
thought to bend his romance material (of which the Victorian
'artificial' plot and its narrower employment in the 'sensation'
novel are late and attenuated derivatives) is to be categorized,
if only roughly, as philosophical and suasive rather than imaginative and aesthetic. Much of the suasive aspect of the novels—
far more than it has been fashionable to recognize—is thoroughly
traditional. Right and wrong, rationality and irrationality,
duty and inclination: we are constantly shown people poised and
struggling between these. At the same time—and surely in some
conflict with this moral vision—another kind of propaganda is
being carried on. New truths, vastly bleak, are inexorably
assailing the human consciousness: the truths of astronomical
space, geological time, man's plight in a neutral and regardless
universe.

If these purposes and persuasions conflict, at least each is highly
serious. And Hardy in his novel-writing practice seems almost
unhesitatingly to assume something really far from clear: that the
elaborately 'made up' plot of the popular Victorian novel could be
manipulated or refined or elevated in such a way as to subserve
both these grave intents. In fact, it was much more fit to be the
vehicle of a different reading of life—and one to which his

temperament rather than his intellect prompted him. The final sentence of *The Mayor of Casterbridge* asserts (although with a faint equivocation in which lurks the ghost even of the Victorian happy ending) that happiness is 'the occasional episode in a general drama of pain'. The conditions amid which consciousness has come into being are so overwhelmingly adverse that if there be a dramatist behind the drama his interest can only be in the creating of suffering. On this view, we are no more than sentient puppets in some cosmic Theatre of Cruelty.

Here, of course, is the interpretation of human existence that much criticism accepts as finally Hardy's own. In fact, he himself usually professes to present this as an abnormal or jaundiced view of life. Again and again, he exhibits the conviction or suspicion of there being an actively malign principle in the universe as something invading the mind of characters who are constitutionally depressive (as he himself appears to have been) or who have fallen into the deepest misfortune, or who are 'fetishistic' and superstitious. All these things are true of Henchard. And we read:

> Misery taught him nothing more than defiant endurance of it. His wife was dead, and the first impulse for revenge died with the thought that she was beyond him. He looked out at the night as at a fiend. Henchard, like all his kind, was superstitious, and he could not help thinking that the concatenation of events this evening had produced was the scheme of some sinister intelligence bent on punishing him.

'Yet they had developed naturally' are the words that follow immediately upon this. The words are not quite true, since the 'concatenation of events' is a product of Hardy's art. Nor is it true, as has been asserted, that multiplied mischances and fatal coincidences are comparatively few in this novel. From the moment that Susan Henchard, in avoiding a booth selling beer, steers her husband into another in which the furmity woman, Mrs Goodenough, proves willing to lace her innocuous concoction with smuggled rum, bad luck makes all the running. Elfride Swancourt's ear-ring, we may say, continues to glint everywhere in these maturer pages. 'The seal had cracked and the letter was open.' 'Much might have resulted from recognition.' 'But the proposal had come ten minutes too late.' The narrative abounds in such small strokes—just as it pivots on larger ones like the furmity woman's turning up (after twenty years) precisely when she does. And here, surely, is the root reason of Hardy's clinging to the highly synthetic plot of the popular novel. All this generating of

great misfortunes out of petty chances ingeniously brought to bear
suggests or insinuates that Henchard at his most cast down (like
Jude Fawley and Sue Bridehead after him) is right, and that we
inhabit a kind of goblin-universe which neither a traditional
Christian nor a respectable nineteenth-century meliorist and
rationalist can at all properly acknowledge. It is arguable that
Hardy's major art pays a heavy price for this species of nervous
release. 'Henchard', we are told upon some occasion, 'was
constructed upon too large a scale to discern such minutiae.' We
end surprised that his largeness survives the press of small
contrivances amid which his story is driven forward. But he *is*
constructed—and by Hardy—upon a very large scale indeed. He
represents Hardy's nearest approach—it may be circumspectly
said—to creating one of the really great male characters in English
literature.

A major character does not make a major novel. And when we
read of Henchard, in a moment of high emotion, 'moving like a
great tree in a wind' the image may bring home to us the slender
proportions and somewhat static quality of everybody surrounding
him. Of his wife it would be unreasonable to expect much. It is
with one of Hardy's most gloomy generalizations that she is first
introduced to us:

> That the man and woman were husband and wife, and the
> parents of the girl in arms, there could be little doubt. No other
> than such relationship would have accounted for the atmosphere
> of stale familiarity which the trio carried along with them like a
> nimbus as they moved down the road.

After that, we shall scarcely think to find Mrs Henchard's company
enlivening, and Hardy himself may be said, perfectly fairly, to take
very little interest in her until she is dead. In terms of any social
context she is completely nebulous, and we find her able to
compose letters in one place, whereas in another her literacy is
confined to writing her own name. But then, as if to make amends,
Hardy creates for her Mother Cuxom's astonishing threnody.
'And all her shining keys', it concludes, 'will be took from her, and
her cupboards opened; and little things 'a didn't wish seen, anybody will see; and her wishes and ways will all be as nothing!'
There is a point early in the book in which Mrs Henchard's
modest attractions in earlier years are described as 'her former
spring-like specialities'. Nothing is odder about Hardy (who is odd
in all sorts of ways) than his weirdly fluctuating command of
English prose.

A little more is made of Lucetta, although she starts off under considerable disadvantages. One of these constitutes, perhaps, no more than a small vexation. Her dilemmas and agonies make sense only if we suppose that she has in fact been Henchard's mistress in Jersey. But there runs through the narrative the reiterated implication that this has not been so. Thus, after her death Farfrae reflects that 'it was hard to believe that life with her would have been productive of further happiness', but this is on the score of her dying confession that she had so comported herself with Henchard as to have made unjust constructions of her conduct possible.[1]

This awkwardness links itself to something else. Hardy, so sensitive alike to the charm and the fatality of women, is regularly uneasy and fumbling when his theme confronts him with their simple sexuality. On this Henry James was to have a mordant word when he read *Tess of the d'Urbervilles*. And Lucetta as a siren produces some singularly helpless gestures. She flings herself on a couch 'in the cyma-recta curve which so became her'—which is also, we must conclude, the 'flexuous position' she tries out on Elizabeth-Jane, and which is further defined as 'the pose of a well-known conception of Titian's'.

Lucetta lacks a further dimension. She is the only character in the novel for whom a genteel or semi-genteel background is posited (her father was an officer, and her money is inherited from a banker), but this class-factor, so significant in the mid-nineteenth century, is scarcely reflected in her relationships with anybody else. The fact, again unimportant in itself, may prove indicative when we come to consider the social background to the novel. More damaging is the pervasive perfunctoriness with which anything that can be called her inner life is exhibited to us. Good critics may insist on the fabular basis of this novel and its affinity with ballad; on Hardy's instinct to 'trust the tale' and the consequent inappositeness of our expecting the penetrations of a developed psychological fiction. All the same, Lucetta is a woman whose past history is important but remains only vaguely defined; whose conduct in Casterbridge, although fateful for others and presented as the issue of a nervous, capricious and largely frivolous temperament, is yet so little elucidated in terms of any real facts of mind that we have difficulty in receiving it as other than the merest function of the plot; and whose death from shock (where

[1] For one commentator, Paterson, Lucetta has 'lived in sin' with Henchard, but for another, Webster, 'she has never done anything to justify society's suspicion'. Hardy himself does not much clarify the matter when he tells us that 'hers had been rather the laxity of inadvertence than of intention'.

we might expect no more than a hysterical fit) is the more palpably a matter of her creator's convenience in that we have already been constrained to witness a similarly compliant demise in the case of Mrs Henchard. Lucetta is subjected to some agonizing moments—as when she is constrained to overhear (*The Mayor of Casterbridge* is a veritable festival of eavesdropping) Henchard reading aloud to her husband from her own compromising letters, knowing that at any moment he may ruthlessly reveal the identity of the writer. 'Her own words greeted her, in Henchard's voice, like spirits from the grave.' We feel with her, even to the extent of resenting Hardy's crude zest in thus squeezing the last drop of melodramatic effect from the whole strained episode. But Hardy feels with her too. As for all her fickle sisterhood in the Wessex novels, his charity grows as he writes. Yet she never becomes, in any meaningful degree, a victim. It is certainly hard to see in her, as one ingenious commentator would have us do, the Gloucester to Henchard's Lear.

Elizabeth-Jane suggests at least a more considered creation. Lucetta is a somewhat untalented hedonist; it is unnecessary to endow her with much beyond this; nor is she so endowed. Basically, Elizabeth-Jane's role is similarly simple, since she is—if within certain limits—an exemplary character. Yet there has been an attempt to model her with a good deal of subtlety. She is sensitive and perceptive, and therefore she develops—but in terms of what has been laid down for her in formative years:

> Knowledge—the result of great natural insight—she did not lack. . . . Like all people who have known rough times, light-heartedness seemed to her too irrational and inconsequent to be indulged in except as a reckless dram now and then; for she had been too early habituated to anxious reasoning to drop the habit suddenly.

We first see her exhibiting an obsessive concern for what she again and again calls the 'respectable'; and this remains with her, in its narrower expression, as a 'craving for correctness of procedure' which is characterized for us as 'almost vicious'. Yet this disposition matures, in the main, into a moral prudence and 'meditative soberness' which is not least admirable in acknowledging the limitations of its own nature. She is not a Cordelia (at least in the final crisis it is not her role) nor even a Dorothea Brooke, but neither is she merely the small person left snug at the end of the tale that she would have been if created to the meagre and functional specifications alone worked to in Lucetta.

When Henchard in his moment of most public disgrace advances upon the King with the scandalous intention of shaking hands, Lucetta is ready to faint but Elizabeth-Jane finds 'her interest in the spectacle as a strange phenomenon' get the better of her fear. She possesses—as her zeal in study shows—intellectual curiosity and something of the dispassionateness without which intellectual curiosity cannot prosper. But Hardy was far from considering curiosity and the speculative mind as blessings. It is these qualities that leave Elizabeth-Jane, from the tranquil haven of her marriage and on the last page of the book, reflecting that there is no occasion for 'effusiveness' in having been accorded 'the doubtful honour of a brief transit through a sorry world'.

3

Such a reflection would not come readily to Elizabeth-Jane's husband and Lucetta's widower, Donald Farfrae, a man unconscious of inner conflict and incapable either of suffering or of much awareness of suffering. This does not prevent his being an excellent citizen: undeviatingly fair-dealing; fair-minded and generous in private relations according to his lights; serious according to these same lights, and always truthful. (When Henchard first says to him 'I want your advice', he replies 'I think I'd run the risk, and tell the truth'—sound counsel which Henchard fatally rejects.) If he shows as obtuse and insensitive, this is at least partly because his fate involves him with such obscure situations and kittle people. But it is impossible much to like him, and simply as a literary creation critics have been prone to disapprove of him on this irrelevant account.

There is a point at which Farfrae is characterized as 'the reverse of Henchard'. The bald statement takes us, clearly enough, to the core of Hardy's dramatic proposal. Moreover it is susceptible of valid interpretation at several levels, of which the first may be called the socio-economic. Henchard himself is made to acknowledge this particular contrast at an early stage of their association:

> In my business, 'tis true that strength and bustle build up a firm. But judgment and knowledge are what keep it established. Unluckily I am bad at science, Farfrae; bad at figures—a rule o' thumb sort of man. You are just the reverse—I can see that.

And when Farfrae takes on the duties of management:

> Letters and ledgers took the place of 'I'll do't', and 'you shall hae't'; and, as in all such cases of advance, the rugged picturesqueness of the old method disappeared with its inconveniences.

It is important to mark the balanced character of this statement. When, at the opening of the main action, Mrs Henchard returns after twenty years to Weydon-Priors, it is to observe that 'the real business of the fair had considerably dwindled'. And the explanation—which would be beyond her view—is that 'the new periodical great markets of neighbouring towns were beginning to interfere seriously with the trade carried on here for centuries'. Mrs Henchard goes straight from Weydon-Priors to Casterbridge, and arrives there, according to Weber's chronology of the novel, on Friday, 18 September 1846. And 1846 is the year in which Peel put an effective end to the Corn Laws. English agriculture is in transition, and is soon to be in decay. This is undoubtedly the setting of *The Mayor of Casterbridge*, and a significant value in the story. But we need not suppose it to be what the story is about, and still less that Henchard and Farfrae have their chief significance as representatives of an old and a new rural economy, with their creator sited well on the nostalgic side of the fence. We may agree with Brown when he tells us that the novel 'acknowledges the bitter situation of agriculture in contemporary England' and even, in a sense, that it 'turns on the situation that led to the repeal of the Corn Laws'. But it is only with some reservation that we can receive it as 'the tale of the struggle between the native countryman and the alien invader' or agree that 'all Hardy's art goes into imagining Henchard's death rather as a loss in community than as the extinction of an individual self'. 'He is agricultural man, defeated,' Brown says, and with him pass 'the older traditional sanctities, now fractured and discarded'.

It is true that 'community' suffers in some respects under the new order for which Farfrae, whether consciously or unconsciously, labours. Hardy dramatizes the point, very effectively, more than once. Farfrae's first disagreement with his employer is over the latter's hauling the sluggard Whittle out of bed and humiliating him by sending him through the town without his breeches. ' "Come," said Donald quietly, "a man o' your position should ken better, sir! It is tyrannical and no' worthy of you." ' Farfrae is right. But Henchard had unobtrusively kept Whittle's mother in coal and potatoes, and it is Whittle who tends the fallen mayor on his death-bed. Again, it is Whittle himself who earlier strikes a balance fairly, if mordantly, enough:

'Yaas, Miss Henchet,' he said, 'Mr Farfrae have bought the concern and all of we work-folk with it; and 'tis better for us than 'twas—though I shouldn't say that to you as a daughter-

law. We work harder, but we bain't made afeard now. It was
fear made my few poor hairs so thin! No busting out, no
slamming of doors, no meddling with yer eternal soul and all
that; and though 'tis a shilling a week less I'm the richer man;
for what's all the world if yer mind is always in a larry, Miss
Henchet?'

The docked shilling is no doubt significant. When, at the end of
the story, his stepdaughter knows that she must seek out Henchard
in his misery and be reconciled to him, Farfrae is 'not the least
indisposed to assist Elizabeth-Jane in her laudable plan', but later
points out that a night away from Casterbridge 'will make a hole
in a sovereign'. Hardy has made Farfrae a Scot partly because of
conventional notions of this kind (including the view that Scots
are particularly good at compartmenting 'the commercial and the
romantic') and partly, perhaps, because the new science of political
economy was still associated, as it is in Peacock's satirical novels,
with ideological percolations from across the Border. But our
main point here must be that the particular sort of 'mortal commercial combat' in which Henchard and Farfrae close is no more
than part of the theatre of their drama. It is possible to urge too
far Hardy's engaged stance as the celebrant of antique rural
sanctities. He had an intimate knowledge of, and a deep affection
for, a passing order. But he had schooled himself in dispassionateness, and believed that he brought to his 'little Exhibition of
Wessex life' his much-prized 'latest illumination of the time'. Yet
again, and above all, the timeless commanded him. The man who
thought of Aeschylus and Shakespeare while writing for the
Graphic had an instinct for grounding his fictions in the universal
and the permanent, and for establishing their significance in terms
of the largest historical perspectives.

It is thus that the scene of Henchard's losing battle against
Farfrae is a town through which have tramped the legions of the
Empire, and this Roman past is emphasized again and again. The
most casual spade may turn up evidence of sepulture so remote in
time as to have lost all common mortuary associations and appear
merely curious. 'Mrs Henchard's dust mingled with the dust of
women who lay ornamented with glass hairpins and amber
necklaces, and men who held in their mouths coins of Hadrian,
Posthmus, and the Constantines.' It is not a mere rural piety that
sees significance in such contiguities. The impulse here is to
set Henchard's story against an appropriate scale of things.
And firmly established as that story is from the first amid the
concrete realities of mid-nineteenth-century Wessex, it is scarcely

fortuitously that Time, Chance, and Fate are invoked for us long before we hear of Casterbridge.

4

The clash, we may at least say, is between men of radically different temperaments rather than between men divided by changing social assumptions and commercial practices. Henchards and Farfraes exist in every age, and this fact enhances the novel's representative quality. But there is surely a further truth about the kind of book Hardy has achieved in *The Mayor of Casterbridge*. Almost everything most worth our observation could be compassed while scarcely taking our eyes off the protagonist. It is true that a number of other people and an unlikely profusion of mischances are involved in the action, but essentially the conflict is within Henchard himself. In his heart there is a kind of fighting. And it is the subject of the book.

After Hardy's usual naïve fashion, we are offered a good deal of direct information about Henchard's nature, beginning on the novel's title-page. He is a man of character. It is a common descriptive phrase, such as we are likely to feel that we understand at once, and yet it is not altogether easy to define. But at least a very brief review of Hardy's 'little Exhibition' will tell us that there is no other 'man of character' of any significance throughout the entire range of the Wessex novels. Active energy, and the impulse to set the impress of one's own volitions upon one's environment; firmness that may modulate into a stubborn continuance in egoism or error; above all, the quality known as presence, with its significant association with the platform and the stage: all these things go towards Henchard's being a man of character. The next thing we are told about him (it comes on page 6) is that he is perverse, and we understand this when we come to sense how often his brutality and even his sins are of a self-lacerating sort. His personal goodness, we are then told warningly, will be of a very fitful cast—'an occasional almost oppressive generosity rather than a mild and constant kindness'. Henchard certainly lives up to this. There is volcanic stuff beneath the rind of the mayor and churchwarden, we next learn—and hard upon this comes the statement that he is like Faust: 'a vehement gloomy being, who has quitted the ways of vulgar men, without light to guide him on a better way'.

The amplification here is without much appropriateness, since quitting the ways of vulgar men is Henchard's course only as the phrase can be made to cover his social ostracism. But the basic

equivalence is valid, if only to the extent that Henchard is
essentially a religious man, inhabiting a world of good and evil.
Here again he is virtually unique among Hardy's creations—and
indeed Hardy is unable to refrain from assuring us, more than
once, that what Henchard is must be termed 'fetichistic' and
superstitious. He is sent to consult the weather-prophet, we must
suppose, to drive this reading of him home. But when he asks
himself, hard upon entertaining one evil design, 'Why should I
still be subject to these visitations of the devil, when I try so hard
to keep him away?' it is possible to feel that he is looking into his
own heart with quite as much perspicacity as is shown by his
creator. And the supreme assertion of his own pride in selfhood
carries a Satanic defiance which places him wholly within a
specifically Christian cosmology:

> I—Cain—go alone as I deserve—an outcast and a vagabond.
> But my punishment is *not* greater than I can bear!

The presentation, unique in Hardy, of a man of powerful will
and feeling, torn between a narrow, thrusting egoism and a
remorseful and resilient sense of violated sanctities, returns us
finally to the issue of the basic intent of the book, and in particular
to what may be called the theory of Henchard as Tragic Hero.
There are certainly kinds of tragedy that the novel is not. It does
not come to us with any conviction as a story of sin and expiation,
such as Dostoevsky is the master of, and Conrad (that hater of
Dostoevsky) achieves in *Under Western Eyes*. Nor does it answer
to that idea of classical tragedy which derives so largely from
Aristotle's fixation upon the *Oedipus Rex*, whereby a man not
pre-eminently virtuous and just yet better than most of us,
prosecuting some endeavour which holds within itself a taint of
moral error, achieves in fact the opposite of the effect he intends.
Nor again can it be elucidated in terms of the same basic theory as
broadened and subtilized under the influence of Hegel in Bradley's
Shakespearean Tragedy. Equally inapplicable is that typically
modern species of tragedy to which Hardy was to address himself
in *Jude the Obscure*, in which the stubborn recalcitrance of social
forces and personal circumstance wears down and destroys the
aspirations of men and women of unusual yet limited lights and
talents who rebel against them. The greatest English novel of this
kind—all the more powerful because the operation of the tragic
principle is exhibited in terms of abrasion and habituation rather
than catastrophe, and because, further, the tragic is so masterfully
interdigitated with other aspects of experience, other tints and

tones of life, evoked in a vivid particularity—is George Eliot's *Middlemarch*. What degree of correspondence—we may pause to ask—is to be found between Middlemarch and Casterbridge?

5

It is commonly said that Hardy knew Dorchester so intimately that he was able to bring its imaginative projection in Casterbridge alive in its every aspect. There is certainly much in the novel that is sheer triumph in this way. Hardy's radical power to make us *see* does not halt at Weydon-Priors (where at dawn the shadows of the yellow and red vans are 'projected far away, those thrown by the felloe of each wheel being elongated in shape to the orbit of a comet'). It comes to town masterfully, and with a technique which *The Dynasts* is to see develop, in the passage beginning: 'To birds of the more soaring kind Casterbridge must have appeared on this fine evening as a mosaic-work of subdued reds, browns, greys, and crystals, held together by a rectangular frame of deep green'. 'Crystals' is as precise as 'frame' is significant. The city's mere Roman angularity; its being 'deposited in the block upon a corn-field' with no 'transitional intermixture of town and down', so that 'the red-robed judge, when he condemned a sheep-stealer, pronounced sentence to the tune of Baa'; the actual close interdependence of territories apparently in such contrast: all this appeals equally to the Hardy who loved a picture gallery and the Hardy who loved a neat coming together of incongruities. The resulting reality comes to us in perfection:

> Casterbridge was the complement of the rural life around; not its urban opposite. Bees and butterflies in the cornfields at the top of the town, who desired to get to the meads at the bottom, took no circuitous course, but flew straight down High Street without any apparent consciousness that they were traversing strange latitudes. And in autumn airy spheres of thistle-down floated into the same street, lodged upon the shop fronts, blew into drains; and innumerable tawny and yellow leaves skimmed along the pavement, and stole through people's doorways into their passages, with a hesitating scratch on the floor, like the skirts of timid visitors.

Skirts no longer behave quite like that, but the suggestion remains vivid. At the same time, a certain significant detachment from the scene is hinted in the whimsicality of much of the description. The old espaliers in Henchard's garden stand 'dis-

torted and writhing in vegetable agony, like leafy Laocoöns'. The
clothes of the male denizens are 'historical records of their wearer's
deeds', and those of the women tend to fall into one of two
categories, 'the simple and the mistaken'. Elsewhere we have
exercises in the Dickensian picturesque:

> Other clocks struck eight from time to time—one gloomily
> from the gaol, another from the gable of an almshouse, with a
> preparative creak of machinery, more audible than the note of
> the bell; a row of tall, varnished case-clocks from the interior of
> a clock-maker's shop joined in one after another just as the
> shutters were enclosing them, like a row of actors delivering their
> final speeches before the fall of the curtain; then chimes were
> heard stammering out the Sicilian Mariners' Hymn; so that
> chronologists of the advanced school were appreciably on their
> way to the next hour before the whole business of the old one
> was satisfactorily wound up.

Dickensian too is the discreet but effective presentation of Mixen
Lane and Peter's Finger, from which we are startled to gather that
something like a brothel quarter is tucked away in Casterbridge.
This exception to the lightly toned character of the general exhibition provides a necessary background for the low brutality of
the skimmington-ride. Yet we do not feel it as a real social force
pressing upon something apprehended as an organic community.
Indeed, no such pressure is felt from either below or above.
When Smith, Elder were considering publishing the novel in
volume form, their reader reported that the lack of gentry among
the characters made it uninteresting—'a typical estimate', Hardy
comments, 'of what was, or was supposed to be, mid-Victorian
taste'. The circumscription, however, is certainly significant for so
long as we are holding any attempted comparison with *Middlemarch* in mind. Henchard and the other characters are, indeed,
borne upon by the conventions and prejudices of their community:
propriety prevents the mayor from simply receiving back Susan as
his wife; a coarse snobbery comes into play when he regards
Elizabeth-Jane's having spent an evening waiting upon the
customers of the Three Mariners as a social catastrophe; the
grossness of the dinner over which he presides as chief magistrate,
when Casterbridge's leading citizens are seen 'searching for tit-bits,
and sniffing and grunting over their plates like sows nuzzling for
acorns', tells us of standards and assumptions which have been at
play upon him for twenty years. But all this is very little when we
set beside it what Howe calls 'that marvellous confrontation of

E

social status and spiritual being' which is *Middlemarch*. The fact is that in Casterbridge Henchard's stark story is merely set against a background; he is not enveloped in a complex moral atmosphere in terms of which, as it were, all his own breathing happens. It is notable that he has no parentage, no affiliations with a personal past extending back beyond the furmity-woman's fatal booth at Weydon-Priors Fair. And all this is relevant at least to some readings of *The Mayor of Casterbridge* as Tragedy.

6

Thus according to a resourceful argument of Paterson's what habitually stood in the way of Hardy's achieving the weight of tragedy was his exposure to metropolitan 'romantic and scientific humanisms' which cut him off from those 'moral and religious universals' in the light of which alone a tragic vision is to be achieved. But, Paterson continues, in *The Mayor of Casterbridge* Hardy of Dorset, who is to be distinguished from Hardy of London, regains contact with a traditional moral wisdom, and Henchard is essentially a man who has offended against a divine order 'whose indignation, once provoked, can neither be appeased nor controlled'. A radical sign of this is the degradation of the city over which Henchard rules. We are called upon to mark

> a brutalized populace bearing witness, like the pimps and whores of *Measure for Measure* and the gravediggers of *Hamlet*, to the moral delinquency of a society that has winked at crime and, in a metaphorical sense at least, offended the gods.

'The denizens of Mixen Lane', in particular,

> express the bitterness and despair of a society whose magistrates, in having offended against justice, have forfeited their clear moral authority to rule. For the demoralization of the city is apparent not alone in the brutalization of the lower orders. It is also apparent in the brutalization of those proud merchant princes who, in having welcomed and celebrated a man offensive to the gods, in having become infected by the mayor's pride and arrogance, have submitted their humanity to base and ugly distortions.

And how significant, we are told, that Mrs Goodenough the furmity woman commits her low offence against the church wall. Hard times in Thebes, where the Sphinx is rampant! Arguments of this sort can be rendered wonderfully persuasive by an earnest manipulation of subsidiary detail, and Paterson's essay makes more stimulating reading than is to be found in most discussions of the novel. Nevertheless, even such a brief glimpse of Casterbridge and its people as we have attempted must make us doubt its validity. We may almost assert that the *finite* is a mark of the novel's character; that it is less Hardy's *King Lear* than his *Othello*. It has very few moments of poetry, or even of strangeness as distinct from sensation; that in which Henchard, thinking to drown himself, is superstitiously checked by the seemingly miraculous appearance of his *Doppelgänger* in the water, is the principal exception. (And this does not quite come off, perhaps because of our instant persuasion that whatever rude effigy of him the rabble had constructed for the skimmington-ride could scarcely retain so recognizable an identity after its immersion.) The imagery seldom carries implications of an outraged or lacerated Natural Order. The setting sun, indeed, once rests upon a hill 'like a drop of blood on an eyelid'. But more commonly sunlight is simply Hardy's sunlight, and is evoked by a man who noticed things:

A yellow flood of reflected sunlight filled the room for a few instants. It was produced by the passing of a load of newly trussed hay from the country, in a waggon marked with Farfrae's name.

There is dramatic implication in the last words. Yet the simple visual beauty of the image reminds us of the restricted sense in which 'dramatic' can be applied to the relationship between Henchard and the city of his mayorality. Casterbridge is a quiet and pleasant place, bustling only in an easy fashion, narrow no doubt in its views and with little refinement in its prosperous quarters. If touched by the beginnings of rural decay, it is not much conscious of the fact, and an active man has no difficulty in making his way in it. What is sombrely toned about it inhabits its fringes only. It has, in short, a character that effectively contrasts with Michael Henchard's character. It is his back-drop.

But if the total statement has not the severely integral cast of Paterson's imagining, what sort of book, once more, is *The Mayor of Casterbridge*? We must adhere to Henchard as tragic hero, even if his is a riddle such as Thebes never knew. But whatever ultimate touchstones towered in the hinterland of Hardy's mind, his story suggests less the Periclean or the Elizabethan than the Napoleonic age. It is to romantic tragedy that Henchard belongs; almost he is a Byronic rather than a Sophoclean or a Shakespearian figure. 'A

vehement gloomy being, who has quitted the ways of vulgar men':
we glimpse, after all, what is here stirring in Hardy's mind. Among
Byron's heroes, as with Byron himself, thrusting egoism, over-
reaching demand, is haunted and thwarted by feelings of guilt
dynamized by apprehensions which, religious in origin, have
shrunk and hardened into superstitious unease. As such, they are
powerless to check the destructive resurgence of the same demand-
ing ego. Michael Henchard is like this.

Hardy had his own retrospective view of the novel. 'I fear it will
not be so good as I meant', he recorded in his diary upon the day
of the first instalment's appearance. And, later, the *Life* records:

It was a story which Hardy fancied he had damaged more
recklessly as an artistic whole, in the interest of the newspaper
in which it appeared serially, than perhaps any other of his
novels, his aim to get an incident into almost every week's part
causing him in his own judgment to add events to the narrative
somewhat too freely. However, as at this time he called his
novel-writing 'mere journeywork' he cared little about it as art,
though it must be said in favour of the plot, as he admitted later,
that it was quite coherent and organic, in spite of its complication.

But despite this routine profession of disregard, Hardy was, of
course, concerned for the artistic worth of his novel, and he took
comfort from the reflection that 'after all, it is not improbabilities
of incident but improbabilities of character that matter'. He rests,
in fact, upon his title-page; upon having written *A Story of a Man
of Character*. And this he has done. Henchard lives for us vividly
throughout his improbable history.

9
The Woodlanders

HARDY'S HUMILITY, AND HIS SIMPLICITY OF MIND, HAVE BEEN MUCH commended by his critics, but there is so frequently a detectable note of irony in his self-appraisals that it is not altogether easy to determine the boundaries of these qualities. When Virginia Woolf visited him in 1926 she was anxious to hear him speak of his preferences among his own novels, and went about it by telling him it was *The Mayor of Casterbridge* which she had herself chosen for reading in the train. 'And did it hold your interest?' Hardy asked courteously, and went on to regret that none of his books were 'fitted to be wedding presents'. When, fourteen years earlier, he had offered a correspondent some confidences in this matter, it was in tones entirely appropriate to an unassuming novelist who would like to be known as 'a good hand at a serial'. (He had already been awarded the O.M., and he was rereading his books in proof-copies for the Wessex Edition.)

I got to like the character of Clym before I had done with him. I think he is the nicest of all my heroes, and *not a bit* like me. On taking up *The Woodlanders* and reading it after many years I think I like it, *as a story*, the best of all. Perhaps that is owing to the locality and scenery of the action, a part I am very fond of. It seems a more quaint and fresh story than the *Native*, and the characters are very distinctly drawn. . . . Seven o'clock P.M. It has come on to rain a little: a blackbird is singing outside.

Thirty-five years before this again, and just after the publication of *The Woodlanders*, he records that it 'enabled me to hold my own in fiction, whatever that may be worth'. Not long afterwards he is saying, in his best take-it-for-granted commercial vein, that it had not been possible to 'accentuate' the true burden of the book's closing scenes 'by reason of the conventions of the libraries, etc'.

Yet in *The Woodlanders*, thus modestly discoursed upon, there
occurs upon an early page—if only by implication—some hint
of that other scale against which Hardy was prompted to measure
his art. The scene of his story, he tells us, is to be 'one of those
sequestered spots outside the gates of the world . . . where, from
time to time, dramas of a grandeur and unity truly Sophoclean
are enacted'. Perhaps here as he began his novel, and with what
he once called his 'original irradiated conception' still unembodied
before him, he saw Grace Melbury's story as one which could be
spoken of in this way. In his next novel he was to be more
circumspect; it is only in the final paragraph of *Tess of the
d'Urbervilles*, and with the greatest of his works securely achieved,
that he evokes the answering name of Aeschylus.

2

Mr Howe has written severely of *The Woodlanders* that 'no
mature mind is likely, after the opening chapters, to pay serious
attention to the plot'. If this be so, it is not because of any extravagance or implausibility in the main story. Hardy's persuasion
that the 'purpose of fiction is to give pleasure by gratifying the
love of the uncommon in human experience' is inoperative in
this novel except in minor and episodic regards, and a perfectly
adequate summary of it can be given which embodies nothing of
the kind.[1] It is even possible to view the book as a casting back

---

[1] George Melbury, a prosperous timber merchant of yeoman stock, has
given his only child Grace an upper-class education, but at the same time
intends that she shall marry Giles Winterborne, a modest forester and cider-
maker: this with a confused notion of making amends to Giles's dead father,
whom he has wronged. The two young people are fond of each other—
Giles indeed to the point of complete and unswerving devotion. But Grace on
coming home is disconcerted and discontented by the simple Hintock ways,
and before a natural readjustment can take place she is a little affected—
and her father is much affected—by signs of favour shown to her by Mrs
Charmond, a woman strange to the district, but now the widowed proprietor
of the local mansion house and estate. While thus unsettled, she comes into
contact with Edred Fitzpiers, a young physician who has taken up an un-
prosperous rural practice, but who is a man of ancient lineage and possessed
moreover of philosophic and scientific pretensions. Grace finds Fitzpiers
sexually attractive and her father is very impressed by what he thinks of as
his social eminence. When Giles has the misfortune to lose nearly all his
small property he ceases to be regarded by the Melburys as an eligible suitor.
Fitzpiers makes advances to Grace—but immediately after definitively doing
so he chases a provocative village girl through the wood and sleeps with her.
Fitzpiers's morals are not good.
    Fitzpiers and Grace marry, and both soon realize their marriage has been
a mistake. It is Giles that Grace really loves. Fitzpiers is quickly disgusted
with the social comedown inherent in his plebeian alliance, and he takes up
with Mrs Charmond. She is amorous in a neurotic fashion and eventually
withdraws to the continent as his mistress; there she is abruptly shot by a

to the modesty of nature exhibited in *Under the Greenwood Tree*; certainly it has even more of the greenwood to it, and it is again the story of a girl of simple background and some acquired sophistication poised indecisively between suitors of widely differing social pretension. But the two novels have a more radical affinity. They are both very little under the oppression of Hardy's normally nagging cosmic overtones. In *The Woodlanders*, indeed, we have a sense of this release as coming about somewhat against his conscious intention. It is clear, for example, that he designs a kind of anti-Arden woodland; the actual trees are to be wrested into a powerful symbol of the human condition as unveiled by Charles Darwin. When Marty South opens her cottage door in Chapter III it is to hear 'the creaking sound of two overcrowded branches in the neighbouring wood, which were rubbing each other into wounds, and other vocalized sorrows of the trees'. This is a constant image. We see the process at work in miniature as we note 'the point of each ivy-leaf on the trunks scratch its underlying neighbour'; or with violence at the crisis of the action, when a bough is seen to smite the roof of Giles Winterborne's hut 'in the manner of a gigantic hand smiting the mouth of an adversary, to be followed by a trickle of rain, as blood from the wound'; or to an effect of mortal disease, as with 'a half-dead oak, hollow and disfigured with white tumours'; or in more expanded passages:

> From the other window all she could see were more trees, in jackets of lichen and stockings of moss. At their roots were stemless yellow fungi like lemons and apricots, and tall fungi with more stem than stool. Next were more trees close together, wrestling for existence, their branches disfigured with wounds resulting from their mutual rubbings and blows. . . . Beneath them were the rotting stumps of those of the group that had been vanquished long ago, rising from their mossy setting like black teeth from green gums.

notably shadowy former lover. Fitzpiers returns to Little Hintock and begins to show signs of reformation. Meanwhile, however, Melbury has been falsely persuaded that a recent change in the law makes a divorce possible, and on the strength of this he has rashly encouraged both Grace and Giles to think that they can soon be married. When the error is revealed Melbury is insistent that his daughter should make the best of things with her more or less repentant husband. She runs away, and places herself under the protection of Giles, who is now a sick man living in a poor hut in the woods. Giles is so mindful of her reputation that he gives up his hut to her entirely and spends several inclement nights in the open, and he succumbs to his illness as a result. Grace is faithful to his memory for a time but is eventually persuaded by Fitzpiers to return to him. Giles continues to be mourned by Marty South, a poor girl who has been his assistant in woodland employments and whose selfless devotion to him has been a percurrent theme of the book.

One has not to probe far into a passage like this to discover the reference to the ruthless action of sexual activity and sexual selection. It is as patent as in Conrad's evocations of the Malayan forests. This is true of the most celebrated of these unusual silvan evocations:

> On older trees still than these huge lobes of fungi grew like lungs. Here, as everywhere, the Unfulfilled Intention, which makes life what it is, was as obvious as it could be among the depraved crowds of a city slum. The leaf was deformed, the curve was crippled, the taper was interrupted; the lichen ate the vigour of the stalk, and the ivy slowly strangled to death the promising sapling.

How authentic and highly charged this writing is appears at once when we turn back a page and find this same woodland being treated in standard uninspired Hardyese:

> Now could be beheld that change from the handsome to the curious which the features of a wood undergo at the ingress of the winter months . . . a change constituting a sudden lapse from the ornate to the primitive on Nature's canvas, and comparable to a retrogressive step from the art of an advanced school of painting to that of the Pacific Islander.

But in general all this anthropomorphous vegetation ('decayed holes caused by old amputations', and the like) takes its high charge rather as a lightning-conductor does; it catches a great deal of inconvenient energy—in this case aesthetically inconvenient energy—and gets rid of it. The personages of the fable, in consequence, have a better chance of going about their business. The images do not, indeed, fail to do their work. They suggest that the same blind drive that maims the oak controls the destinies of the people of Little Hintock. At the same time, they concentrate and localize this large philosophic reference, and thus in a sense free the artist for other things.

But there is more to be said about the arboreal background. As in a great place in *The Prelude*, what we are made aware of is 'woods decaying, never to be decayed'. The strong pulse of the seasons beats in the book, and what winter announces is spring. In one aspect the timeless cyclic drive enhances our sense of the tragic quality of human destiny. But in another it is consolatory, as all intimations of rebirth must be. Hardy is breaking no new ground here. Nor is he doing so, except in one crucial instance, in his evocation of rustic life. This is still rendered largely in his pastoral-sentimental mode. Simple and unambitious and un-speculative people—those immersed in the primary tasks of an agricultural or at least rural economy—are the people best circumstanced in the end. This has held true in all the novels so far, and we cannot be unconscious that a good deal of hard fact has been withheld in the interest of the proposition. Such tasks as we see Hardy's peasantry engaged upon are commonly agreeable and often idyllic: in *The Woodlanders*, for example, the communal activities of the barking season described in Chapter XIX. It is almost fair to say that Hardy has not yet taken us really down to the soil.

But he himself mentioned, and others have emphasized, that *The Woodlanders* is at least the novel in which he comes closest to the terrain of his own childhood. And there is one fact of that childhood which it is useful to recall here. We are perhaps inclined to think of Hardy's immediate forbears as being, what-ever the social elevation of their ancestors, as near peasants as makes no matter. This we have already noted as not wholly accurate; it reflects only what is indeed the substantial truth that, at least from the point of view of a nineteenth-century gentry, all persons lacking gentle birth are much of a muchness. The Hardys belonged to a class which, at a peak of its prosperity, would produce men like Melbury—a substantial employer of labour in one kind of rural concern or another, who would yet, when he went to the 'big house', enter by the tradesmen's door and be addressed firmly as 'Melbury' as he stood respectfully before the local landowner. It was no doubt the very prosperity of this class that made its members resentful (as Hardy himself clearly was) of the rigidly maintained gulf between themselves and their betters. But they were at least not unconscious of a corresponding gulf between themselves and their labourers—only the more so because it was a gulf crossed frequently enough by the less fortunate of their own order.

The point here is that Hardy had no immediately inherited sense of what it is like to walk at a plough-tail. It was only with maturity (which came to him late) that he began to take a hard look at the bases of rural life. Commencing novelist, he had no difficulty in seeing his rustics much as Shakespeare (who was of similar social origin) had seen his: splendid material for a comic turn. It is true that by the time of *The Woodlanders* he has become tired or chary of deploying this resource in set scenes. But he still presents his labourers almost as if they were a leisure class. We commonly view them after or between working hours, quaintly discoursing in malt-houses and ingle-nooks over pots of cider or ale.

What there is of this in *The Woodlanders* does at least lighten its tone. Yet it is not markedly a *dark* book at all. The narrative moves with a fluent ease, a lack of architectonic anxiety, which some critics have reprehended as an abnegation of drama and a regression upon mere chronicle. It is true that the narrative method is very much a wandering from brief episode to brief episode, and that the point of view also strays regardlessly from place to place. In these particulars one can certainly establish no very favourable comparison with Stevenson, James, Conrad and others. But this is to miss a point. The relaxation reflects, and in an aesthetically advantageous way, something like an interval of confidence and ease in the personal life of its author. As Weber points out, *The Woodlanders* is the first novel written at Max Gate, that eminently respectable suburban home of an established writer, whose financial corner has been turned, and whose publisher henceforth—Alexander Macmillan—is eminently respectable too. There is a temperance of emotion in the book, a sparing exhibition of harsh extremities, a clarity in the statement and treatment of subject which reflects this situation, and at least conduces to an effect of notable professional competence. It must have been this aspect of the book that prompted Arnold Bennett to describe it as 'the finest English novel'.

It is rather far from being that. Indeed, on a first consideration we might think to distinguish in it elements foreboding the decline of Hardy's power over, or at least interest in, the novel form. Alert after the event, we may detect how often the mind of the writer reveals itself through passing references as turning to the English poets. And on this hint we may go further, discovering that a significant number of Hardy's own poems show some relationship with the novel—two of them to the extent of explicit statement by the writer.[1] Another, and this time disconcerting, indication of a shift of interest is the facility with which he accommodates the final stages of his story to 'the conventions of the libraries, etc.'. He had already done something of the kind with *The Return of the Native*, but in this later book the manipulations appear more radical. If a remark made in 1893 is to be accepted at its face value, he permitted calculations of this sort

---

[1] 'In a Wood' and 'The Pine Planters'. The first of these is still sub-titled erroneously in the edition of 1965 as 'From "The Woodlanders"'—'From' being a misreading of 'Vide' in Hardy's manuscript.

to affect his whole conception of his heroine's actions and character. He said that Grace Melbury

> never interested him much; he was provoked with her all along. If she would have done a really self-abandoned, impassioned thing . . . he could have made a fine tragic ending to the book, but she was too commonplace and straight-laced and he could not make her.

This, of course, is open to the interpretation that Grace, to her creator's exasperation, simply went her own way—a power which it is popularly believed that the characters of fiction occasionally command. But there is nothing involuntary about the dogged craftsmanship with which, in the closing chapters, Hardy sets about a superficial credibilizing of that moral rehabilitation of her worthless husband which Grace's final reconciliation with him requires. 'He saw how deep had been his offence': there is much in this vein that we do not believe—or believe that Hardy believes. It is true that Hardy finds a means of intimating as much:

> 'Let her take him back to her bed if she will! . . . But let her bear in mind that the woman walks and laughs somewhere at this very moment whose neck he'll be coling next year as he does hers to-night; and as he did Felice Charmond's last year; and Suke Damson's the year afore! . . . It's a forlorn hope for her; and God knows how it will end!'

But lest we should pay too much attention to this sombre prophecy—'accentuate' it, in Hardy's word—it is placed in the mouth of Melbury, whose obstinate follies and misjudgements have been the mainspring of almost everything disastrous in the story. We are free to think of his as a discredited voice, if we will. 'Cynicism' is perhaps too strong a word justly to characterize this acquiescence of Hardy's in the popular canons of Victorian fiction. He is doing no more, after all, than follow through the common course of things in closing his story, as he does, not upon some large tragic or romantic resonance but upon a muted world of compromise and fatigue and disillusion. So it is hard to see just where the falseness lies. It is there in some degree, nevertheless.

3

But if we sense in *The Woodlanders* the presence of an artist who has grown impatient with some of the circumscriptions of his

medium, we are aware that the book evidences at the same time a
strong principle of growth—and of growth still capable of
operation within the boundaries of prose fiction. If we compare
Grace Melbury's story with that of Elfride Swancourt in *A Pair of
Blue Eyes* we shall find obvious similarities. But Grace, while
being much less poetic a creation than Elfride, is at the same
time a great deal more real. And this seems to be because, as we
have remarked, Hardy has been content a little to let up on the
theme of some vast cosmic malignity. Elfride is caught again and
again in Fate's gins and toils and booby-traps—this to the
impairment of our sense that she effectively enjoys any free
agency at all. This technique of distortion and intensification is
not brought to bear upon Grace to anything like the same extent.
The climax to which her story mounts, indeed, is one in which she
quite literally *escapes* being caught in such an engine. An actual
man-trap is placed in her husband's path as a consequence of
actual and finite human spite; it is Grace who is in danger of
being maimed by it; but Grace is swift and light-footed and
escapes. She is merely stripped of her skirt, and thus disrobed
finds herself clasped in her husband's arms. The man-trap is in
the story, no doubt, chiefly because Hardy had hit upon it early
in the course of his design as a useful means of generating a long
moment of suspense and sensation at the close.[1] It has its crude
effectiveness in this way, although there are few places in the
novel in which Hardy's prose is so astray. Fitzpiers, finding the
skirt in the trap, supposes Grace to have been 'taken out mangled
by some chance passer':

> Of all the degrees and qualities of punishment that Fitzpiers
> had undergone since his sins against Grace first began, not
> any even approximated in intensity to this. 'O, my own—my
> darling! O, cruel Heaven—it is too much this!' he cried,
> writhing and rocking himself over the sorry accessories of her
> he deplored. . . . Right and left of the narrow pass between the
> oaks were dense bushes; and now from behind these a female

[1] Near the start of the novel, Grace is shown a collection of man-traps by
Mrs Charmond. Mrs Charmond says with arch vulgarity: 'Man-traps are of
rather ominous significance where a person of our sex lives, are they not?'
And Grace responds primly: 'They are interesting, no doubt, as relics of a
barbarous time happily past.' Since *The Woodlanders* was written for publication in monthly parts in the common Victorian hand-to-mouth fashion we
know that this proleptic touch was not a late interpolation. And similarly
with Mrs Charmond's fatal and improbable former lover, the 'Italianized
American'. In Chapter XLIII he has all the appearance of a reckless im-
provization. But in fact he has made a conscientious, if unpersuasive,
personal appearance in Chapter XXI, and he is heard of again in Chapter
XXXII.

figure glided, whose appearance even in the gloom was, though graceful in outline, noticeably strange.

She was white up to the waist, and figured above. She was, in short, Grace, his wife, lacking the portion of her dress which the gin retained.

In spite of the high absurdity of this, the man-trap that has failed of its prey is not unimpressive as an oddly concretized metaphor. And that Grace's command of herself as instanced in her mere fleetness of foot has for once thwarted the mere cruelty of things is an index of the manner in which in *The Woodlanders* Hardy has, for the time, freed himself from an overplus of fatality.

But if in this novel the President of the Immortals is being allowed forty winks (or perhaps thirty) the reason is that Hardy's apprehension of injustice has shifted elsewhere. He had by now, we must suppose, received more occasion than John Milton ever did to meditate grimly on the doctrine and discipline of divorce. But although the President may be blamed for bringing unhappy marriages into being, it is intellectually unpersuasive to arraign him for their enforced continuance. Upon this it is rather his self-appointed priests and presbyters who insist—or if not these the prejudices and irrationalities of human society as a whole. Hardy had already written novels in which, in Edmund Gosse's phrase, he had shaken his fist at his Creator. It was the turn of his fellow-citizens now. The preface which he wrote for the novel's publication in book form contains what is virtually an explicit avowal of his intention:

It is tacitly assumed for the purpose of the story that no doubt of the depravity of the erratic heart who feels some third person to be better suited to his or her tastes than the one with whom he has contracted to live, enters the head of reader or writer for a moment. From the point of view of marriage as a distinct convenant or undertaking, decided on by two people fully cognizant of all its possible issues, and competent to carry them through, this assumption is, of course, logical. Yet no thinking person supposes that on the broader ground of how to afford the greatest happiness to the units of human society during their brief transit through this sorry world, there is no more to be said on this covenant; and it is certainly not supposed by the writer of these pages.

The irony here is designed to declare rather than to mask a didactic purpose. And that the novel is really *about* marriage as a social and legal institution claiming some divine sanction and immunity plainly appears as its close, when Grace is considering whether she has a duty to return to her husband:

> Impelled by a remembrance she took down a prayer-book, and turned to the marriage-service. Reading it slowly through she became quite appalled at her recent off-handedness, when she rediscovered what awfully solemn promises she had made him at Hintock chancel steps not so very long ago. She became lost in long ponderings on how far a person's conscience might be bound by vows made without at the time a full recognition of their force. That particular sentence, beginning, 'Whom God hath joined together,' was a staggerer for a gentle woman of strong devotional sentiment. She wondered whether God really did join them together.

'Whom the Archbishop of Canterbury hath joined together let no man put asunder.' Bernard Shaw was to complete Grace's thought.

It is not at a jump that Hardy thus shifts the emphasis of his intellectual interest and emotional concern to the evils of man-made ordinances; nor in doing so is he falling back upon some late-romantic derivative of the thought of Rousseau. Grace at one point displays 'her revolt for the nonce against social law, her passionate desire for primitive life'. But her creator is under no impulsion to carry a doctrine of primitivism very far. The corruptions and irrationalities of complex society may be responsible for much ill, but if we trace our way back through history there is no Noble Savage at the end of the road. Men are best circumstanced when they live and die within the matrix of some stable and enduring culture. But even such men as these are not in fact innocents simply borne upon hard by fate. Often enough—in the phrase of another great novelist and poet of the age—'we are betrayed by what is false within'. That the imperfection of the universe is miniatured in the hearts of individual men had been a main burden of *The Mayor of Casterbridge*, and is what makes that novel a greater novel than *The Woodlanders*, which succeeded it. In *The Woodlanders* the indictment takes a step forward, and in doing so seems to enter a narrower space. Michael Henchard has suffered indeed beneath the institutions of society, or at least from changes in the English rural economy which he has failed to understand. But for what is more elemental in Henchard's tragedy—for the man's mere inches, we may say—

there would be no room in *The Woodlanders*, which is the least poetic of Hardy's major productions.

4

Guerard is saying something like this when he declares that *The Woodlanders* and its immediate successor are Hardy's 'closest approaches to orthodox realism: to an impression of life as an unselective flow of plausible events', and adds that 'the margin of chance is reduced almost to nothing as against the margin of error'. The novel is in a sense a tragedy or quasi-tragedy of errors; all the principal characters except Marty South (against whom the entire action is counterpoised) miscalculate more or less fatally under the interacting pressures of individual inclination and 'social law'. Melbury is at the head of them; it is chiefly against his folly that we find ourselves inwardly exclaiming again and again as we read.

The prosperous man late-risen from the people, who has given his daughter a superior education and is intent upon marrying her out of her class, is a familiar figure in Victorian fiction, and his portrait is commonly the portrait simply of a snob. But the word by no means fits Melbury; its associations are quite wrong. It is the pressure of a traditional and essentially unemulous social attitude that deflects the timber merchant from his sensible and honourable hope that Grace will marry Giles Winterborne. 'That touching faith in members of long-established families as such, irrespective of their personal condition or character, which is still found among old-fashioned people in the rural districts, reached its full perfection in Melbury.' This is a reiterated note. 'The Hintock woodlanders held with all the strength of inherited conviction to the aristocratic principle'—to the extent that when Dr Fitzpiers, understood to be descended from a line 'once among the greatest', does in fact marry Grace Melbury, he falls sharply in their esteem. 'They won't believe'—a candid old woman tells him—'you know such clever doctrines in physic as they once supposed of ye, seeing as you could marry into Mr Melbury's family, which is only Hintock-born such as I be meself.'

Knowledge of such a context of social feelings as this might have given any man pause. But Melbury—as much as Dr Sloper in Henry James's *Washington Square*—is the very type of the parent in a fatal relationship with his child. His weakness is in part temperamental and innate—that of the insecure man who must assert himself through the successes of his children. But we see how this is played upon at an early stage not only by chance (the chance that a gentleman takes a fancy to his daughter) and class-feeling (the simple fascination of the big house, whether it be Mrs Charmond's to which he hopes Grace may gain entrance as a kind of companion, or that vanished one in which Fitzpiers's ancestors lived long ago), but also by the profit-and-loss calculations which become second nature to the small merchant. Melbury feels that he has sunk good money in Grace, and because of this he has reservations about Winterborne from the start. 'Since I have educated her so well'—he says to his second wife in Chapter III—'and so long, and so far above the level of the daughters hereabout, it is *wasting her* to give her to a man of no higher standing than he.'

It is essentially Melbury's want of judgement that first puts Grace's happiness at risk, and that twice bears disastrously upon it later on. Rashly taking for granted the feasibility of a divorce, and prompted by a sort of acquisitiveness which is reluctant to let Winterborne slip, he edges the two—largely against the better judgement of each—into an impasse from which the major catastrophe proceeds. And equally fatal here is the anxious social conformity with which, when the possibility of divorce has been exploded, he urges Grace to take her husband back. Even when she cries out against this, 'turning white with dismay', he pushes heavily ahead with it:

'Surely it is the most respectable thing to do?' he continued. 'I don't like this state that you are in—neither married nor single. It hurts me, and it hurts you, and it will always be remembered against us in Hintock. There has never been any scandal like it in the Melbury family before.'

It is because Grace is thus thrust—or at least is thus too precipitately thrust—towards a re-established union which is nervously intolerable to her that she obeys what is called her 'Daphnean instinct' and makes that flight into 'the depths of the woods' which in fact ends in Winterborne's hut.

Almost equally with her father, of course, Grace Melbury's conduct is controlled by notions of social status. But although her errors lie in the same broad field as his they do not alienate our sympathies to anything like the extent that his do. She is considerably more sensible, for one thing, and for a time at least becomes 'more and more uneasy at being the social hope of the family'. Nevertheless, her fashionable (or at least expensive) boarding-school has done its work, and as she is driven home by Winterborne on the last stage of her return from it there is no surprise in her reflecting that her late companions have been girls 'whose parents Giles would have addressed with a deferential Sir or Madam'. It is, we are told, her 'delicate femininity' that makes it impossible for her to lose sight of this, and she remains to the end liable to be offended by company or even mere table-appointments of the homelier sort. Her excitement at the promise —deceitful, as it turns out—of Mrs Charmond's patronage is 'a species of exaltation'; and is indeed what makes the level-headed Giles first fear that 'this engagement of his was a very unpromising business'. In itself it is innocent and inevitable enough. Yet Grace's real mistake lies back here, as it were, near the start of the story. Equally near the end, it is true, we hear of her 'timid morality'—hear of it, we may say, from that Hardy who told Miss Rebekah Owen of New York City that more might have been contrived with a Grace who could manage some 'really self-abandoned, impassioned thing'. 'How selfishly correct I am!' Grace tells herself, and it is easy to feel today that she would have done better to coax Giles back into his hut, nurse him until he was strong enough to possess himself of her, and then depart with him for other territories. D. H. Lawrence's Connie Chatterley would have made no bones about this. Nevertheless Grace is right—if only because Giles is not a Mellors. To take him would have been a kind of rape—a violation of his personality.

Giles's first renewed encounter with Grace when she returns from school, given in Chapter V, is one of those scenes in Hardy which we think of as visually memorable, and which are so because of the high felicity of their imaginative implication. Giles has taken a specimen apple-tree to market in Sherton Abbas, and it is under it that they meet. There would be difficulty in conceiving a setting more to be approved by those who admire the archetypal in fiction. Yet it is not very definitely our First Parents who are in question. Of course the tree is a phallic tree, and Beach is no doubt right when he tells us that all the trees in the novel 'are like sacred beings; and Winterborne is their priest or tutelary god'. But the tree is the symbol, too, of something related indeed to this but more generalized; it stands for what another critic, Mr Brown, calls 'intimacy with the plenitude of the natural order'. When Grace's first misfortune has overtaken her, and she sees her husband ride off to visit Mrs Charmond on the very

horse that Giles had bought for her own use, she meets Giles and
takes a walk with him:

> He looked and smelt like Autumn's very brother, his face
> being sunburnt to wheat-colour, his eyes blue as corn-flowers,
> his sleeves and leggings dyed with fruit-stains, his hands clammy
> with the sweet juice of apples. . . . Nature was bountiful, she
> thought. No sooner had she been cast aside by Edred Fitzpiers
> than another being, impersonating chivalrous and undiluted
> manliness, had arisen out of the earth ready to her hand.

And later we are told of Grace that Giles

> rose upon her memory as the fruit-god and the wood-god in
> alternation: sometimes leafy and smeared with green lichen,
> as she had seen him amongst the sappy boughs of the planta-
> tions: sometimes cider-stained and starred with apple-pips, as
> she had met him on his return from cider-making in Blackmoor
> Vale, with his vats and presses beside him. . . . She thought
> of that time when he had been standing under his apple-tree on
> her return from school, and of the tender opportunity then
> missed through her fastidiousness.

It is not for nothing, we may feel, that Hardy has been turning
again to the poets, Keats among them. And we may recall the
place in E. M. Forster's *A Room with a View* in which Lucy
Honeychurch, having with something much like Grace Melbury's
social fastidiousness turned down George Emerson (a young
man obscurely connected with railways), next sees him thrown
on the ceiling of the Sistine Chapel by Michelangelo—where he
is carrying a burden of acorns.

There is one regard in which we should not be misled by the
feel of all this imagery. Grace's error in marrying Fitzpiers
(and his in marrying her) is not being viewed, in any narrow
sense, as a matter of the absence of a mutual sexual responsiveness.
The Woodlanders, indeed, like most novels of its period, is in-
explicit here. But our predominant impression is of a relationship
quickly crippled rather by disparities of habit and culture the
significance of which has been badly underestimated by the
people concerned. It is Fitzpiers who miscalculates most. He is
accustomed to a certain freedom of moral stance: otherwise he
could scarcely so off-handedly pursue and possess Suke Damson
within minutes of first declaring himself to Grace. The lamp-light
by which he is supposed to be poring over 'the books and *matériel*

of science' as frequently illuminates 'rank literatures of emotion and passion'. 'The love of men like Fitzpiers', we hear, 'is unquestionably of such quality as to bear division and transference.' And of particular significance in relation to all this is his total divorce from the activities and assumptions of the community among which he has chosen to come and live. Like Mrs Charmond (who owns most of what, in the Hintocks, one can survey) he is a total stranger to the place, and in general habit he is like her totally incurious about it. He is foolish to suppose that a man of his temperament, and thus circumstanced, is likely to make anything stable out of the marriage he undertakes. His entanglement with Mrs Charmond fails to impress us, partly, no doubt, because Hardy manages such things badly. (The polite characters are seldom much good when alone in each other's society, and least of all when they are squaring up to make love.) But chiefly we are unimpressed because the couple are failing to make something essentially spurious at all impressive or convincing between themselves; and the episode must thus in some degree be accounted an artistic success. Mrs Charmond's error, quite a considerable one, lies in believing in the reality of her own postures.

5

We are left with Giles Winterborne and Marty South. They are, in differing degree, the book's exemplary characters. Because one of Hardy's most powerfully apprehended conceptions was that of Consequence—of all the increasing and narrowing compulsion that will flow from some initial action or failure to act—it is commonly in the early part of a story that the fateful moments come. Giles, like Grace, makes his error at the start. It is the not ungenerous error of overestimating the obstacles which Grace's genteel accomplishments and recently acquired habits of mind must place in his path as a suitor. He may reckon that something of this will wear off, as indeed it does, when Hintock life again becomes familiar to her. He is chargeable with being too passive, all the same, and in a sense his passivity lets Grace down. But this censure, even if just, cannot be directed upon him in the closing scene of his life. When Howe says of his shivering with fever outside his own hut that 'no one, neither man nor dog, should have to be that loyal', he is perhaps regarding the matter from an insufficiently historical point of view. It is not a shallow propriety that is involved, and Grace in her last desperate cry to him knows as much. What Hardy characteristically calls 'the present trying conjuncture' brings up for Giles a question of honour. The passage continues with that awkward strength which is so seldom to be laughed at:

> There was one man on earth in whom she believed absolutely, and he was that man. That this crisis could end in nothing but sorrow was a view for a moment effaced by this triumphant thought of her trust in him; and the purity of the affection with which he responded to that trust rendered him more than proof against any frailty that besieged him in relation to her.

As a background to this we may recall earlier scenes in the recesses of this wood: 'the subdued screams and struggles audible from neighbouring brakes', for example, which reveal to Fitzpiers as he takes Grace in his arms for the first time 'that there had been other lurkers thereabout for a similar purpose'. The near-promiscuity of such a rural Saturnalia as this (it is Midsummer night), and those miserable herdings of families in mere hovels which led to the same or graver ills such as confront us in speculations on the parentage of Rebecca and Tryphena Sparks: these conditions in the lives of the rural poor required to be countered by stringent rules of conduct. And Giles Winterborne's life, we are told, had been thus 'ruled by household laws'. Something like tabu is operative, if we care so to express it, when Grace passes within the protection of Giles in his hut. We must recall that such is the hinterland of the situation before we are amused or shocked by Grace's pushing Giles's supper through the window and in a ritual fashion bolting the door at his command.

It is Marty South who represents the chief growing-point in *The Woodlanders*. The action opens and closes on her; and if what she chiefly exhibits in the interim is, as somebody has said, 'mournful passivity', she is at least constantly exhibited as a stoic who goes determinedly about the day's work. And that Marty has, beyond everything else, a day's work to perform is the cardinal point, for in exhibiting it as harshly as he does Hardy is effectively closing his account with his whimsical cider-drinking peasantry. These, led by Winterborne's faithful and Shakespearian Robert Creedle ("tis well to think the day *is* done, when 'tis done'), still linger nostalgically in the corners of this book. But Marty is never shown in direct contact with their diversions.

She is first shown in the cottage of her dying father, endeavouring to hold things together by toiling far into the night at the man's craft of making spar-gads for thatchers. And Hardy at once pauses upon a paragraph which is almost a formal indictment of social injustice:

> The young woman laid down the bill-hook for a moment and examined the palm of her right hand, which, unlike the other, was ungloved, and showed little hardness or roughness about it. The palm was red and blistering, as if her present occupation were as yet too recent to have subdued it to what it worked in. As with so many right hands born to manual labour, there was nothing in its fundamental shape to bear out the physiological conventionalism that gradations of birth show themselves primarily in the form of this member. Nothing but a cast of the die of destiny had decided that the girl should handle the tool; and the fingers which clasped the heavy ash haft might have skilfully guided the pencil or swept the string, had they only been set to do it in good time.

'The cast of the die of destiny' is a phrase which might suggest that resigned melancholy of acquiescence in extreme inequality which the poet Gray insinuates so skilfully into his *Elegy*. But it is at once brilliantly followed by a passage of different implication. The barber Percomb appears with his design upon Marty's 'one bright gift of Time', her hair. Since Mrs Charmond will buy the tresses, he can afford a good price; and to tempt Marty (who describes him as behaving 'like the Devil to Doctor Faustus in the penny book') he leaves on her chimney-piece a couple of sovereigns 'in such a manner as to suggest a pair of jaundiced eyes on the watch for an opportunity'. It is just over the page from this that Melbury is found saying of his expensively educated daughter that 'it is *wasting her* to give her to a man of no higher standing' than Giles Winterborne. But Giles is to be of a standing too high for Marty. And, in any case, when she does part with her hair, she seems practically as well as symbolically to be accepting sexlessness. Sheer economic oppression has robbed her even in this way, and it is as a kind of disnatured dryad that she moves through the rest of the book to her moving apotheosis in its final paragraph. Few critics have found this conclusion other than beyond praise. It is less commonly acknowledged that in beginning with Marty as it does *The Woodlanders* is not very far behind *The Mayor of Casterbridge* itself.

But we distort in some measure the total impression made by the novel if we concentrate upon its principal characters and main design. When Hardy said that he liked *The Woodlanders* best '*as a story*', and that the story struck him as commendably 'quaint and fresh', he was no doubt setting (or affecting to set) principal emphasis upon all those elements of oddity and ingenuity which he never ceased to see as essential to popular fiction. *The Woodlanders* is very adequately enlivened in this way; and it also continues to provide, with some appearance of artless counter-balance to all this, the customary quota of culture-references in literature, philosophy, the sciences, and the arts.

These last frequently seem, in the individual instance, incongruous and even absurd. On the third page we find the reins of a carrier's van described as forming a catenary curve; and when we have considered the word we see that they could scarcely form anything else. The barber, fixing his gaze through a window on Marty's hair, is contemplating 'an impression-picture of extremest type': this is an almost up-to-the-minute reference, since the term came into being only after the first Impressionist Exhibition in Paris in 1874. Grace's eyebrows, if painted, would probably have to be done 'in Prouts's or Vandyke brown'; at Giles's unfortunate supper-party there is a tablecloth 'reticulated with folds as in Flemish Last-Suppers'; Fitzpiers, diminishing in distance on Grace's mount Darling as he goes off on the hunt of Mrs Charmond, is 'a Wouvermans eccentricity reduced to microscopic dimensions'; and when, after an accident and with his face covered in blood, he presents himself at Mrs Charmond's window, his appearance 'as disclosed in the square area of the pane . . . met her frightened eyes like a replica of the Sudarium of St Veronica'.

This last image joins the artistic with the macabre and bizarre, and these elements are elsewhere scattered about the book: sometimes in passing imagery, as when 'the bleared white visage of a sunless winter day' emerges 'like a dead-born child' or we view a pack of cards stained 'by the touch of generations of damp and excited thumbs, now fleshless in the grave'. Again, Fitzpiers at the window is but one instance of a device to which the action has constant recourse; the clandestine or the unexpected is regularly thus being spied on, just as numerous revealing if improbable soliloquies are being overheard. The action is frequently prodded or jerked forward by small ingenuities, as when a tell-tale turnpike ticket drops from Fitzpiers's pocket or Suke proves still to own the tooth he has claimed to draw; or it exhibits a chancy kind of nemesis: 'I foredoomed my revived girlhood's romance', Mrs Charmond has to tell herself, realizing that her depriving Winterborne of his small house-property made him ineligible as a suitor of Grace, and that as a consequence

Grace has become the wife of Fitzpiers, whom Mrs Charmond has lately discovered to be the young man with whom she once had an abortive love-affair in Germany. Similarly, her final and fatal break with Fitzpiers is the consequence of his discovering, through the instrumentality of a belatedly opened letter from Marty, the truth about his mistress's hair, and that 'he had stroked those false tresses with his hand many a time without knowing them to be transplanted'. Than this final ingenuity, nonsense could not farther go.

Yet we have to admit—pausing on this last point—that Hardy's world is not one in which the likelihood or unlikelihood of such a deception surviving sustained sexual intimacy very much matters. The episodes of sensation and melodrama still scattered over the great canvases of his maturity have something of the function—to use a comparison he might have approved—of Constable's snow: the glint of these highlights has an animating effect on the composition as a whole. It is improbable that Fitzpiers, perched in front of Melbury on Darling, should on the strength of a swig of spirits pour out to the supposed stranger the evil talk he does. It is improbable that, Fitzpiers being injured in his chamber, Grace should cry out to Mrs Charmond and Suke, 'Wives all, let's enter together!' It is improbable, a little earlier, that she and Mrs Charmond, being lost in the woods, should suddenly behave like Cytherea and Miss Aldclyffe in *Desperate Remedies*:

> They consequently crept up to one another, and being in the dark, lonely, and weary, did what neither had dreamed of doing beforehand—clasped each other closely. Mrs Charmond's furs consoled Grace's cold face; and each one's body, as she breathed, alternately heaved against that of her companion; while the funereal trees rocked, and chanted dirges unceasingly.

It is even more improbable that, hard upon this, Grace should be seizing for the first time on a truth which should long have been apparent to her. But the distortion of sober likelihood makes possible a startling (and, for its time, most audacious) effect:

> Grace started roughly away from the shelter of the furs, and sprang to her feet.
> 'O, my great God!' she exclaimed, thunderstruck at a revelation transcending her utmost suspicion. 'He's had you! Can it be—can it be!'

Extravagances of which these are random samples are not, as has been remarked earlier, prominent in *The Woodlanders*. But it is clear that Hardy had no thought of eliminating them even from his most serious fiction. They have an integral place, indeed, in his aesthetic.

10
Minor Fiction

'HARDY'S MINOR FICTION' IS PERHAPS A POLITE WAY OF SAYING 'Hardy's less successful fiction'. The term may be taken to cover more than forty short stories (some of them mere anecdotes), four novels of varying length, and *The Well-Beloved*. *The Well-Beloved* is the most interesting work in this group; it fails to come off, but is almost unique in Hardy's writing as being essentially a fable— and a substantial one at that. So odd a performance could not conceivably have been written with any pot-boiling intent. The short stories *are* pot-boilers. And the four novels—*The Hand of Ethelberta, The Trumpet-Major, A Laodicean,* and *Two on a Tower* —at least come to us as distinguishably the product of Hardy's struggle with what Coleridge once called 'those two giants linked together: bread and cheese'. This does not mean that we should disregard them. In the heat—or at least the dust—of that struggle there sometimes emerges what is most native to a writer's mind: those basic interests and humbly diurnal concerns which in his more dedicated creations are disciplined and distorted into the proper deliverances of art. It would be absurd to assess Hardy on the strength of this writing (which is what T. S. Eliot came near to doing in his celebrated attack), and unprofitable to linger over it for very long. But it does present us, in brief, with certain of the rudiments of his imagination.

If we begin with the first volume of short stories, *Wessex Tales*, we find the first story, 'The Three Strangers', to be constructed round a song. It is a ballad-like song, and we might suppose it to be traditional, did we not find it reprinted as Hardy's own, with the title 'The Stranger's Song', in *Wessex Poems*:

> O my trade it is the rarest one,
> > Simple shepherds all—
> > My trade is a sight to see;
> For my customers I tie, and take 'em up on high,
> > And waft 'em to a far countree!

My tools are but common ones,
          Simple shepherds all—
     My tools are no sight to see:
A little hempen string, and a post whereon to swing,
     Are implements enough for me!

To-morrow is my working day,
          Simple shepherds all—
     To-morrow is a working day for me:
For the farmer's sheep is slain, and the lad who did it ta'en,
     And on his soul may God ha' mer-cy!

The hangman is on his way to Casterbridge on professional business. Caught in a rainstorm, he finds shelter in a shepherd's cottage in which a christening-party is going on; prompted by curious questioning, and encouraged by plenty of strong mead, he announces himself in what is represented as an extemporary composition. He does so, as it happens, in the presence of the escaped prisoner he is due to hang on the morrow—and indeed sings the third verse after the arrival of yet another stranger at the party: the condemned man's brother. 'The Three Strangers' is an admirably dramatic little story, and, although in places ponderous in the telling, ends deftly enough on a note of mild comedy and the successful get-away of the fugitive, whose crime had indeed simply been that of stealing a sheep. But we may recall as we lay it down that Hardy as a child had twice witnessed public hangings. And we may recall, too, the spectacle upon which *Tess of the d'Urbervilles* was to close.

   The second of the *Wessex Tales*, 'A Tradition of Eighteen Hundred and Four', we may think of, if we please, as looking forward to *The Dynasts*; it represents Napoleon as engaged upon a most improbable reconnaissance of the Wessex countryside. The third, 'The Melancholy Hussar', returns us to the theme of judicial execution; a girl looks over her garden-wall and sees her lover despatched by a firing party while kneeling on his own coffin. The fourth, 'The Withered Arm', has as its scene 'the same heath which had witnessed the agony of the Wessex King Ina, presented to after-ages as Lear'—the fancy to which Hardy was to recur when he wrote a preface for the 1895 edition of *The Return of the Native*—and as its climax a woman's attempt to cure her magically induced malady by the answering magic of touching the neck of a man who has just been hanged—the man turning out at the last to be her husband's illegitimate son. Two other stories are ironic rather than macabre. In 'Interlopers at the Knap' a simple tale of

a marriage prevented at the last moment by the return of a former
sweetheart from abroad is complicated by various quirks of
fortune, including an ingeniously contrived first reappearance of
this woman in a gown which had been intended for the other.
'Fellow-Townsmen' is a more developed story of the same order;
we may feel it to be related, rather more substantially than by the
suggestion of its title, to *The Mayor of Casterbridge* of six years
later. The prosperous Barnet has failed to gain his true love, Lucy
Savile, and has made a most unfortunate marriage instead. His
more modestly circumstanced friend Downe is married very
happily indeed. The two wives go out in a boat; Mrs Downe is
drowned; Mrs Barnet is resuscitated by her husband after the
doctor has given her up, and the issue is that she deserts him.
Barnet persuades Downe to engage Lucy (who lives in reduced
circumstances) as governess to his motherless children. Later, he
receives a letter announcing Mrs Barnet's death, and realizes that
he is now free to marry Lucy. But a second letter arrives hard upon
the first; it is from Downe and announces that he and Lucy are to
be married that morning. And here the author of this sad tale
makes his point with sufficient emphasis:

> Barnet was a man with a rich capacity for misery, and there
> is no doubt that he exercised it to its fullest extent now. The
> events that had, as it were, dashed themselves together into one
> half-hour of this day showed that curious refinement of cruelty
> in their arrangement which often proceeds from the bosom of
> the whimsical god at other times known as blind Circumstance.
> That his few minutes of hope, between the reading of the first
> and second letters, had carried him to extraordinary heights of
> rapture was proved by the immensity of his suffering now.

It seems fair enough that the remaining story in *Wessex Tales*,
'The Distracted Preacher', should be humorous in intention. But
Hardy appears not to have been satisfied with it; he added to an
edition of 1912 a note to the effect that the story ends as it does
only to please the taste of a magazine public. He makes a similar
comment, indeed, on 'The Withered Arm': there is something
wrong about it, and 'readers are therefore asked to correct the
misrelation'. This somewhat cavalier attitude occurs most famously
in the note of similar intent about the close of *The Return of the
Native*.

2

The stories brought together as *A Group of Noble Dames* are
based upon antiquarian research of a not altogether amiable

150

MINOR FICTION

sort. Asked by the *Graphic* for a 'short novel', Hardy turned
to Hutchins's *The History and Antiquities of the County of
Dorset* and assembled from it (and also, we are told, from the
confidences of aged persons who had known 'old family
servants of the great families') a sufficient pageant of disastrous
marriages, confessed and unconfessed adulteries, complicated
illegitimacies, sudden deaths, suspected crimes, bizarre cruelties
and the like among the Wessex gentry of some generations
back to provide material for a sequence of ten short stories.
They are in the main sensational and perfunctory narratives,
hastily and carelessly written. Yet they have interest for us
if only as showing how willing was the imagination of the
mature Hardy (for *Tess of the d'Urbervilles* is now behind him)
to entertain kinds of fantasy which must have been familiar
to him in boyhood. The figures in these stories luxuriate alike in
the sorrows and in the polished ungodliness of an aristocracy
viewed from the cottage or the servants' hall. The most celebrated
of them is that unfortunate wife of Lord Uplandtowers (a fictional
version, it seems, of the fifth Earl of Shaftesbury) whose fate
Hardy recounts in the very ugly tale called 'Barbara of the House
of Grebe'.

Rather more considerable than this extravagance is 'Squire
Petrick's Lady'. Petrick, an heir to large estates, is horrified when
his wife confesses on her deathbed that the son to whom she has
just given birth is not his. But Petrick's lineage is by no means
equal to his acres, since his father has been merely a lawyer and
agent to several noblemen, and when he finds reason to believe
that the intruder in his bed was the young Marquis of Christminster, son of the Duke of Southwesterland, he comes to dote on
the boy as a scion of nobility, and looks eagerly and happily for
the emergence in his features 'of those historic curves and shades
that the painters Vandyke and Lely had perpetuated on canvas'—
including, in particular, 'the elegant knife-edged nose' of a true
Southwesterland. Eventually, however, he learns that his wife came
of a stock subject to delusions, and that the paternity of young
Lord Christminster, indeed, is a chronological impossibility. The
boy is, after all, his own—and Petrick is at once disenchanted and
disgusted with him.

The story is very briefly told, and with no attempt to realize or
credibilize the characters in a manner incompatible with its fabular nature. Yet an abundant credibility is present, and the absurdity of Petrick's successive attitudes constitutes a mordant ironic
anatomy of a type of English social consciousness by no means
confined to the Late Victorian age.

3

Of Hardy's remaining short stories, brought together in *Life's Little Ironies* and *A Changed Man*, several treat the consequences of social disparity, not through fantasy but with a sombre realism. In 'The Son's Veto' (which Hardy is said to have judged the best of his tales) a vicar marries his parlourmaid and later dies. The widow is left with a single son, who is sent to a public school and Oxford, himself becomes a clergyman, and eventually makes his mother swear upon the holy cross that she will never marry her first love, a market-gardener's assistant who has some hope of setting up as a greengrocer. 'His education', we are told rather heavily of this disagreeable young man, 'had by this time sufficiently ousted his humanity to keep him quite firm; though his mother might have led an idyllic life with her faithful fruiterer and greengrocer, and nobody have been anything the worse in the world.' A more substantial story, 'A Tragedy of Two Ambitions', combines a similar anti-clerical animus with a certain balance of sympathy, and has the interest of looking forward to *Jude the Obscure*. It opens upon two brothers of humble station 'plodding away at the Greek Testament', and follows the bitter struggle by which they make their way to a clerical career and are on the verge of marrying their adored sister to a landowner. But they have a chronic liability in a drunken and disreputable father, and when he turns up disastrously at the very crisis of their fortunes they fail to hasten to his help as he flounders in a weir and drowns. The marriage takes place, and the brothers continue in their clerical functions. But they remain somewhat uneasy and depressed in mind. On a subsequent occasion they visit the scene of the fatality, and find that their father's walking-stick, which one of them had hastily concealed in the mud, has rooted itself and now become 'a straight little silver-poplar'. This dubious concluding symbolism was an afterthought on Hardy's part. The turning of strange or melodramatic action to the purposes of poetry which is one of Hardy's notable powers in the novels seems to elude him, for the most part, in the short stories. There is an attempt at it in 'The Romantic Adventures of a Milkmaid', a kind of fairy-story expanded to the length of a *novella*; as an ambiguous presentation of what may or may not be supernatural it compares unfavourably with Henry James's *The Turn of the Screw*. But there is a notable success in a much shorter story, 'The Fiddler of the Reels'.

The fiddler like the hangman had been a potent figure in Hardy's childish imagination—but with the difference that Hardy

had precociously become a fiddler himself. In 'The Fiddler of the
Reels' we have an instance of something basic in his sensibility
declaring itself in a work of minor compass written for an unassuming occasion—the publication by *Scribner's Magazine* of a special
'Exhibition Number' in connection with the Chicago World's
Fair of 1893. Hardy manages to bring the Great Exhibition of
1851 in London into his narrative. But for him a 'Fair' meant
something rather different: a rural occasion the mild excitement of
which might be vastly heightened by music and dancing. In the
story this heightening is raised to possession and frenzy. Wat
Ollamoor has come to Mellstock from nobody knows where, and
he is a fiddler of preternatural power. 'He could make any child
in the parish, who was at all sensitive to music, burst into tears in
a few minutes', and he is not averse from exercising the same effect
upon 'young women of fragile and responsive organization'. One
of these is Car'line Aspent; under Wat's fascination she throws
over her honest lover Ned Hipcroft, who in consequence departs
disconsolately to seek employment in London. Four years later,
Ned receives a repentant letter from Car'line, and he agrees to
marry her. When she joins him she brings a small daughter whom
she confesses to be Wat's child. The marriage nevertheless takes
place, and eventually the little family thus constituted return to
Wessex. On their arrival in Casterbridge Ned decides at once to
spend an hour or two seeking work, and to catch up with Car'line
and the child as they make their way on foot to their destination.
But when the wayfarers reach the Quiet Woman Inn on the lower
verge of Egdon Heath Wat is there playing his fiddle. Car'line is
drawn into the dance; under the compulsion of Wat's fiddling she
dances on and on and on until she drops senseless to the floor;
when Ned arrives it is to find that Wat and the child have disappeared together. Nothing beyond rumour is ever heard of them
again, although Ned, who has come to love the little girl, makes
many efforts to recover her.

What renders this simple-seeming story perhaps the best Hardy
ever wrote is the delicacy and certainty with which it projects and
balances its mundane and preternatural elements. Car'line and
Ned have nothing of the overemphatic quaintness of some of the
Wessex rustics; the account of their reunion in London is writing
with perfect fidelity to all that is limited yet touching in the
relationship; we accept them, without need of nudging, as
symbolic of the modest security to be won on earth through the
exercise of good feeling and the affections. But it is a frangible
security, a reasonable order of things which yet remains at the
mercy of the irruptive Dionysiac power which Wat and his fiddle

represent. Yet the myth only moves disturbingly beneath the surface of the tale. In this its art is perhaps surer and stronger than that found in, say, those short stories of E. M. Forster's in which the myth, as it were, breaks cover and prances around.

4

There is general agreement that *The Hand of Ethelberta* is not a very successful novel, and the basic reason for its failure lies in Hardy's proposal to treat in the key of comedy those chasms between gentle and simple, rich and poor, which it was his more genuine inclination to exhibit in a sombre and serious light—even in such minor pieces as 'The Son's Veto' and 'A Tragedy of Two Ambitions'. The book's main interest for us is as exhibiting a struggling young novelist's ingenious if ill-conceived attempt to extend his range and command some new field of interest. He could not, he believed, write about sheepfarming for ever—so what was he to do? Professional opinion on *The Poor Man and the Lady*, however tactfully delivered, must have convinced him of the difficulty of writing knowledgeably about good society. Yet one sort of knowledge of that society existed in his family. His father the master-mason had been in a superior line of business which had brought him some contact with the gentry; more significantly, his mother, before her marriage, had spent some time as cook in a noble household, and was said to have contrived to have several brothers and sisters living with her during this employment. Might it not be possible to tackle from such a viewpoint a more extended social scene? George Meredith, the grand personage who had discussed *The Poor Man and the Lady* with him, had contrived something of the sort when he traced in *Evan Harrington* the ascending fortunes of his three 'Daughters of the Shears'. Hardy is unlikely to have been possessed of the interesting fact that the grand personage's grandfather had himself been a tailor. But a glance at the chapter-headings of *Evan Harrington* shows us where *The Hand of Ethelberta* came from.

We are told in the *Life* of 'one experienced critic going so far as to write that it was the finest ideal comedy since the days of Shakespeare', but Hardy has to add that the novel was greeted, on the whole, without 'cordiality'. He shows himself a little sore about this:

It was, in fact, thirty years too soon for a Comedy of Society of that kind—just as *The Poor Man and the Lady* had been too soon for a socialist story, and as other of his writings—in prose and verse—were too soon for their date. The most impossible situation in it was said to be that of the heroine sitting at table at a dinner-party of 'the best people,' at which her father was present by the sideboard as butler. Yet a similar situation has been applauded in a play in recent years by Mr Bernard Shaw, without any sense of improbability.

There may be a grain of truth in this arraignment of the *Zeitgeist*, but the more relevant fact is that *You Never Can Tell* is very good of its kind and *The Hand of Ethelberta* is very bad. Mrs Hardy, who seems not quite to have understood such point as the novel has, disapproved of it on the ground that too many of the characters were servants.

It has been the opinion of a number of commentators that Hardy's resentment at the rejection of *The Poor Man and the Lady* (which sounds in the passage I have just quoted) coloured his attitude to the writing of fiction to the end of his days. He certainly seems to have taken small satisfaction in his eventual fame as a novelist, or even to have been convinced that he had attained it. In his old age, it has been recorded, almost the only bitter feelings he ever expressed were directed, not very rationally, against the critics of his novels. But if we are seeking for turning-points in his manner of regarding his craft we ought not wholly to neglect the history and character of *A Laodicean*.

The Hand of Ethelberta, distinctly feeble in its earlier chapters, improves later on, when the heroine's character hardens, sharpens, and defines itself. In *A Laodicean* quite the opposite occurs; as Guerard has it: 'As the book proceeds . . . the charmingly modern and ambiguous Paula degenerates into a paragon of Victorian smugness and evasion.' But more degenerates than this. The novel begins as a far more serious attempt upon something like Meredithian comedy than Hardy elsewhere ventures upon; it disentegrates into melodramatic nonsense such as it would be idle to summon before the court of criticism. The most villainous of its villains, William Dare, has indeed been solemnly enrolled by Professor J. O. Bailey in the philosophical category of Hardy's 'Mephistophelian visitants'. This, I think, is to consider a little too curiously.

It is well known that the crumbling of this book was coincident with, and due to, Hardy's suffering a severe physical illness. Most of it had to be dictated to his wife while he lay uncomfortably immobilized in bed. Valiantly trying to keep up with the demands of serial publication, he fell back on concocting sensational incidents such as clutter *Desperate Remedies*, upon travel-notes made on the Rhine and elsewhere, and even (it seems) upon mild plagiarism. All this was just a matter of Crass Casualty at work upon him. But the question we are tempted to ask is whether the pattern thus enforced by illness does not repeat itself under different circumstances later on, so that early proposals and ambitions for a book do not quite fulfil themselves in the writing. *Two on a Tower*, in particular, raises this issue. But first we may briefly consider *The Trumpet-Major*, which was the novel immediately preceding *A Laodicean*.

5

Guerard declares that Hardy's early critics 'preferred the worst books, *The Trumpet-Major* in particular', and Howe calls this novel 'the one among his books that is most clearly meant as an entertainment'. *The Trumpet-Major* must certainly disappoint readers whose estimate of the worth of a work of fiction depends chiefly upon the earnestness of its endeavour to reach deep into human experience or to persuade us towards one or another philosophic reading of life. Moreover, the novel is not an instance of such ambitions being distinguishably present but in the issue unfulfilled. From the outset the story has no serious designs upon us. It is indeed an entertainment, and one carefully confined within the boundaries of traditional literary expectation. That our chief sense of *The Trumpet-Major* should be of something missing is no doubt an index of the high seriousness of Hardy's major art.

What makes the relaxed character of this particular book surprising is the fact of its being the first direct issue of what we think of as a powerful and brooding historical imagination. The action is set amid 'our preparations for defence against the threatened invasion of England by Buonaparte'. For Hardy as a boy it was clearly Napoleon and his legend that *was* 'history', and we are made aware of Hardy the man intermittently throughout his career as keeping with Napoleon that date which was eventually to be honoured in *The Dynasts*. We therefore expect the novel to be a kind of prolegomenon, and we know that Hardy went to considerable pains to collect material which would enable him to get his period right. Yet the book cannot be said to re-create what must have been the actual tensions of the time in which it is set. The evocation, such as it is, is antiquarian rather than historical in temper.

One factor here may be the circumstances in which the story was written. Hardy hoped to sell it to the *Cornhill*, but

F

when he told Leslie Stephen of his project it was to be informed
that 'a historical character in a novel is almost always a
nuisance'. Eventually he found himself writing his story for
Good Words, a periodical then under the editorship of Dr Donald
Macleod, who was a presbyterian minister in Glasgow. Macleod
was to censor the use, by various soldiers and sailors in the novel,
of such expressions as 'Good God!' and 'O Lord!', and to insist
on one episode being transferred from Sunday to Saturday.
Confronted by this sort of thing, Hardy may well have decided
to construct his book in terms of the conventionally pleasing and
innocuous.

It is a shade ironical that so pervasively accommodating a work
as *The Trumpet-Major* should have got its author into trouble
after all, and significant that the trouble should take the form of
a charge of plagiarism. The specific point at issue has been elucidated by Weber, and is of very minor significance. But the novel
considered in larger terms reveals itself as a deft mingling of
the highly derivative (as in the character, for example, of Festus
Derriman, a pure *miles gloriosus*) with aspects of Wessex life
and feeling which only Hardy could have compassed. The story
concerns the rivalry of two brothers—John and Robert Loveday,
respectively a soldier and sailor—for the hand of the village
beauty, Anne Garland. Anne cannot make up her mind, but in the
end it is the more volatile and light-hearted Robert who wins her,
while the staunch and self-sacrificing John goes to his death in the
Spanish campaign. As in so many of Trollope's domestic novels,
the vacillations of the herione are somewhat tiresomely exploited
to spin out the tale, but Hardy here employs other traditional
resources as well: rustic humour, local colour, and—what is quite
outside Trollope's range—a certain amount of rough-and-tumble
chasing around. In its unassuming way the whole mixture blends
very well, and we are aware in the end that, despite the book's
being so little marked by what is most arresting and compulsive in
Hardy's vision, the harmonizing agent at work is in fact a subdued
but pervasive illumination from his own authentic temper.

6

Two on a Tower is a more unequal novel than *The Trumpet-Major*,
more definitely a failure, and a good deal more interesting. Hardy
was to speak of it in a preface as 'the outcome of a wish to set the
emotional history of two infinitesimal lives against the stupendous
background of the stellar universe'. Lord David Cecil tells us that

this wish was a mistake, since 'the contrast between the stellar
universe and human passion is too simple a theme', and Hardy has
been led 'to choose fiction as the vehicle for an inspiration which
is appropriate only to a lyric—a lyric such as Hardy's own 'At a
Lunar Eclipse' or 'In Vision I Roamed'. But in fact 'the contrast
between the stellar universe and human passion' is *not* Hardy's
theme, although it was no doubt a value in the projected book.
The actual theme derives from two early works of Shakespeare,
Love's Labour's Lost and *Venus and Adonis*. Lady Constantine, a
mature woman of nearly thirty who has been deserted by her husband, patronizes a rural youth of intellectual habit called Swithin
St Cleeve, provides him with astronomical instruments in a tower
on her estate, and falls in love with him. Swithin is slow to remark
the fact. He 'did not observe the tender reproach in Viviette's eyes
when he showed . . . his decided notion that the prime use of dark
nights lay in their furtherance of practical astronomy.' To this
central conception—the conflict between purposive masculine
activity and distracting feminine emotion as focused in the rival
attractions of study and courtship and in a symbolism of the stars
and of a woman's eyes—Hardy was almost certainly led when he
took up Shakespeare's play for the purpose of writing a scene of
amateur theatricals into *A Laodicean*, the novel which came immediately before *Two on a Tower*. But Swithin starts off as a
reluctant lover of a more archetypal order than Berowne and his
companions, and the book's *donnée* requires a simpler and more
straightforward development than it in fact receives. Guerard
ascribes its declining into artificially complex situations of conventional intrigue to 'fatigued evasion'. And indeed here, as with
A Laodicean, we may feel ourselves to be witnessing a failure of
nerve or stamina, an inability to hold on to a new and exploratory
form of ironic comedy. The book has to get itself written; it has
to get itself written at a fixed and very considerable length; basic
situations and ideas must be tinkered with until they are unlikely
too much to offend an editor's or publisher's sense of the pro-
prieties of fiction. Under these depressing constraints Hardy's
inspiration falters and founders. Invention has to take over, and
it is invention of a commonplace sort. The book displays two
characters keenly observed; and one of them, the woman, hints
at some of her creator's largest powers. But the story, scratching
around amid unlikelihoods and absurdities, sadly lets them down.
These are not unfair judgements. Yet, when one has forgotten
most of the action, *Two on a Tower* lingers in the memory as
possessing something of the elusive poetry which Hardy first
brought into the novel in *A Pair of Blue Eyes*.

7

The Well-Beloved, published in 1897 and thus the last of Hardy's prose works to appear as a book, is a revised version of a hastily written short novel dating from four years earlier. Hardy appears not to have thought highly of it, and in this estimate most of his critics have vigorously concurred; among the more recent of them Howe will be found to ignore the book and Guerard to devote to it several paragraphs of vigorous censure. It has considerable interest, nevertheless.

When, in 1889, the firm of Tillotson & Son decided that they could not face up to serializing the novel we know as *Tess of the d'Urbervilles* they seem to have been anxious to remain on good terms with its author, and they made an agreement to purchase from him, at some future date, 'something light', of the order of 60,000 words. Hardy named this projected work *The Pursuit of the Well-Beloved*, and provided the Tillotsons with what Purdy justly calls 'the following reassuring prospectus':

> The novel is entirely modern in date and subject, and, though comparatively short, embraces both extremes of society, from peers, peeresses, and other persons of rank and culture, to villagers.
>
> The principal male characters are: the leading personage— a young sculptor of gradually increasing fame; a landscape painter; one or two [men of rank *deleted*] luminaries of science and law, titled politicians, &c. Those of the opposite sex include an attractive, educated country girl, a rich merchant's daughter of city tastes and habits, the wife of a political peer, her friends, a fashionable London hostess, an aristocratic widow, a village sylph-like creature, &c.
>
> The story, though it deals with some highly emotional situations, is not a tragedy in the ordinary sense. The scenes shift backwards and forwards from London studios and drawing-rooms of fashion to the cottages and cliffs of a remote isle in the English Channel, and a little town on the same.
>
> There is not a word or scene in the tale which can offend the most fastidious taste; and it is equally suited for the reading of young people, and for that of persons of maturer years.

What this rather notably fails to communicate is the basic idea of the novel, of which Hardy had in fact made a note about a year before:

The story of a face which goes through three generations or more, would make a fine novel or poem of the passage of Time. The difference in personality to be ignored.

To this note Hardy added at a later date: 'This idea was to some extent carried out in the novel *The Well-Beloved*, the poem entitled "Heredity", etc.'. 'Heredity', which is to be found in *Moments of Vision*, runs thus:

> I am the family face;
> Flesh perishes, I live on,
> Projecting trait and trace
> Through time to times anon,
> And leaping from place to place
> Over oblivion.
>
> The years-heired feature that can
> In curve and voice and eye
> Despise the human span
> Of durance—that is I;
> The eternal thing in man,
> That heeds no call to die.

The Well-Beloved starts from this notion of genetic immutability, and sets over against it the mutability of human love as that love operates beneath the sway of so subjective a mental phenomenon as the sense of beauty. The fabular character of the story is disguised, perhaps not altogether judiciously, beneath the commonplace realism of its presentation. The structure, on the other hand, is rigidly schematic.

Jocelyn Pierston is a twenty-year-old sculptor obsessed by the notion of ideal beauty—which he has already fleetingly glimpsed (not, we suspect, to any great practical effect) in a dozen women:

> To his Well-Beloved he had always been faithful; but she had had many embodiments. Each individuality known as Lucy, Jane, Flora, Evangeline, or what-not, had been merely a transient condition of her. . . . Essentially she was perhaps of no tangible substance; a spirit, a dream, a frenzy, a conception, an aroma, an epitomized sex, a light of the eye, a parting of the lips.

In this oppressively Shelleyan frame of mind the young man comes home to the remote Wessex peninsula which Hardy calls the Isle of

Slingers, where his people have for long lived in simple but prosperous circumstances. He is promptly kissed by a childhood friend,
Avice Caro, and to his own confusion perceptibly winces on the
occasion. He is far from certain that the Well-Beloved inhabits
Avice, and although he becomes engaged to her after an uncertain
fashion it is only to run away with a more opulent island beauty,
Marcia, who however leaves him before he has married or possessed her. Twenty years later Pierston returns to the island for
Avice Caro's funeral, and finds her daughter, also Avice Caro,
who is physically indistinguishable from her mother. This time
there is no doubt about the Well-Beloved's embodiment in an
Avice. But the second Avice turns out to go in for Well-Beloveds
herself; she has had fifteen of them, and eventually turns out to
be already married. With her daughter, Avice the third (who is
indistinguishable alike from her mother and her grandmother),
Pierston duly falls in love twenty years later still. She agrees to
marry him, but thinks better of it on learning of his former
attachments, and elopes with a young man who proves to be the
son of that Marcia with whom Pierston had less effectively run
away forty years earlier. Pierston suffers a serious illness, and its
consequence is the 'strange death' of the entire sensuous side of
his nature:

> The malignant fever, or his experiences, or both, had taken
> away something from him, and put something else in its
> place. . . . The artistic sense had left him, and he could no
> longer attach a definite sentiment to images of beauty recalled
> from the past. His appreciativeness was capable of exercising
> itself only on utilitarian matters. . . . At first he was appalled;
> and then he said 'Thank God!'

The reversal is absolute, so that Pierston's responses to experience
pass into what Pavlovian neurology was long after Hardy's time
to term the 'ultra-paradoxical' phase. Pierston pays a visit to his
former studio and surveys his own works, 'the Nymphs and Fauns,
Eves, Avices, and other innumerable Well-Beloveds'. And he cries
out:

> I want to see them never any more! . . . 'Instead of sweet
> smell there shall be stink, and there shall be burning instead of
> beauty,' said the prophet.

Eventually he reconciles himself to marriage with Marcia. Now
decrepit, she has to be wrapped up and wheeled into the church
for the ceremony in an invalid chair.

What are we to make of this bizarre story? Guerard reflects, with undeniable truth, that it 'might have provided material for another short novel by Peacock', but is shocked that a major poet and novelist such as Hardy should treat it in a manner suggesting compliance with a debased and sentimental view of the artistic temperament. 'The book could have been saved by a genuinely critical irony', but this its creator culpably fails to provide. Morrell, on the other hand, declares that the novel 'seeks to show that the beautiful appearances which glamorize our lives are devices of cowardice; and that reality is life, and life is courage'. These are markedly divergent views. Perhaps it is worth while remarking that an older critic, Beach, simply declares *The Well-Beloved* to be 'good fun'. There is certainly an attempt on Hardy's part to lend the working out of what he calls his 'fantastic tale' a certain lightness of air. Yet he intends something basically serious, and in the *Life* we are bidden to notice that the book's 'theory of the transmigration of the ideal loved one, who only exists in the lover, from material woman to material woman' was 'exemplified also by Proust many years later'.[1] Finally we may notice that a poem to which we are referred on the same page of the *Life*, itself entitled 'The Well-Beloved', presents the central idea of the novel in a visionary or ghostly setting.

[1] In one of the last notes reproduced in the *Life* (July 1926) Hardy observes that 'the theory exhibited in *The Well-Beloved* in 1892 has been since developed by Proust still further', and in support of this claim he transcribes two short passages from *A l'Ombre des Jeunes Filles en Fleurs*. Proust was, in fact, a reader of Hardy, surpassing even Tennyson and Patmore in admiration for *A Pair of Blue Eyes*, which he declared (Harold Nicolson records in his diary on 21 June 1933) to be 'of all books the one which he would himself most gladly have written'.

11

Tess of the d'Urbervilles

TO THE END OF HIS NOVEL-WRITING CAREER HARDY CONTINUED TO take for granted the economic necessity of serial publication. Unfortunately both in England and America the magazines willing to publish fiction and able to make adequate payment for it were 'family' magazines. This meant that nothing could be admitted to them which the most restrictive opinion of the time judged unfit for perusal by children. Editors had to be on the look-out even for stray expressions which might, if come upon during reading aloud, occasion embarrassment in a domestic circle. The test was quite simply Mr Podsnap's test in *Our Mutual Friend*: 'The question about everything was, would it bring a blush into the cheek of the young person?' Nowadays Mr Podsnap is hard to believe ĩn. But there is abundant evidence of how seriously the cardiovascular system of his proverbial girl had to be reckoned with by Victorian writers—and this in relation not merely to magazine or newspaper publication but to book publication as well.

Thus in 1890 the *New Review* printed a symposium on 'Candour in English Fiction'. Walter Besant, a popular novelist and miscellaneous writer much concerned with the practical problems of the literary profession, was for making the best of things. What the young person's mama would not permit to be exposed in circulating libraries or upon railway bookstalls it was futile to produce, for 'he who works for pay must respect the prejudices of his customers'. But happily, Besant declared, the novelist might at least deal fairly faithfully with the English upper classes, since they were by no means so black as they were painted—gentlemen rarely continuing to lead irregular lives after marriage and ladies never doing so at any time. Mrs Lynn Linton, another popular novelist, was a little less easily daunted than Besant. She saw hope in the locked bookcase. 'To whom ought Fiction to be addressed?— exclusively to the Young Person? or may not men and women, who know life, have their acre to themselves where the *ingénue* has no business to intrude?' Hardy, coming in his turn to consider this 'lording of nonage over maturity', was equally without confidence in any head-on confrontation with current convention. He too was inclined to seek an out-of-bounds solution—such as had been successfully applied, we may reflect, by the same age to the public house. The 'explicit' novel might, he thought, be published in *feuilleton*, as in France, so that it could be removed from the family reading-matter. There should be 'magazines for adults', and even 'at least one magazine for the middle-aged and old'.

Hardy, as we have seen, had long been accustomed to trouble on this front. Sometimes he had merely been judged insufficiently edifying, as when the *British Quarterly Review* declared that the author of *The Trumpet-Major* failed 'to encourage high ideals of manhood' and evinced 'a dislike to look high in the field of motive-elements from which the loftiest workers in the creative field have always drawn the materials for their best and most influential effects'. More commonly—as when the *Spectator* condemned his first novel on the score of its downright immorality—it was his handling of sexual situations that was denounced. Publishers, and more particularly periodical editors, became so apprehensive here that they frequently queried the merest *minutiae* of vocabulary with all the anxiety of modern broadcasting authorities confronted with four-letter words. 'I doubt', Leslie Stephen as editor of the *Cornhill* wrote to Hardy during the serializing of *The Hand of Ethelberta*, 'whether a lady ought to call herself or her writings "amorous". Would not some such word as "sentimental" be strong enough?'

When we come on records like this we are inclined to judge that the moral disapproval which Hardy's novels first met with was largely comical. Nevertheless, there was reason beneath the Victorian panic in matters of sex. To Mrs Lynn Linton, once more, it appeared paradoxical that we should 'cut ourselves off from one of the largest and most important areas of that human life we pretend to portray' while at the same time throwing 'the limelight of fancy on crimes which are of comparatively rare occurrence, and which consequently excite but little living sympathy'. But the fact, of course, is simply that censorship falls most heavily in the field where there is a really powerful prompting. And when Hardy declared to a startled clergyman that with the acceptance of Darwinism there ceased to be any logical reason why the young of the human species ('the smaller children, say, of overcrowded families') should not be hunted or shot by sportsmen he was saying by implication that there had ceased to be any logical reason why, if they escaped this Swiftian fate, they should not grow up to the exercise of a happy sexual promiscuity. But few intellectual people

approved of anything of this sort—and prudently, if it be true that
advanced cultures do not develop except on the basis of one or
another strict sexual morality. Thus it was not merely bigoted
persons (such as we shall encounter when we come to the outcry
against *Jude the Obscure*) who were anxiously repressive of all
enquiry tending to innovation in the sexual sphere. It was often, on
the contrary, those of Hardy's contemporaries who most un-
reservedly accepted the new rationalism, and who had the mental
equipment to realize its full implications. The age, like Stephen
blue-pencilling the mildest suggestions of amative behaviour at a
desk elsewhere piled with what are, even today, hair-raising
guffaws at the central tenets of the Christian civilization of Europe,
was prepared for panic resistance to all suggestions of sexual
heterodoxy; yet it had largely submitted to a drastic reassessment
of the human situation upon which such heterodoxy, with much
else that was, and is, alarming, must almost inevitably follow in
many minds. What was felt as potentially subversive in Hardy was
not his universe—for this he shared with most of his professional
critics—but his predisposition to let his sense of that universe
act, however cautiously, upon areas of experience hitherto fenced
off because of the explosive material apprehended as buried
there.

These are considerations which we must bear in mind if we are
to understand either the shifts to which Hardy was constrained
when giving his last two novels to the world or the abuse which
greeted them notwithstanding.

2

The Woodlanders in its three-volume form had been published
with fair success early in 1887; later in the same year Macmillan
reissued it in a single volume, and this sold widely. It could be seen
that Hardy was perhaps on the way to gaining a large public, and
he himself must have felt that he had at last attained a position of
substantial professional security. When, shortly before his forty-
eighth birthday, he returned with his wife from a holiday in Italy it
was to find a small queue of editors and publishers anxious to do
business with him. Thus in a position to pick and choose, he
contracted with the Lancashire firm of Tillotson & Son of Bolton
to provide in a year's time a novel which should, in the first
instance, be syndicated in serial form in a number of newspapers.
The title was to be *Too Late Beloved*, and the story was to concern
a milkmaid. Hardy, we are told, clarified his thoughts by re-reading
Sophocles.

Such was the inception of what became *Tess of the d'Urbervilles*.[1] Half the novel was completed by the late summer of 1889, and despatched to Bolton in order that illustrations might be put in hand. At once its troubles began. Tillotson's, we learn from Professor Purdy, did not require any prospectus of a forthcoming work in their contracts, and what they now received from Hardy took them by surprise. W. F. Tillotson, the recently deceased head of the firm, had been a prominent Congregationalist and Sunday

[1] Tess Durbeyfield is the eldest child of an improvident haggler (or carrier in a small way of business), John Durbeyfield, in the village of Marlott. At the opening of the story he learns from a clergyman with antiquarian interests that his family name is a corruption of d'Urberville, and that he is himself a lineal descendant of Sir Pagan d'Urberville who came from Normandy with William the Conqueror. The discovery drives Durbeyfield into further laziness and inebriety, so that his family's position becomes desperate. They hear of rich people called d'Urberville in another part of Wessex, and conclude that they are blood-relations: in fact these d'Urbervilles are upstarts who have adopted the name almost at random after having bought property in the region. Tess is persuaded to go and make an appeal to the d'Urbervilles, her mother in particular indulging foolish and uninformed notions of what may come of the connection. Alec d'Urberville, an idle and lecherous young man, makes plans to seduce her. These succeed and Tess, although little more than a child in years, becomes for a short time Alec's mistress. She breaks away from him on becoming pregnant, returns home, and bears a child who dies shortly after. Tess rallies, and takes employment as a dairymaid in a part of the country where her story is unknown.

Angel Clare, a clergyman's son with advanced ideas which preclude his taking orders, is working in the dairy by way of preparing for a career as a farmer. He is attracted by Tess, and Tess falls deeply in love with him. They get married—without Tess's being presented to Angel's parents, since Angel feels that this will be easier when she has been further polished by his conversation. Tess's attempts to tell her story have been prevented partly by her own reluctance to confess and even more by mischance and Angel's obtuse disregard. But when they return from church Angel himself confesses to 'eight-and-forty hours' dissipation with a stranger', and Tess in turn gives an account of her misfortune. Angel is horrified, makes some perfunctory financial provision for her, forbids her to take any initiative in communicating with him, and goes away to Brazil.

John Durbeyfield dies, and Tess becomes her family's only means of support. She works under conditions of indescribable hardship through a winter on an upland farm. Her misery is increased by the reappearance of Alec d'Urberville as a tempter; after an episode of religious fanaticism he has returned to his libidinous courses. Tess holds out, hoping against hope for some sign from her absent husband. The Durbeyfields are evicted from their cottage in utter destitution, and Tess succumbs to Alec's offers of help. He sets her up as his mistress in a smart seaside resort.

Angel Clare, meanwhile, has had some serious conversation with a chance acquaintance in Brazil, and as a result returns to England intending to receive back his wife. He traces Tess, learns the truth of her situation, and goes away again. Tess kills Alec and overtakes Angel. His realization of what she has done is also his realization of her love for him and his for her. They flee across country, spending some nights together in a deserted house. Tess has regained her husband, and is fulfilled and happy. They are discovered, and have to flee again. They find themselves at Stonehenge, upon the sacrificial altar of which Tess falls asleep. She awakens only to be apprehended by the police, and some weeks later she is hanged.

School worker, who 'held strong views as to the tone of all material in his own papers and the family newspapers that were his clients'. His successors, confronted with Tess Durbeyfield's seduction by Alec d'Urberville, with her spirited denunciation of a clergyman who refuses Christian burial to her illegitimate child, and with the yet more disconcerting fact that she was plainly to be the heroine of the whole work, felt it due to the tradition of their firm to ask for at least drastic alterations and deletions. When Hardy refused these conditions they declared themselves unable to issue the story, which they would nevertheless pay for as arranged. Upon this Hardy suggested that their agreement should be cancelled, and thus the matter ended on a reasonably amicable note. Hardy had some later, if unimportant, dealing with the firm, which was building up a substantial empire in syndicated fiction.

So a publisher for *Too Late Beloved* (now become *A Daughter of the d'Urbervilles*) was yet to seek. While Hardy was still at work on the later chapters, the editors of both *Murray's Magazine* and *Macmillan's Magazine* were constrained to decline it also. In point of serial issue, at least, the position had now become serious. It was also humiliating, and we need not be surprised that a certain reticence and even contradictoriness attend the account given in the *Life*. In particular it is not clear to what extent the bowdlerizing process to which Hardy subjected his manuscript was dictated by the *Graphic*, the weekly paper in which the novel eventually appeared, and to what extent it was prudentially carried out by Hardy before approaching the editor. But the main course of his action was simple enough. He finished the novel without compromise in the form in which we read it today, and then cut and altered it ruthlessly for the serial market.

Two main excisions Hardy thriftily disguised and adapted for use elsewhere. Alec's seduction of Tess appeared as 'Saturday Night in Arcady' in a Special Literary Supplement of the *National Observer*, and for the *Graphic* Hardy (recalling an abortive plan for *The Return of the Native*) substituted a short passage in which Tess tells her mother how she was deceived by a mock marriage-ceremony. The baptism and death of Tess's baby appeared similarly as 'The Midnight Baptism, A Study in Christianity' in the *Fortnightly Review* (and actually two months before the serial publication of the novel began). There were many minor changes—of which we can hardly believe that the most celebrated could have come to Hardy unprompted. In the serial version of the story Angel Clare is not permitted to pick up Tess and her companions in order to carry them across the flooded lane. He is made to say to the stranded milkmaids: 'I'll wheel you through the pool—all of you—with pleasure, if you'll wait till I get a barrow.' And he gets a barrow.

When *Tess of the d'Urbervilles* was eventually published in volume form Hardy covered all this in what he called an 'Explanatory Note'. It reads, in part:

> The main portion of the following story appeared—with slight modifications—in the *Graphic* newspaper; other chapters, more especially addressed to adult readers, in the *Fortnightly Review* and the *National Observer*, as episodic sketches. My thanks are tendered to the editors and proprietors of those periodicals for enabling me now to piece the trunk and limbs of the novel together, and print it complete, as originally written two years ago.

This was to make the best of an awkward business. It might be maintained that the episode of Tess's baptizing her baby had been constructed merely to carry a certain animus against institutional Christianity (the priest to whom Tess appeals is described as 'having the natural feelings of a tradesman at finding that a job he should have been called in for had been unskilfully botched by his customers') and could well be omitted without essential disadvantage to the novel as a whole. And Angel's fetching the wheel-barrow, although it detracts from the delicately created picture of the girls' relationship with him, remains a very minor matter. But the mock-marriage is different, since it significantly distorts the character of both people concerned. A young man who seduces a girl on a nocturnal jaunt—even if he has been deliberately planning something of the sort—is one thing; a young man who rigs up a false marriage ceremony for the purpose is quite another. And to a girl who has been 'betrayed' only as a consequence of not spotting that falsity there inevitably attaches, even if unfairly, a certain air of Pamela-like calculation. In general, we cannot avoid the conclusion that Hardy, under what he conceived to be a financial compulsion, laboured to sell the purchasers of the *Graphic* what he knew to be inferior goods. In the *Life* he describes himself as having 'carried out this unceremonious concession to conventionality with cynical amusement'. Whether or not he was, in fact, thus amused, he had the satisfaction of knowing that the authentic text of the novel would be available (to anybody caring to pay 31*s* 6*d* for it) some weeks before the *Graphic* issued its final instalment of the bowdlerized version.

But the book's worst ordeal was yet to come, since when it was so made available its reception by the critics was in the main unfavourable and censorious. Hardy found one of the reviews so 'fiendish' that he wrote to Besant for advice as to whether he should resign from the Savile Club. And when he read in the *Quarterly Review* that 'Mr Hardy has told an extremely disagreeable story in an extremely disagreeable manner' he confided to his diary (on Good Friday of 1892): 'Well, if this sort of thing continues no more novel-writing for me. A man must be a fool to deliberately stand up to be shot at.'

Meanwhile, *Tess of the d'Urbervilles* was enjoying what its detractors could readily represent as a *succès de scandale*. It sold as nothing of Hardy's had sold before. Podsnap notwithstanding, the common reader approved it. It has remained by far the most generally acclaimed of the Wessex Novels.

3

The story told in *Tess* is extremely sombre, and as the telling is achieved with tremendous power the novel is not one to which anybody will think to return in the expectation of pleasure in the narrow sense. There is perhaps no other English novel the reading of which so matches the reading of *King Lear* as described in Keats's sonnet:

> once again, the fierce dispute
> Betwixt damnation and impassion'd clay
> Must I burn through; once more humbly assay
> The bitter-sweet of this Shakespearian fruit. . . .

Yet it is not in the final issue a depressing book. The reviewer who said that *Tess* 'except during a few hours spent with cows, has not a gleam of sunshine anywhere', was saying a smart and silly thing. And this is because Tess Durbeyfield herself is as the sun at noon.

She can, of course, be taken in other ways. Brown tells us that Tess is 'the agricultural community in its moment of ruin'. And Holloway, coming in a brilliant essay to the novel as Hardy's 'vision of the passing of the old rhythmic order of rural England', sees her as exemplifying her creator's ultimate and most desolating discovery: 'that that earlier way did not possess the inner resources upon which to make a real fight for its existence'. 'The springs of goodness are now no longer the springs of strength'—and hence in Tess Durbeyfield 'an alienation, a dreaminess' constituting a radical weakness of character.

It is certainly true that Tess's story is told to us against a background of humble Wessex life from which every softening veil has been stripped remorselessly away. For example, those dream-rustics untouched by time, uncrippled by labour, ceaselessly aphoristic over their inexhaustible cider and ale, 'pastoral' to their very bone and marrow, cunningly fabricated for urban delight: they are gone for ever; gone, we may say, with the bitter wind which in *The Woodlanders* blew upon Marty South. In place of the golden malt-house we have, typically, the Rolliver, that sleazy and clandestine drinking-shop where topers perch on a four-poster bed until strained and frightened children come to lead them home. 'Her mother's fetching'—the young Tess knows— 'simply meant one more to fetch'. John Durbeyfield, fatuously exposed in the depths of his ignorance to the folly of Parson Tringham's meaningless genealogical disclosure; his 'poor witless wife', incompetent at household tasks to the pitch of 'flinging the baby from side to side like a weaver's shuttle' in its cradle, and whose maternal care sums itself in the proposition that 'if he don't marry her afore he will after': these have taken the place of the Dewys and other rude forefathers abounding in a quaint immemorial wisdom. 'My life looks as if it had been wasted for want of chances,' Tess says sadly at one point, and despite her Sixth Standard in the National School we are allowed no sense either that this is a mending matter at the end of the nineteenth century or that Tess and her kind are really fortunate in being destined to blush unseen. We are spared little of what is degraded and degrading in the condition of the labouring poor. In place of those seemly wedding parties and harvest festivals of which we used to hear there is the disordered revel which preludes Tess's undoing, with the dancers 'a sort of vegeto-human pollen . . . the indistinctness shaping them to satyrs clasping nymphs—a multiplicity of Pans whirling a multiplicity of Syrinxes; Lotis attempting to elude Priapus, and always failing'—and with Alec d'Urberville, the predatory upstart gentleman, looking on amused as his cast trollop Car Darch strips to the waist to confront her rival. 'A sense of awe, in the presence of a landscape filled with immemorial signs of age; a sense of tranquillity in the presence of human toil, so bound up and associated with the venerable needs of human life'—so Lionel Johnson wrote, in a splendid phrase, of what comes to us from the Wessex novels as a whole. But it is not thus that we respond to Tess's winter of servitude at Flintcomb-Ash, working from dawn to dusk amid the half-eaten turnips with a hacker, or in stupified subjection to the pitiless steam-engine which now gives its tempo to the 'venerable needs'—and again with Alec prowling on the fringe, waiting to take his other toll of helpless poverty.

But if there is Flintcomb-Ash there is also the Valley of the

Great Dairies, and over against the low revel at Chaseborough has to be set the 'club-walking' at Marlott. This mild festival, it is true, is a mere lingering remnant of an occasion the true significance of which has passed out of mind. The decay of English agriculture consequent upon the opening up of the great wheat-growing areas of North America was significant for Hardy the countryman in terms not merely of its immediate economic implications but of that breaking up of broad cultural patterns which both that decay itself and indeed the very efforts being made to counter it were steadily bringing about. The harmless-seeming mechanical contraption which the progressive Donald Farfrae brings to Casterbridge breeds the sinister steam-engine for which Tess must slave, and the increasingly migratory character of the labourer and the desuetude of small trades and crafts which bring final disaster to her family on Old Lady-Day have their place in the alarming picture. Yet in face of all this we do not feel that Hardy, so celebrated as a 'pessimist', is precisely giving up. Here as in his essay on 'The Dorsetshire Labourer' he denounces the urban writing-off of the farm-hand, the substituting for the real man of 'the pitiable dummy known as Hodge'. (So seriously is he engaged here, indeed, that he actually incorporates several passages from the essay in the novel.) The Valley of the Great Dairies, we may repeat, remains—and Angel Clare would be a better man had he learnt more from it. As it is, he becomes 'wonderfully free from the chronic melancholy which is taking hold of the civilized races with the decline of belief in a beneficent Power'. The young and spuriously emancipated prig who lectures his pious and gentle father on his Church's 'untenable redemptive theolatry' comes to glimpse 'something new in life and humanity' while working for Dairyman Crick. Above all, it is her background in the essentially unchanging solidities and sanctities of rural England which we feel as sustaining Tess—as giving her, indeed, 'the "appetite for joy" which pervades all creation' and which, inseparably mingled with her suffering, establishes her so unshakably among the very greatest characters in English fiction.

But about the background—if that is indeed the right word—of the novel there is something further to be said. Its several contrasting terrains are, of course, exploited in the interest of demonstrating the impact upon individuals of their natural—as in some degree distinguishable from their resulting economic and social—environment. This Hardy had already achieved powerfully enough in *The Return of the Native*. There the fact of Budmouth, the dream of Paris, are set over against Egdon Heath. But the Heath is the single overwhelmingly important place, and Hardy's road to asserting this is to present the region in terms of the largest cosmic implications. Authentic as is much of the detailed evocation, Egdon remains essentially a country of the mind: to this day it returns some echo of this condition to the wayfarer who would seek out its vestiges in the county of Dorset. The Heath as metaphysical statement, that is to say, tends to swamp the Heath as terrain in the strictest sense: so many soils, so many acres, such and such a route with its several prospects, levels, descents and acclivities to tramp. But now we have something different. Tess tramps as even Mrs Yeobright on her fatal last journey does not quite tramp. Sheer measured muscular effort is a controlling factor in *Tess of the d'Urbervilles*. The boots which Tess sheds before venturing to present herself to Angel's parents (and which Miss Mercy Chant makes off with to present to the deserving poor) may almost stand as the central symbol of the book.

There is a great deal that is symbolic in *Tess*, much episode and action the impact of which is expressionistic and poetic rather than persuasively realistic. The thrust of this is sometimes carried to a bold extreme. There is the sleep-walking scene which George Moore was to find so eminently absurd: Angel Clare has not merely to pick up his rejected bride and deposit her in a stone coffin; his route must be across the 'giddy pathway' of a footbridge above waters 'voluminous and deep'—and from which 'the autumn flood had washed the handrail away'. And as immediate hinterland to this we have had the Conan Doyle-like legend of the d'Urberville Coach and the sheer gothic of the portraits of sinister d'Urberville women which so improbably bar Angel's way when he earlier makes an irresolute waking progress towards his wife's bedroom. One might suppose that matter of this sort would have its theatricality enhanced and exposed by the closely textured circumjacent modesty of nature and sober realism the pressure of which we feel everywhere in the book. But it is not so. On the contrary the realism floats or sustains the melodrama. We suspend our prosaic disbelief in Alec's blood seeping copiously through a solid floor and solid ceiling, or in Tess and Angel as traversing undetected and on foot a large tract of southern England to be overtaken only as Tess lies sleeping (and 'at home', as she expresses it) on the sacrificial altar of Stonehenge. These large audacities (and also the little ones, such as Clare's Christian name and the fact that he plays a harp—rather badly) are supported, not undermined by their generous context in simple rustic reality.

There is a further audacity which is similarly fortified and controlled by the predominant sobriety of the book. 'In general,' we are told of Mr Crick's dairy, 'the cows were milked as they presented themselves, without fancy or choice.' But this humdrum information, with much else of the same sort, comes in the middle of Hardy's establishing the first of two steeply contrasting congruities between Tess's destiny and her natural environment. To the Var Vale (or Valley of the Great Dairies) she comes in renewed hope—mastered at length, after her first misfortune, by 'the irresistible, universal, automatic tendency to find sweet pleasure somewhere, which pervades all life'. Approaching this new scene, we are told, 'her spirits, and her thankfulness, and her hopes, rose higher and higher. She tried several ballads, but found them inadequate.' Instead, she chants, as she walks, the *Benedicite*: 'Praise Him and magnify Him for ever!' 'But perhaps,' she breaks off to murmur to herself, 'I don't quite know the Lord as yet.' (It is, one supposes, the prerogative of great writers to be as terribly moving as this.) And then the life of the Great Dairies receives her:

> Amid the oozing fatness and warm ferments of the Var Vale, at a season when the rush of juices could almost be heard below the hiss of fertilization, it was impossible that the most fanciful love should not grow passionate. The ready bosoms existing there were impregnated by their surroundings.

It is in this environment that Angel Clare, while still unstirred himself, becomes so potent an object of desire to the milkmaids:

> The air of the sleeping-chamber seemed to palpitate with the hopeless passion of the girls. They writhed feverishly under the oppressiveness of an emotion thrust on them by cruel Nature's law—an emotion which they had neither expected nor desired.

And it is here that we see Angel and Tess 'converging, under an irresistible law, as surely as two streams in one vale'. The theme of human sexuality responding to the influence of a richly procreant natural world has been rehearsed a thousand times; the power of the recital here is in the high authenticity of the scene—as when the lovers go out together in the dawn:

> At these non-human hours they could get quite close to the waterfowl. Herons came, with a great bold noise as of opening doors and shutters, out of the boughs of a plantation which they frequented at the side of the mead; or, if already on the spot, hardly maintained their standing in the water as the pair walked by, watching them by moving their heads round in a slow, horizontal, passionless wheel, like the turn of puppets by clockwork.

They could then see the faint summer fogs in layers, woolly, level, and apparently no thicker than counterpanes, spread about the meadows in detached remnants of small extent. On the gray moisture of the grass were marks where the cows had lain through the night—dark-green islands of dry herbage the size of their carcases, in the general sea of dew. . . . Or perhaps the summer fog was more general, and the meadows lay like a white sea, out of which the scattered trees rose like dangerous rocks. Birds would soar through it into the upper radiance, and hang on the wing sunning themselves, or alight on the wet rails subdividing the mead, which now shone like glass rods. Minute diamonds of moisture from the mist hung, too, upon Tess's eyelashes, and drops upon her hair. . . .

This is the Hardy who could so finely see and hear. In other passages the implication with great creating Nature becomes indefinably ominous. Tess, attracted by the notes of Angel's harp, draws covertly close to him in the dusk:

The outskirt of the garden in which Tess found herself had been left uncultivated for some years, and was now damp and rank with juicy grass which sent up mists of pollen at a touch; and with tall blooming weeds emitting offensive smells—weeds whose red and yellow and purple hues formed a polychrome as dazzling as that of cultivated flowers. She went stealthily as a cat through this profusion of growth, gathering cuckoo-spittle on her skirts, cracking snails that were underfoot, staining her hands with thistle-milk and slug-slime, and rubbing off upon her naked arms sticky blights which, though snow-white on the apple-tree trunks, made madder stains on her skin; thus she drew quite near to Clare, still unobserved of him. . . .
The floating pollen seemed to be his notes made visible, and the dampness of the garden the weeping of the garden's sensibility. Though near nightfall, the rank-smelling weed-flowers glowed as if they would not close for intentness, and the waves of colour mixed with the waves of sound.

There is indeed 'a pollen of radiance over the landscape' in all this writing, and when at length Angel's 'heart had outrun his judgment' it is inevitable that Miss Chant should stand small chance as compared with 'the impassioned, summer-steeped heathens in the Var Vale', and with Tess pre-eminent in their midst, 'warm as a sunned cat'.
But the whole great hymn to fecundity sinks to the minor when

contrasted with the stark power with which Hardy evokes winter at Flintcomb-Ash, 'a starve-acre place'. First we have the sheer bleak brute tillage to which the women are set, with its sudden flash of a bold and brilliant symbolism breaking surface through some stray geological remarks:

> But Tess set to work. . . . The swede-field in which she and her companion were set hacking was a stretch of a hundred odd acres, in one patch, on the highest ground of the farm, rising above stony lanchets or lynchets—the outcrop of siliceous veins in the chalk formation, composed of myriads of loose white flints in bulbous, cusped, and phallic shapes. The upper half of each turnip had been eaten off by the live-stock, and it was the business of the two women to grub up the lower or earthy half of the root with a hooked fork called a hacker, that it might be eaten also. Every leaf of the vegetable having already been consumed, the whole field was in colour a desolate drab; it was a complexion without features, as if a face, from chin to brow, should be only an expanse of skin. The sky wore, in another colour, the same likeness; a white vacuity of countenance with the lineaments gone.

Upon this vision of sex petrified amid a vast sterility the march of winter succeeds. In the passage beginning with the 'non-human hours' in the Valley of the Great Dairies the herons are not without their hint of threat ('a slow, horizontal, passionless wheel, like the turn of puppets by clockwork'). But there are other birds at Flintcomb-Ash:

> There had not been such a winter for years. It came on in stealthy and measured glides, like the moves of a chess-player. One morning the few lonely trees and the thorns of the hedge-rows appeared as if they had put off a vegetable for an animal integument. Every twig was covered with a white nap of fur grown from the rind during the night, giving it four times its usual stoutness; the whole bush or tree forming a staring sketch in white lines on the mournful gray of the sky and horizon. . . .
> After this season of congealed dampness came a spell of dry frost, when strange birds from behind the North Pole began to arrive silently on the upland of Flintcomb-Ash; gaunt spectral creatures with tragical eyes—eyes which had witnessed scenes of cataclysmal horror in inaccessible polar regions of a magnitude such as no human being had ever conceived, in curdling temperatures that no man could endure; which had beheld the

crash of icebergs and the slide of snow-hills by the shooting light of the Aurora; been half blinded by the whirl of colossal storms and terraqueous distortions; and retained the expression of feature that such scenes had engendered. These nameless birds came quite near to Tess and Marian, but of all they had seen which humanity would never see, they brought no account. . . .

Then one day a peculiar quality invaded the air of this open country. There came a moisture which was not of rain, and a cold which was not of frost. It chilled the eyeballs of the twain, made their brows ache, penetrated to their skeletons, affecting the surface of the body less than its core. They knew that it meant snow, and in the night the snow came.

What we are afforded in such a passage as this is not a mere evocation of hard times, or a notably stiff torment in the history of a patient Griselda. It is rather a vision—and moreover it is writing of an order which admits no comment except from genius:

This is the wonder of Hardy's novels, and gives them their beauty. The vast, unexplored morality of life itself, what we call the immorality of nature, surrounds us in its eternal incomprehensibility. . . . And this is the quality Hardy shares with the great writers, Shakespeare or Sophocles or Tolstoi, this setting behind the small action of his protagonists the terrific action of unfathomed nature; setting a smaller system of morality, the one grasped and formulated by the human consciousness within the vast, uncomprehended and incomprehensible morality of nature or of life itself, surpassing human consciousness.

Thus D. H. Lawrence. It is because Tess accepts this greater morality that she endures as she does. She 'trudged on', we have been told in the passage which brings her in bad weather to Flintcomb-Ash, 'the honesty, directness, and impartiality of elemental enmity disconcerting her but little'.

4

Hardy, like Shakespeare, works with the often artistically and psychologically crude materials of popular entertainment, and his transmutation of this material, again as with Shakespeare, is radical but not pervasive. *Tess of the d'Urbervilles* is the extreme instance in his writing alike of hazard and success in the process. A good deal has been written of the extent to which the world of this novel is close to the world of the traditional ballads. An affinity is undeniable, and even the theme of the wronged maiden driven to kill and be killed can be shown often enough to have haunted the mind of the folk. But between such a remote ancestry on the one hand and the progeny of Hardy's imagination on the other stand rank upon rank of crude performers in sheerly melodramatic fictions. Gothic romances, vulgar theatrical entertainments, street-ballads, even 'penny dreadfuls': the line is long enough. And every now and then genius—Dickens's, Hardy's—touches it.

The story told in *Tess of the d'Urbervilles* has its origin here. An innocent maiden is seduced (or raped: 'There were they that heard a sobbing one night last year in The Chase; and it mid ha' gone hard wi' a certain party if folks had come along'), and this misfortune introduces her to a long course of mischances which culminate in her being hanged. The dire issue is not brought about by some single large catastrophe, whether verisimilar or not. It advances (perhaps because Tess's story has to be a *long* story) as we have seen winter advance upon Flintcomb-Ash, 'like the moves of a chess-player'. With Tess everything goes wrong, step by step, as her destiny fulfils itself. In her progress the incidence of accident is sharply stepped up again, so that in places we feel ourselves to be back with Elfride Swancourt. It is so when the letter conveying her confession to Clare goes not only under the door but also under the carpet. It is so when Clare's obtuseness is screwed to a point at which uttering the truth becomes a mere nervous impossibility. 'A d'Urberville!—Indeed!'—Clare says, at once amused and impressed—'And is that all the trouble, dear Tess?' The tone of light condescension, as to a child, is fatal:

'Yes,' she answered faintly.

We still do not quite feel that Tess need be on her way to the gallows, and we may find ourselves wondering whether a national morbidity (reflected in Hardy) rather than a tragic necessity dictates this end. The English are attached to hangings; every now and then their gutter journals and many of their members of parliament are to be heard howling for them. Perhaps it is significant that Tess's killing of Alec is the weakest moment in the fable. 'The murder is badly done,' Lawrence says. In fact it is not, in the artist's sense, 'done' at all. If we are in any doubt about this, we need only turn to Winnie Verloc's killing of her husband in Conrad's *The Secret Agent*. That—quite supremely—is 'done'.

It is certainly true that Tess's deed lands Hardy with a ticklish task in the concluding phase of his story. When first working out his plot he had jotted down this note:

> When a married woman who has a lover kills her husband, she does not really wish to kill her husband; she wishes to kill the situation. Of course in Clytaemnestra's case it was not exactly so, since there was the added grievance of Iphigenia, which half-justified her.

If this tells why the novel concludes upon an 'Æschylean phrase', it tells us, too, that Hardy early saw something of his problem. 'If he were dead it might be different', Clare is made to say hard upon Tess's eventual revelation of Alec's place in her life, and this reverberates when Tess, catching up with Clare after her deed, speaks as she does:

> 'Angel, will you forgive me my sin against you, now I have killed him? I thought as I ran along that you would be sure to forgive me now I have done that. It came to me as a shining light that I should get you back that way. I could not bear the loss of you any longer—you don't know how entirely I was unable to bear your not loving me! Say you do now, dear, dear husband; say you do, now I have killed him!'

Whatever may be Tess Durbeyfield's psychological, or her spiritual state here and during the strange fulfilment of her love for Angel that follows, there can be little doubt that the interposition, between her deed and its expiation, of this tragic idyll around which is finally so audaciously drawn, as if in an ironic pastoral, the vast druidic sheepfold of Stonehenge, does achieve at the conclusion of the story that sort of intensity (for it is dreamlike and intense at once) which, in Keats's phrase, is 'capable of making all disagreeables evaporate, from their being in close relationship with Beauty and Truth'. And stirring in the novel's close—if almost, perhaps, beyond its creator's ken—is truth, or myth, as venerable as any from the Attic stage. Tess is hanged and Angel, who has at last believed in her, is redeemed after a fashion. The presence of Tess's sister, 'Liza-Lu, as a kind of bequest from Tess to her husband has been censured as a sentimental intrusion of evolutionary hope. ('Furthermore,' one severe critic says, 'we do not believe that young girls make ameliorated lives out of witness of a sister's hanging.') Yet as these two, in the book's last sentence, join hands and turn from Wintoncester Gaol to pursue what path they can they are like persons who walk away from a Tomb.

5

The process by which a mature graphic art arrives at a high degree
of successful illusion is that known to art historians as schema and
correction. The artist requires, as starting-point, a hieroglyph,
stereotype or the like upon which he can work with the aim of
'bringing it to life'. It is part of Hardy's basis in unsophisticated or
naïve art that in his characterization he is often thus distinguishably at work upon stock figures. Tess Durbeyfield herself can be
considered in this way as built upon a schema of outraged virtue or
injured innocence. More persuasively, but by a similar genetic
criticism, she can be derived from antecedent and less complex
women in the earlier novels. Guerard makes a notable attempt at
this by looking back no farther than *The Woodlanders*:

> Tess herself is directly descended from Marty South, and even
> perhaps from Suke Damson. Suke merely stands on the squalid
> fringes of the story, a highly sexed and unreflective hoyden who
> casually gives herself to the rakish Dr Fitzpiers. Marty, on the
> other hand, is a 'pure woman' as well as a hard-working and
> unselfish child of the soil; she is betrayed only in the sense that
> Giles never appreciates her solid worth and fidelity. But what
> would have happened had Marty been endowed with Suke's
> sensuous nature as well as her own purity and faithfulness?
> What would have happened had *she* been seduced by an
> intruding Dr Fitzpiers? And what, finally, would have been the
> inner life of such a simple and pure child of the soil, seduced or
> unseduced? To answer these questions about Marty South,
> consciously or unconsciously, is to conceive of Tess Durbeyfield.

Not quite, perhaps—and it is certainly not to achieve her. The
men—with whom we come at once to minor creations—are
another matter. They extend from Angel's brothers, who are as flat
as pancakes ('We must get through another chapter of *A Counter-
blast to Agnosticism*', one of them says in his first utterance, as he
seeks to hasten Angel out of the presence of the dancing maidens),
to Angel's father, in whom there is a little light and shade, and
Tess's father, who has a rather rusty command of the old rustic
comedy, and then to Angel himself and to Alec d'Urberville.
These last two are of not quite the same order of creation. With
Alec it is possible to feel that Hardy too hastily planted a merely
stock figure on his stage. With his 'bold rolling eye', and his cigar

('D'Urberville mechanically lit a cigar'), and his 'Well, my Beauty'
he seems beyond redemption pasteboard from the start; his
religious conversion and backsliding are a mere puppetry dictated
by the fable; and so, more fatally, is his manner of resolving once
more to be Tess's master, since a single reassertion of his will
would be the natural measure of the slack and slothful womanizer
he is. Howe says that Alec 'can be likable, simply because commonplace vice is easier to bear than elevated righteousness'. But this
is a muddle. That need not be likable which is less dislikable
than Angel Clare. Hardy himself tries to give Alec a leg up by a
method other than that of Tom-Jonesing him. Tess in a fit of
feverish imagining thinks of her unbaptized child 'consigned to
the nethermost corner of hell . . . the arch-fiend tossing it with
his three-pronged fork'. Long afterwards, Alec, the child's father,
appears in the middle of a burning field, just such a fork in his
hands—and the symbolic significance (in which, calling himself
the old Other One, he takes pleasure) is reinforced by our
recalling another scene, only a little way back, when he has
presented himself to Tess very decidedly as the devil quoting
scripture. Yet not much can be done for Alec d'Urberville, even
when raised to the status of a Mephistophelean visitant. The
catastrophe is perhaps impaired by our feeling that he is only
worth walking out on, not killing. Tess contrives, after a fashion,
both these actions.

Angel Clare, that 'advanced and well-meaning young man',
among his various other misfortunes has been hardly dealt with by
time. What Hardy's preface calls 'views of life prevalent at the end
of the nineteenth century' are in Angel's head a conflicting crew
sadly in need of sorting out. So much is he a child of his age that
the passing of that age has incredibilized him. We cannot see him
even as a gentle and generous lover weak enough to be thrown
fatally off balance by a revelation which the whole tradition and
culture which he so idly and complacently thinks himself to have
escaped from declare to be a very dreadful revelation indeed.
We see him as something worse (or at least something even
more impossible) than Elfride Swancourt's fatal Henry Knight,
with his indecent insistence upon 'untried lips'; we see him
rather as a man unscrupulously and hypocritically grasping
at an unexpected chance of escaping from a false position. He
ought never to have become Tess's admirer, much less have
stood beside her at the altar, taking tremendous vows. For
some deep morbidity, less inversion of any sort than what
Lawrence calls 'ascetic revulsion', surfaces in him as soon as
sex threatens to harbour anywhere except in his head. We are

wrong thus to see him, no doubt—but no more wrong than Tess was, after another fashion:

> She had not known that men could be so disinterested, chivalrous, protective, in their love for women as he. Angel Clare was far from all that she thought him in this respect; absurdly far, indeed; but he was, in truth, more spiritual than animal; he had himself well in hand, and was singularly free from grossness. Though not cold-natured, he was rather bright than hot. . . .

Angel loves Tess, then, 'ideally and fancifully'. Tess herself knows this, even in her first hour as a bride:

> 'O my love, my love, why do I love you so!' she whispered there [in her bedroom] alone; 'for she you love is not my real self, but one in my image; the one I might have been!'

The words hold a truth beyond the stiff circumstances to which they immediately refer. Angel would subdue 'the substance to the conception', and deep in him there is struggle that is fatal and false. 'It is in your own mind what you are angry at, Angel; it is not in me.' Tess could not speak more truly. And so lost do we feel Angel to be that we find it difficult to believe in the good influence over him of that 'large-minded stranger' with whom he holds enlightening conversations—not reported to us—in the depths of Brazil. We are unfair to him, perhaps—as Hardy is not.

6

Tess of the d'Urbervilles is not merely an emotional novel; it is one of the greatest distillations of emotion into art that English literature can show. We do not know what so moved Hardy in the contemplation of Tess's story. But at one point we are told something about the quality of her voice 'which will never be forgotten by those who knew her'. There can be no doubt of the deliberateness with which Hardy thus in a single phrase accords Tess Durbeyfield a status unique in his fiction. Yet biographical delving is surely idle. There are those who see some special and apt relationship between Tess and Tryphena Sparks. Is not the warning clear?

At least we can say that of all Hardy's books this, his greatest book, is most a work of art. More than in any other, that is to say, the art has absorbed the emotion—so that we comparatively seldom have any sense of the writer's directly airing or relieving his feelings at our expense. It is true that when in the preface to the fifth impression (1892) he declares himself to be 'a mere tale-teller . . . without any ulterior intentions whatever' we are inclined to respond that both the title-page and the last paragraph of the book quite plainly declare designs upon us as moral, or sadly immoral, beings. There are matters upon which *Tess of the d'Urbervilles* is very clearly intended to bring us to a better mind. The curse upon Hardy as an artist was perhaps his persuasion that, virtually within his lifetime, cosmic discoveries had been made which rendered it incumbent upon artists to take a gloomy view of things—and even to distribute over the human spectacle in general a proper quota of downright atrabilious and conscien-tiously irreverent remarks. The authorial voice will be raised under some such primitive disguise as 'Some people would like to know' or 'Some people might have cried', and what follows is a swipe at the optimism of Browning or at 'the last grotesque phase of a creed which had served mankind well in its time'. Or Christ is casually referred to as one of 'two great thinkers' to whom it might be enlightening to appeal 'as fellow-men to fellow-men'; or again we are informed (in a thought Hardy plays upon elsewhere) that 'the mill still worked on, food being a perennial necessity; the abbey had perished, creeds being transient'. Sallies of this kind are not always artistically harmless:

> The only exercise that Tess took at this time was after dark; and it was then, when out in the woods, that she seemed least solitary. She knew how to hit to a hair's-breadth that moment of evening when the light and the darkness are so evenly balanced that the constraint of day and the suspense of night neutralize each other, leaving absolute mental liberty. It is then that the plight of being alive becomes attenuated to its least possible dimensions. She had no fear of the shadows; her sole idea seemed to be to shun mankind—or rather that cold accretion called the world, which, so terrible in the mass, is so unformid-able, even pitiable, in its units.
>
> On these lonely hills and dales her quiescent glide was of a piece with the element she moved in. . . .

Tess is here about to bear an illegitimate child, and her crepuscular excursions are natural enough. The passage, indeed, is a very fine one, but into it has been inserted, with 'the plight of being alive', something that we may feel as being thrust at us by the author once too often.

Or again there is the place, late in the story, in which the younger Durbeyfield children, who will be homeless on the day following, sing a hymn learnt at Sunday-school:

> Here we suffer grief and pain,
> Here we meet to part again;
> In heaven we part no more.

The passage is extremely moving, and it is also finely realized:

> The four sang on with the phlegmatic passivity of persons who had long ago settled the question, and there being no mistake about it, felt that further thought was not required. With features strained hard to enunciate the syllables they continued to regard the centre of the flickering fire, the notes of the youngest straying over into the pauses of the rest.

We read on:

> Tess turned from them, and went to the window again. Darkness had now fallen without, but she put her face to the pane as though to peer into the gloom. It was really to hide her tears. If she could only believe what the children were singing; if she were only sure, how different all would now be; how confidently she would leave them to Providence and their future kingdom! But, in default of that, it behoved her to do something; to be their Providence; for to Tess, as to not a few millions of others, there was ghastly satire in the poet's lines—

> > Not in utter nakedness
> > But trailing clouds of glory do we come.

> To her and her like, birth itself was an ordeal of degrading personal compulsion, whose gratuitousness nothing in the result seemed to justify, and at best could only palliate.

In a passage so fine as this the reference to Wordsworth is a false note. Tess is being used, not quite as she ought to be used, by her creator.

Yet such flaws—as we may venture to think them—are unimportant and infrequent. *Tess of the d'Urbervilles*, unlike most of Hardy's novels, is not notably an uneven book. It is tauter than the others, and although it is not without the kind of awkwardness of language censured by Vernon Lee and made fun of by George Moore (Tess is at one point described as 'an almost standard woman'), it is in some mysterious way better written. Above all, when Hardy's dramatic imagination is fully engaged with Tess, and his emotion confined within the bounds of his creative purpose, he writes with unexampled certainty as well as power. Tess's long letter (it comes at the end of Chapter XLVIII) to the husband who has deserted her is an instance of this. Only in Richardson's *Clarissa*, indeed, are we likely to find anything of its kind that comes near it.

12

Jude the Obscure

THE PREFACE TO THE FIRST EDITION OF *JUDE THE OBSCURE* BEGINS thus:

The history of this novel (whose birth in its present shape has been much retarded by the necessities of periodical publication) is briefly as follows. The scheme was jotted down in 1890, from notes made in 1887 and onwards, some of the circumstances being suggested by the death of a woman in the former year. The scenes were revisited in October 1892; the narrative was written in outline in 1892 and the spring of 1893, and at full length, as it now appears, from August 1893 onwards into the next year.

Some further chronological information is then provided before Hardy moves on to his main business of briefly vindicating the moral propriety of his book.

These opening sentences are worth pausing on. The chief 'scene' of *Jude the Obscure* is Oxford, which Hardy calls Christminster. But it seems reasonably certain that Hardy, far from having 'revisited' Oxford in October 1892, arrived there for the first time in June 1893, when already his novel had been 'written in outline'—whatever that may mean. This is a curious circumstance. Some thirty years earlier Hardy, as a young architect in London, had written to his sister Mary: 'Oxford must be a jolly place. I shall try to get down there some time or other.' Whether jolly or not, Oxford is certainly of interest to architects, and its distance from London is fifty-five miles. For many years before he came to write *Jude the Obscure* Hardy, far from being the reclusive countryman of popular imagination, had been moving freely about England and the Continent, and freely amid both fashionable and intellectual society. Yet he first saw Oxford twenty years after he had first seen Cambridge. He was first able (we may reflect) to imagine Sue Bridehead in an Oxford setting on an excursion during a London season in which he had witnessed *Hedda Gabler, Rosmers-*

holm, and *The Master Builder*. His fighting shy of the university city tells us something already perhaps intimated in the jaunty tone of his reference to it in the letter to Mary.

And what are we to make of the statement about 'the circumstances being suggested by the death of a woman in the former year [1890]'? In itself this might lead us to expect that a woman's death has an important place in the novel, but the only woman whose death we hear of is Jude's great-aunt Drusilla, a very minor character. So what Hardy is presumably saying is: 'The death of a woman in 1890 brought back to me memories which suggested this novel'. And we know that Tryphena Sparks died in 1890—thereby occasioning in Hardy that 'curious instance of sympathetic telepathy' recorded in the *Life*. There is nothing in *Jude the Obscure* which, so far as we can discern, could have been 'suggested' by Tryphena except the character of Sue Bridehead, and parts of Sue Bridehead's story. Admitting this much, we may still be troubled by the phrase: 'suggested by the death'. Was it, after all, Tryphena's *death* which suggested something? There is a macabre sense in which Sue *may* be said to *die* in the novel. It is when she finally drags herself in loathing into the embrace of her deeply unfortunate husband, Richard Phillotson.

However this may be, Hardy, after all, is saying no more than that 'some of the circumstances' of the story were suggested by a woman's death. Do we learn anything further about the origins of the novel from the 'notes made in 1887 and onwards'? Only one relevant note appears in the *Life*. It was written in April 1888:

A short story of a young man—'who could not go to Oxford' —His struggles and ultimate failure. Suicide. There is something the world ought to be shown, and I am the one to show it to them—though I was not altogether hindered going, at least to Cambridge, and could have gone up easily at five-and-twenty.

Here, then, and accompanied once more by suggestions of enduring personal feeling, is a hint of the novel as first conceived; it was to present, in a context of academic ambition, what Hardy later in the preface calls a 'tragedy of unfulfilled aims'. But the preface does not suggest this as the novel's *principal* intention. Primacy is given to an attempt 'to deal unaffectedly with the fret and fever, derision and disaster, that may press in the wake of the strongest passion known to humanity'. This, whether for good or ill, is obviously not the passion to go to Oxford. It is the passion to mate and go to bed.

Beginning from these two centres of interest—and perhaps from a poignantly felt sense of personal deprivation in each—Hardy devised a fable which was to represent them in a dramatic inter-relationship. There is a point, half-way through the novel, in which its conceptual basis is exhibited in one of those summaries—in themselves bleakly undramatic—to which Hardy is prone. Jude is musing:

> Strange that his first aspiration—towards academical profic-iency—had been checked by a woman, and that his second aspira-tion—towards apostleship—had also been checked by a woman.

Here are the bare bones of the story as any brief abstract must reveal them.[1] The baker's boy teaches himself Latin and Greek—without, so far as we are told, a single lesson, so much as a single encouraging word, from another human being: an almost super-human achievement. But he is himself human enough; a first upsurge of sexual feeling betrays him into the arms of Arabella Donn, and his marriage to a woman so ignorant and crudely sensual wrecks his career at the moment when, conceivably, he

---

[1] Jude Fawley, a poor orphan who finds rural Marygreen ugly and sleepy, sets his heart on going to Christminster, a great university city just visible on the horizon. He devotes his boyhood to solitary study directed to this end, being encouraged by the example of the village schoolmaster, Richard Phillotson, who has gone off to Christminster with the intention of taking a degree. But Jude attracts the interest of Arabella Donn, a coarse and ignorant girl in search of a husband, and is placed in a situation in which he feels bound to marry her. The marriage turns out so badly that Jude makes an indecisive attempt at drowning himself (as his mother had actually done), and then finds that Arabella has left him, declaring that she will not come back. A few years later he makes his way to Christminster, believing that he can earn his living as a stone-mason there while continuing his plan to enter the university. At Christminster he meets for the first time a cousin, Sue Bridehead, and falls in love with her. She works at the lettering of religious texts, but is in fact sceptical and 'modern', shocking Jude's orthodox piety by declaring, for example, that the railway station and not the cathedral is 'the centre of the town life now'. Jude and Sue have an extraordinary affinity for each other, which is remarked both by themselves and by others. This, however, seems in part a consequence of their blood relationship, and unfortunately theirs is a family in which 'marriage usually meant a tragic sadness'. Sexually, more-over, Sue is extremely reticent, and there is something 'epicene' about her tenderness. Jude renews his acquaintance with Phillotson, who has been thwarted in his academic ambitions and is now the village schoolmaster at Lumsdon (which is Cumnor near Oxford). Phillotson accepts Sue as a pupil-teacher. Jude's approaches to the colleges of the university meet with no more success than Phillotson's have done, and he begins to find inter-mittent solace in drink.

Jude goes to Melchester (Salisbury) in the hope of studying for the ministry in a more humble way, and Phillotson, who is also attracted by Sue, secures her entry into a teachers' training college in the same city. Sue is punished for an innocent escapade with Jude, and runs away to him. She tells him of her living, when eighteen, in close intimacy with a Christminster student whom she had nevertheless never admitted as a lover. But when, soon after-wards, Jude confesses to her his married state she makes a hasty and un-might have decisively furthered it. Seemingly freed from Arabella, he falls in love with his cousin Sue Bridehead, who has some appearance of being the ideal mate for such a man. Sue too has rebelled against her inherited station in life; she is intellectual and clear-sighted; she knows that Jude's Christminster is a mirage, but knows too that Christminster is the just birthright of such as Jude; she is fire where Arabella is earth, and she can thus command such a man's imagination as well as his senses. Yet Sue's fatality is far deeper than Arabella's. Her fascination is the product of a diffused and nervous sexuality which has nothing to give. In an elusive and quasi-genetic fashion she is not her cousin's complement but his mirror-image. Each is eventually the destruction of the other.

At the end of a much later prefatory note, written in 1912, Hardy observes that 'no doubt there can be more in a book than the author consciously puts there, which will help either to its profit or to its disadvantage as the case may be'. In proceeding even thus far with a preliminary analysis, I may have proceeded a little

considered marriage with Phillotson. At about this time, Arabella turns up again; still finding Jude attractive, she succeeds in sleeping with him once more, and then tells him how she has contracted a bigamous marriage in Australia.

Sue's marriage is a disaster. She cannot bear the thought of physical relations with Phillotson, and begs to be allowed to leave him. He agrees, and she goes to live with Jude, who decides that, an unlicensed love being necessarily the end of his ambition towards the ministry, he had better burn 'all the theological and ethical works that he possessed'; in fact, however, Sue has little more disposition to sleep with him than with Phillotson. Phillotson, unaware of this legal insufficiency, frees Sue by securing a divorce—an honourable and rational course of conduct which loses him his job.

Jude in turn secures a divorce from Arabella. But Sue refuses to submit to a ceremony of marriage with him, and only after a long and uncertain interval is their union consummated, with the result that two children are born. Meanwhile Arabella, legally married and living in London, has placed in their care an older child, hers and Jude's, who is preternaturally joyless, is described as 'Age masquerading as Juvenility', and announces upon arrival that he is commonly addressed as Little Father Time. This unnerving boy and Sue hold lugubrious conversations together.

Jude moves his household back to Christminster. They arrive just in time to witness some grand academic occasion. Jude harangues the populace on his own defeated ambition. Father Time finds that the Doctors in their 'blood-red robes' suggest the Judgment Day and supposes that the colleges must be gaols. Accommodation for so strange a family is hard to find, and when 'this too reflective child' learns that Sue is to have another baby he hangs the other children and himself in despair; as Jude and Sue confront their tragedy a college organ is heard playing 'Truly God is loving unto Israel' and two clergymen of differing views argue about 'the eastward position'. What is the final blow to Jude's already shaken faith has the opposite effect on Sue—whom Arabella, who is hovering again, reports to be 'took in a queer religious way'. Sue marries Phillotson for the second time, and drives herself to go to bed with him. Hearing that Arabella's husband is dead, she tells Jude it is his duty to remarry too. He does so, but fails long to survive his degradation, inebriety and misery. Arabella says that he is 'a 'andsome corpse.'

G

beyond what Hardy 'consciously' proposed for his book. Hardy taught himself Greek, Hardy wanted to go to Oxford (or 'at least to Cambridge'), Hardy had profoundly disillusioning experiences in the sphere of sexual relationships—and these facts prompted him to write *Jude the Obscure*. Yet, viewed as centred upon Jude Fawley, *Jude the Obscure* is a fatigued and awkward and really rather dismal performance. Viewed as centred upon what the impressed but scandalized Edmund Gosse called Sue's *vita sexualis*, there can be no doubt that *Jude the Obscure* stands among the most impressively exploratory and intuitive of modern English novels. But the manner in which—if at all—Tryphena Sparks acted as catalyst in this achievement seems likely for ever to elude the curiosity of biographers.

2

It has become a common contention of the critics that *Jude the Obscure* is not fully viable as a 'realistic' novel. They point out that it is the last labour of prose fiction Hardy brought himself to achieve; that a growing interest in poetry is seeping into it even in the unassuming form of scraps of Browning, Swinburne, Barnes, Drayton and others dragged not always very appositely into the text; more significantly, that its essential power is less fictional than poetic. 'The feelings', Mr Alvarez remarks in an acute essay, 'are those which were later given perfect form in Hardy's best poetry.' At least it looks forward to kinds of fiction which break away from the Victorian norms in order to admit effects of expressionism, symbolism, and significant distortion.

Yet the novel renders certain impressions running quite counter to this. In moving from the heartland of Wessex to Christminster and Aldbrickham, from the labourer to the artisan, from the cycle of the seasons and immemorial toil to 'problems' and 'questions' currently at issue in late-nineteenth-century England, Hardy is in an obvious sense drawing closer to 'realistic' fiction as it was then conceived. In turning from Tess Durbeyfield to Jude Fawley he is forsaking a figure of heroic proportions for one anxiously cut down to life size. Above all, in eschewing all excursus into those heightened and dreamlike episodes in which melodrama turns to poetry—and they have occurred in every major novel hitherto—he seems determined faithfully to render nothing except the common textures of everyday. Our awareness of intermittent failures in verisimilitude and persuasiveness is no sufficient warrant for supposing that departures from 'realism' had any place in his conscious intentions.

Perhaps no work of the English imagination since *Samson Agonistes* at once suggests so much power and so much fatigue. One observation set down in Hardy's notebook is of significance here: 'On account of the labour of altering *Jude the Obscure* to suit the magazine, and then having to alter it back, I have lost energy for revising and improving the original as I meant to do.' In letters to friends, moreover, he more than once asserted his disappointment with the finished novel. 'You have hardly an idea how poor and feeble the book seems to me, as executed, beside the idea of it that I had formed in prospect.' 'Alas, what a miserable accomplishment it is, when I compare it with what I meant to make it!' Such feelings, indeed, are common to artists, and Hardy had expressed them before. Yet they are answered by our recurrent sense as we read that much in the novel has been merely stated, rather than— again in the artist's word—'done'.

This holds of the very important matter of Jude's intellectual bent. We are nowhere made to *feel* what brought him his Greek and Latin; he is seen in virtually no concrete situation relevant to it—unless it be 'returned home from hearing a lecture on ancient history' in a public hall. (The point will become apparent if one compares Jude's struggles for self-cultivation with those—less ambitious but much more closely observed—of Arnold Bennett's young Edwin Clayhanger.) Again, the extended passage in which Jude is represented as wandering about Christminster and hearing the ghostly *ipsissima verba* of departed Oxford men ('Then the sly author of the immortal Chapter on Christianity', etc.) is a poor and even embarrassing substitute for something not really created in the book. A similar unsatisfactoriness attends the handling of Jude's son by Arabella, Little Father Time. The child arrives magnificently in his railway carriage (the passage is matched by the remarkable poem 'Midnight on the Great Western'), and the 'steady mechanical creep' with which he sets off to seek out his destination is eerie enough. But he scarcely murders his siblings in the closet more effectively than his creator murders him with deadly prose. We hear of 'the quaint and mysterious personality of Father Time', of 'a boy with an octogenarian face', of 'this too reflective child' and so on. What we do *not* hear of is so much as the names of the children he kills; instead, we have portentous remarks from Jude about the catastrophe instancing 'the beginning of the coming universal wish not to live'. Pretty well everything is unrealized throughout this dimension of the novel.

Next we must notice that a high proportion of both the dialogue and the interior monologue is implausible even beyond Hardy's common licence. It is, of course, a well-established, if odd, feature of English fiction that the language of simple people should approximate more closely to the language of the cultivated in proportion as they are presented in serious or elevated situations. (This is sometimes called the convention of heroic speech.) Hardy had here always been in a position of peculiar linguistic difficulty, since he had an uncertain sense of the tone and idiom of polite speech itself; and he was more likely to go wrong with characters in so curiously *déraciné* a situation as Jude and Sue. It may be that in some measure the absence of any authentic colloquial note between these two is deliberately contrived to convey the difficulty of their relationship. On the other hand, we are frequently told that their ordinary companionship is marked by total unconstraint, 'delightfully unreserved intercourse', and this renders puzzling their manner of addressing each other so much in the spirit, as it were, of public occasions. Jude lectures Sue on the Tractarians and Sue lectures Jude on architecture; Sue talks of the house of Atreus and Jude immediately comes back at her with the house of Jeroboam. On the whole, Sue has the edge on Jude, as she has too on Phillotson: having spent a night in a cupboard in order to express her feelings about this unhappy man, she quotes John Stuart Mill *verbatim* to him next morning, and follows this up with a series of missives (delivered from classroom to classroom by infant hands) quoting from Humboldt ('your Humboldt,' she points out), and citing appositely from the beliefs of the primitive Christian communities.

Such exercises may be thought of, no doubt, as the characteristic exchanges of well-read people. But Jude, at least, talks in much the same way to the uninstructed, offering Arabella thoughts from the *Antigone* and discoursing to a casually encountered rustic on 'the stillness of infinite motion—the sleep of the spinning-top, to borrow the simile of a well-known writer'. Yet this too can be justified; here, we may say, is the habitual pedantry of the autodidact—which is similarly evidenced when, on some ceremonial Christminster occasion, Jude exhorts a gaping crowd to 'perceive there is something wrong somewhere in our social formulas'. Nevertheless there seems to be a flagging or disregard of the imagination in the unvaried employment of an idiom skimmed, as it were, from the mere surface of the writer's mind. And an equally flattening effect attends the spilling over of this into the unspoken meditations of the characters, as when Jude realizes that his marriage is a disaster:

> Their lives were ruined, he thought; ruined by the fundamental error of their matrimonial union: that of having based

a permanent contract on a temporary feeling which had no necessary connection with affinities that alone render a life-long comradeship tolerable.

This is merely the notation of a novelist making jottings for his private use; we are afforded no sense of following the contours of Jude Fawley's mind. And in the same area of inadequate and imprecise expression must be reckoned the manner in which Jude is frequently represented as addressing Sue or as characterizing her in his thought. She is his 'impatient little dear', his 'curious little comrade', his 'ever evasive companion'. 'O you darling little fool,' he says to her near the end, and goes on: 'You dear, sad, soft, most melancholy wreck of a promising human intellect that it has ever been my lot to behold!' Surely no man ever uttered such words to a woman—just as no man ever (as Jude is made to do a few pages earlier) ended a bitter speech by saying 'Ha-ha-ha!'

Dialogue and interior monologue aside, there is a good deal of perfunctory cliché-writing in *Jude the Obscure*—far more than in *Tess of the d'Urbervilles*. We are told that Melchester Cathedral is 'the most graceful architectural pile in England', that Jude succumbs to Arabella's 'midnight contiguity' and is conducted by her 'through the varieties of spirituous delectation', that Sue 'blinked away an excess of eye moisture', and that in her relations with Jude 'the antagonisms of sex to sex were left without any counterpoising predilections'. Those who amuse themselves with the oddities of Hardy's prose style have a happy hunting ground in this final novel.

Any extended consideration of comparatively superficial aspects of the book must appear trivial. Yet it is conceivable that the effect of these apparent insufficiencies and infelicities is not wholly negative, nor indeed wholly inadvertent. Hardy may well have believed himself to have 'lost energy for revising and improving'. But there is something about the dogged awkwardness and charmlessness of the narrative which surely suggests a conscious design upon the reader. The traditional canons of romance are flouted rather as in an *anti-roman*. We are denied much of the aesthetic pleasure associated with fully realized imaginative creation. The writer is determined, beyond everything else, that his vision shall grate on us. He exploits whatever will grate.

3

We have seen Jude himself stating in bleakly conceptual terms the theme of the story his creator has devised for him: successive

aspirations checked by successive women. At the close of the
novel Jude is employed to make another of these summary
statements: this time, not on the book's theme but, in effect, on its
form. He laments to a useful confidante, Mrs Edlin, Sue's final
return to Phillotson. 'Then bitter affliction came to us,' he says,
'and her intellect broke, and she veered round to darkness.
Strange difference of sex, that time and circumstance, which
enlarge the views of most men, narrow the views of women
almost invariably.'

It is this proposition, whether true or false, that dictates the
formal organisation of *Jude the Obscure*.

Jude Fawley starts out as a pious youth. He is going to become a
great scholar, but also a Doctor of Divinity. (He is planning his
road to this at the very moment in which Arabella so fatefully
throws the pig's pizzle at him.) It is a great day when he finds in a
bookseller's at Alfredston 'some volumes of the Fathers which had
been left behind by an insolvent clergyman of the neighbourhood'.
When he first becomes aware of Sue lettering texts in an ecclesiastical warehouse he is particularly pleased that such 'a sweet
saintly Christian business' is hers. He is further edified when he
finds her shepherding a group of children 'to see an itinerant
exhibition, in the shape of a model of Jerusalem, to which schools
were admitted at a penny a head in the interests of education'.
Later, he is mildly scandalized to find that she has cut up and
reassorted the books of the New Testament according to the
chronological findings of the higher criticism, and he judges her
remarks on the Song of Solomon 'quite Voltairean'. Later still,
however, he can ask if she knows of 'any good readable edition of
the uncanonical books' and be duly referred to Cowper's *Apocryphal Gospels*. Hardy, we may remark in passing, cannot resist
making Jude's pious conformity and theological interests absurd,
and this has the unfortunate effect of suggesting that Jude is really
rather a stupid young man.

Sue, of course, is not in fact 'saintly' at all but a total unbeliever
who likes to think of herself as liberated into a neo-pagan condition, and who signalizes the fact by buying two plaster casts of
heathen divinities—an Apollo and 'a Venus of standard pattern'—
and concealing them in the room in which she entertains herself
with Gibbon, Swinburne and other heterodox writers. We are told
that she is deeply interested in Jude (who has recently hired a
harmonium and begun practising chants) 'as one might be interested in a man puzzling out his way along a labyrinth from which
one had one's self escaped'.

But Sue is to re-enter the labyrinth—and by the same route, as it were, which eventually takes Jude out of it. The identical disasters which cause Jude to lose his faith engulf Sue in a pit of morbid religiosity. Time and circumstance, it is implied, have indeed enlarged his views and narrowed hers. Certainly the man and woman have exchanged stances with a kind of formal obtrusiveness which may be said to take the place in this novel of the strongly accented artificial, melodramatic, or sensational elements upon which Hardy had been accustomed to rely. We do not need to turn to any of the acknowledged masterpieces of this 'hourglass' structure—say Henry James's *The Ambassadors*—to conclude that Hardy arrives at only indifferent success with it. Yet although we feel too much of a *parti pris* operative in the last stages of the fable, we are certainly not unconvinced by the deeper motivations of Jude's and Sue's final tragedy.

It is possible to view *Jude the Obscure* as a 'purpose novel'. In the preface (or 'postscript') of 1912 Hardy speaks of 'the marriage laws being used in great part as the tragic machinery of the tale', and goes on to give his own views on a rational attitude to divorce. But it is not really true that the marriage (or divorce) laws are of prime importance, or that the novel is at all like the many which were then beginning to be published with the 'marriage question' as a central theme. In *The Woodlanders* mischief is caused by the folly of George Melbury in concluding without proper enquiry that his daughter Grace can obtain a divorce from Dr Fitzpiers. But in *Jude the Obscure* nothing of this kind is at issue, and the two divorces described go through with a minimum of fuss. What causes real trouble is not the fact but the absence of a marriage, or ceremony of marriage. When Jude and Sue are at length free to marry, Sue hangs back. Having already, while Phillotson's wife, concluded marriage to be 'only a sordid contract, based on material convenience in householding', been 'certain one ought to be allowed to undo what one has done so ignorantly', and suggested that 'domestic laws should be made according to temperaments, which should be classified', she is chary about submitting once more to the unreformed institutions of her country. When 'the decree *nisi* in the case of Phillotson *versus* Phillotson and Fawley' has been made absolute, Jude is sufficiently optimistic to 'put on a lighter tie'. (It is one of the most exuberant actions recorded of him.) But Sue feels that 'an iron contract' may extinguish his tenderness for her:

'I think I should begin to be afraid of you, Jude, the moment you had contracted to cherish me under a Government stamp, and I was licenced to be loved on the premises by you—Ugh,

how horrible and sordid! Although as you are, free, I trust you
more than any other man in the world.'

She goes on to entertain Jude with the paradoxical proposition
that a marriage vow would do less harm if it were an undertaking
to cease loving. Jude admits 'this, or something like it, to be true',
but points out that 'people go on marrying because they can't
resist natural forces'. This is not a proposition that means much to
Sue, who is presently saying how a glimpse of Arabella has made
her 'feel more than ever how hopelessly vulgar an institution legal
marriage is'.

Jude nevertheless makes several attempts to marry Sue. They
must 'pluck up courage', he says. He gets her into a registry office,
but there is a bride with a black eye and the place is ugly. They go
on and witness a wedding in a church, but this is just as bad. Sue
points out that Jude and she are 'horribly sensitive . . . folk in
whom domestic ties of a forced kind snuff out cordiality and
spontaneousness'. Jude, who himself seems unenthusiastic, eventually gives in, declaring that what she calls her 'whims' accord
very much with his own. But some sort of show has to be put up:

> The result was that shortly after the attempt at the registrar's
> the pair went off—to London it was believed. . . . When they
> came back they let it be understood indirectly, and with total
> indifference and weariness of mien, that they were legally
> married at last. Sue, who had previously been called Mrs
> Bridehead, now openly adopted the name of Mrs Fawley. Her
> dull, cowed, and listless manner for days seemed to substantiate
> all this.

The imposture proves not convincing, all the same, and it is from a
resulting social near-ostracism that the catastrophe—at least at
the surface level of the narrative—is supposed to proceed. Jude
had been making some progress as a stonemason, in an independent if humble way. But now 'the headstone and epitaph orders fell
off'. Penury lies ahead.

That a 'dull, cowed, and listless manner' should give colour to
the conjecture that a woman has just been married is a proposition
cohering with a good deal said about marriage in the novel in an
incidental or *obiter dictum* fashion. We hear of the 'antipathetic,
recriminatory mood of the average husband and wife of Christen-
dom', and at the point at which Jude is lured back to Arabella we
have this:

The landlord of the lodging, who had heard that they were a queer couple, had doubted if they were married at all, especially as he had seen Arabella kiss Jude one evening when she had taken a little cordial; and he was about to give them notice to quit, till by chance overhearing her one night haranguing Jude in rattling terms, and ultimately flinging a shoe at his head, he recognized the note of genuine wedlock; and concluding that they must be respectable, said no more.

This, from near the end of Jude's and Arabella's story, echoes the tone in which we are told that story's beginning:

And so, standing before the aforesaid officiator, the two swore that at every other time of their lives till death took them, they would assuredly believe, feel, and desire precisely as they had believed, felt, and desired during the few preceding weeks. What was as remarkable as the undertaking itself was the fact that nobody seemed at all surprised at what they swore.

But all this of the unreasonableness of the marriage bond—the expression of which, whether by Sue or by Hardy himself in his familiar passing sarcasms, is commonplace enough—is not really deeply woven into the imaginative fabric of *Jude the Obscure*. In this it twins with the 'young man who could not go to Oxford' theme. Here again is something clearly potent with Hardy himself, but equally clearly it has ceased much to command him in this novel as it develops, so that it is brought in only intermittently, as when Hardy invents the absurdly named Sarcophagus College and credits it with 'four centuries of gloom, bigotry, and decay'. At the close, indeed, the theme has to be given a stiff rhetorical boost if its presence is to be felt at all, so Jude's Henchard-like commination out of *Job* is punctuated by the hurrahs of what are presumably privileged young men on and around the playing-fields of Christminster. Jude is not, in fact, snuffed out because he has been denied the diploma of a Doctor of Divinity, nor essentially because of anything in his personal history that changed legal ordinances could have altered. When Hardy talks about his novel in terms of such conceptions, he is doing so because there existed still, in the 1890s, topics which even a writer in an exacerbated and un-compromising mood could not quite nerve himself to air—except, indeed, in confidential correspondence or conversation. From cover to cover, *Jude the Obscure* is concerned as preponder-antly with problems of intimate sexual relationship as is *The*

Rainbow or *Women in Love*. Much of it is concerned with what—conventionally, at least—is regarded as sexual pathology.

4

Hardy is a writer belonging to a popular tradition, and behind the characters in this, in fact, most innovatory novel there lies much literary stereotype, which he had to penetrate and which, in a sense, we have to penetrate too.

The first of these stereotypes is Jude Fawley as hero. He is clever, purposeful and tenacious; he formulates honourable goals; he is physically attractive and sexually straightforward; this straightforwardness makes him vulnerable in an earthy yet essentially wholesome Tom Jones fashion. Arabella Donn, who manages to tumble him into bed and so to marry him, is a second stereotype, full of sensual appeal, but for a hero too earthy altogether. Jude then finds Arabella's antitype in Susanna Bridehead. Sue is not earthy enough; she prizes spiritual and intellectual qualities and is therefore 'good' where Arabella is 'bad'; but she lives to an exaggerated degree at that sort of fastidious remove from physical sex which constrains the heroes of ordinary Victorian novels to be as wary as they invariably are in making advances to virtuous girls.

All three of these characters clearly enough crack their respective moulds. In Fielding's world Jude would be left standing at the post, since he possesses even more than a common share of that passivity which is a regular feature of Hardy's male characters. This is true of more than his mere sexual comportment, for as well as being pushed around by his women he is very much pushed around by life at large. As Blunden has said, he regularly renders the effect of one 'altogether sent here below to accumulate bitter disasters about him'. Yet within this somewhat inert stance he is in fact a complex and disturbing character. Some recent commentators assert that Arabella was really the girl for Jude; that he needed quick and unassuming sex, just as he needed an occasional quart of ale, to cheer him up on his lonely intellectual road. His passion for Arabella, Alvarez remarks, 'is considerably more human and spontaneous' than his passion for Sue.

There is perhaps no more than a half-truth in this. Jude certainly needs sex, and he gets it from Arabella whereas Sue denies it to him. But within Jude himself there is some principle of sexual revulsion; it is hard to isolate yet unmistakably there, and connects with the *Doppelgänger* theme—Jude as his cousin Sue's mirror-image—which is one of the most insistently reiterated ideas in the novel; 'the extraordinary sympathy, or similarity, between the pair' is as apparent to Phillotson, for example, as it is to the cousins themselves. 'A little chill overspread him at her first unrobing' is what we learn of Jude as a bridegroom, and it takes only the business of killing the pig (about which Arabella is inadequately squeamish) and a quarrel over his books for Jude to make an ineffectual attempt at suicide, and discover immediately thereafter that Arabella has had enough of him and departed. Arabella is not a fool; indeed, it is in the possession of considerable intelligence that her own divagation from a traditional role is most apparent; we must suppose that she had good ground for writing off Jude at this time, and it is to be only under the prompting of jealousy that she goes after him again.

There was no impossible degree of scandal in the characters of either Jude or Arabella, although much of their behaviour did, of course, strike refined readers as low. Sue was a different matter, and Hardy is distinguishably nervous about her. In 1912 he cites, or invents, 'an experienced reviewer' in Germany, who

> informed the writer that Sue Bridehead, the heroine, was the first delineation in fiction of the woman who was coming into notice in her thousands every year—the woman of the feminist movement—the slight, pale 'bachelor' girl—the intellectualized, emancipated bundle of nerves that modern conditions were producing, mainly in cities as yet; who does not recognize the necessity for most of her sex to follow marriage as a profession, and boast themselves as superior people because they are licenced to be loved on the premises. . . . Whether this assurance is borne out by dates I cannot say.

Here is a new stereotype for Sue—or rather here is Sue as an archetype in England of that 'New Woman' whom Ibsen is supposed to have been the first to distinguish. And the 'experienced reviewer' is indeed producing a recognizable portrait of Sue—as she would be, we may say, had it been Bernard Shaw who invented her and given her some such name as Vivie Warren. We only have to read this little piece of obfuscation (for it is that) put up by Hardy, and then think of Hardy's actual Sue, to realize the astonishing triumph of intuitive psychology that the portrait represents.

Writing to Gosse a few weeks after the publication of the novel, Hardy offers a somewhat different account of Sue, admirable so far as it goes, which he would probably not at the time have cared to put into print.

You are quite right; there is nothing perverted or depraved in
Sue's nature. The abnormalism consists in disproportion, not in
inversion, her sexual instinct being healthy as far as it goes, but
unusually weak and fastidious. Her sensibilities remain painfully
alert notwithstanding, as they do in nature with such women.
One point illustrating this I could not dwell upon: that, though
she has children, her intimacies with Jude have never been more
than occasional, even when they were living together (I mention
that they occupy separate rooms, except towards the end), and
one of her reasons for fearing the marriage ceremony is that she
fears it would be breaking faith with Jude to withhold herself at
pleasure, or altogether, after it; though while uncontracted she
feels at liberty to yield herself as seldom as she chooses. This has
tended to keep his passion as hot at the end as at the beginning,
and helps to break his heart. He has never really possessed her
as freely as he desired.

Sue is a type of woman which has always had an attraction
for me, but the difficulty of drawing the type has kept me from
attempting it till now.

But this in itself does not do justice either to the scope of Hardy's
conscious proposal or to the depth and delicacy of his perception.
A sexual habit such as is here described may be innate, one
imagines, or a product of peculiar nurture or early traumatic
experience. But, however derived, it is certain to be played upon,
as is every emotional predisposition, by complex social forces
through life. Hardy designs to exhibit the fortunes of both his
principal characters as moulded by the pressures of the age in
which they live. And although Weber assures us that the action of
Tess of the d'Urbervilles opens a decade after that of *Jude the
Obscure* closes, it is of course the latter that is by far Hardy's most
aggressively 'contemporary' book. The immemorial walks and
ways of his earlier imagination have been put aside as if almost
suddenly revealed as wholly of the past and no more affording a
relevant arena for the presentation of vehement real life. Coming
from ancient Wessex to the modern city, Jude and Sue exchange
an environment the traditional stabilities of which have been
ceasing to stabilize and sustain in favour of one more complex,
abrasive, and isolating.

Hardy's anatomy of this new social context is not particularly
searching and certainly not sympathetic; he obviously disapproves
of what he calls 'the modern vice of unrest' and sees it as something with 'no foundation in the nobler instincts' which is reflected
in the less worthy side of Jude's ambition. And it is upon Sue far

more fully than upon Jude that we see it effectively bearing. As a young workman with intellectual ambitions, Jude could readily have been put in relation with others of like mind, and also with some of those practical measures for self-improvement, social reform, and political effectiveness which were vigorously in being in what was, after all, the heroic age of the British working class. Jude's remove from all this renders the pathos of his 'case' slightly factitious; he cherishes Christminster as a kind of all-or-nothing dream which is in fact insidiously disabling and immobilizing. There is surprisingly little intimacy in Hardy's entering into the humbly born Jude's personality at grips with an alien and baffling environment. That it should be otherwise in Sue's case is an index of the imaginative depth from which the more powerful parts of this novel come.

Sue, who is far more intelligent, daring, and original than Jude, has at the same time—simply because she is a woman—far less power to take her destiny into her own hands. Social ordinances press upon her much more intimately and hardly. Jude can work at his masonry—a craft the superior branches of which he likes and respects—whereas Sue must hold down jobs she despises or is superior to. She is under a strong economic compulsion to exploit her sex, and the idiosyncratic character of such sex as she possesses is at once a special asset and a special hazard. Her whole fatality exposes itself in the brilliant passage which begins with her reeling off to the plodding Homer-and-Horace Jude the long list of authors she has read (she might be a courtesan ticking off her eminent lovers) and then entering casually upon her more personal history. The power of this sharp and compressed retrospection proceeds, of course, from our instant knowledge that it is prospective as well. The recital must be compressed:

'You have read more than I,' he said with a sigh. 'How came you to read some of those queerer ones?'

'Well,' she said thoughtfully, 'it was by accident. My life has been entirely shaped by what people call a peculiarity in me. I have no fear of men, as such, nor of their books. I have mixed with them—one or two of them particularly—almost as one of their own sex. . . . When I was eighteen I formed a friendly intimacy with an undergraduate at Christminster, and he taught me a great deal. . . . We used to go about together—on walking tours, reading tours, and things of that sort—like two men almost. He asked me to live with him, and I agreed to by letter. But when I joined him in London I found he meant a different thing from what I meant. He wanted me to be his mistress, in fact, but I wasn't in love with him—and on my saying I should go away if he didn't agree to *my* plan, he did so. We shared a sitting-room for fifteen months; and he became a leader-writer for one of the great London dailies; till he was taken ill. . . . I hope he died of consumption and not of me entirely.'

. . . Jude looked round upon the arm-chair and its occupant, as if to read more carefully the creature he had given shelter to. His voice trembled as he said: 'However you have lived, Sue, I believe you are as innocent as you are unconventional!'

'I am not particularly innocent, as you see, now that I have

> "twitched the robe
> From that blank lay-figure your fancy draped," '

said she, with an ostensible sneer, though he could hear that she was brimming with tears. 'But I have never yielded myself to any lover, if that's what you mean! I have remained as I began.'

. . . Jude felt much depressed; she seemed to get further and further away from him with her strange ways and curious unconsciousness of gender.

Upon the ill-fated undergraduate poor Phillotson succeeds; Sue, having got herself expelled from the training college she had entered through his interest, resolves what she calls 'the awkwardness of my situation' by marrying him out of hand—and is presently jumping through the window when he inadvertently enters her room. 'The dreadful contract to feel in a particular way in a matter whose essence is its voluntariness' is too much for her—besides which (her ghoulish great-aunt Drusilla has encouraged her to believe) there is some specific physical revoltingness about the schoolmaster. There is nothing of the kind about Jude, whose turn comes next. Nevertheless, when she runs away to him, and he takes a room (very characteristically) in a Temperance Hotel, she explains at once that she 'didn't mean that!' 'My nature is not so passionate as yours,' she announces simply—but is very offended when the hotel they eventually find separate rooms in turns out to have been the scene of Jude's and Arabella's 'midnight contiguity'. Jude, told that she doesn't like him as well as she did, and that he, her last hope, has been false to her, answers with a flash of spirit that he has never known such an unreasonable, such a dog-in-the-manger, feeling. But his fate is sealed. 'You ought not to be touchy about that still', is her subsequent instant reply to his referring even 'mischievously' to her steady refusal to go to bed with him. That children are eventually born to Jude and Sue is to be accounted for (we are tempted to feel) merely by the fact that Father Time must have children to hang when the moment comes.

Yet through all this, Sue Bridehead remains attractive—both to the two men who are sufficiently unfortunate as to fall in love with her and to ourselves as we follow her appalling history. 'She was so vibrant that everything she did seemed to have its source in feeling', we are told, and we do come to acknowledge that—at least until her final disaster—there is nothing merely hysterical about her. Her 'tight-strained nerves' are very honestly tight-strained; she has to do battle with a deeply insulating egoism or narcissism which is all the more overwhelming in that there is obscurely something of the same quality in Jude. Tediously much is made in the novel of a 'Curse of the Fawleys' theme; it is one of the blights set going by great-aunt Drusilla, and it runs not only to a hereditary disastrousness in marriage but even to a family gibbet; the cousins Jude and Sue are made to reflect that a union between them would mean 'a terrible intensification of unfitness—two bitters in one dish'. Hardy himself appears to have attached emphasis to this idea; protesting to Gosse that his novel was not 'a manifesto on the "marriage question" ', he wrote:

> It is concerned first with the labours of a poor student to get a University degree, and secondly with the tragic issues of two bad marriages, owing in the main to a doom or curse of hereditary temperament peculiar to the family of the parties.

Accepted *tout court*, this must suggest the importation into the novel of a theme which remains equally inapposite whether it is conceived as arriving from Greek drama or sensational romance; the representative character of the fiction is impaired by the introduction of an inherited psychopathology. Yet what the theme really expresses is valid enough, perhaps even at a genetic level. In-built in both Jude and Sue is something which prompts them to elect frustration and self-destruction; this is what unites them, and at the same time confines them in an inalienable loneliness.

Sue's is spiritually a more dreadful end than Jude's, because it is blinder. She believes that religious enlightenment has come to her. It tells her that her children have not died in vain, since their killing has been divinely appointed to bring home to her the error of her views and achieve a 'first stage' of her 'purification'. It makes her reject Jude's supreme plea that abandonment of him will mean his certain destruction. Yet this whole frame of mind is no more than a dire instrument to achieve both that destruction and her own. Its basis is a terrible vanity, an unyielding self-regard. 'Don't criticize me, Jude—I can't bear it!' she says at one point—and adds, 'I have often told you so'. All she possesses *is* her self-regard, and she elects alike Jude's destruction and her own self-immolation in order to cling to it. There is no difficulty in being alarmed by her, even in loathing her:

> It was natural for Sue to read and to turn again to:

> > Thou hast conquered, O pale Galilean!
> > The world has grown grey from Thy breath.

> In her the pale Galilean had indeed triumphed. Her body was as insensitive as hoar-frost. She knew well enough that she was not alive in the ordinary human sense. . . .

D. H. Lawrence can combine this kind of panic-reaction to Sue with a sensitive responsiveness to the deepest implications of her character. But Jude, who does not die blind, gives his life in the performance of an act of devotion to her. Nor does Hardy condemn her, perhaps because he has discerned in her a quick spirit of joy, an impulse to wring something from life however burdened without and within, such as his compassion has always responded to.

It is probably wholly idle to attempt to identify or quantify the autobiographical elements in *Jvde the Obscure*. Hardy issued an unusually categorical denial that there were any at all. No doubt this is suspicious. And there are several places in the book in which we feel the presence of material, irrelevant to the progress of the narrative, of a kind which is likely to percolate into fiction when the writer is recalling personal experience, or perhaps family tradition. Sue's training college at Melchester (which is Salisbury) was in fact that attended—the *Life* tells us—by Hardy's two sisters, and it may also reflect Stockwell College at Clapham, where it is not improbable that Hardy visited Tryphena Sparks. The passage of interest here is that describing at some length the behaviour of the students upon the occasion of Sue's being punished for her truancy. It has an irrelevant circumstantiality which inescapably suggests an anecdotal origin. There may also be significance in the first Mrs Hardy's extraordinary dislike of the book, which took her to the British Museum under the persuasion that Richard Garnett might have the power to contrive its suppression: a sad and funny episode suggesting some more specific cause of disapprobation than that to be found in coarse expressions and a jaundiced view of matrimony.

The introduction of Mrs Hardy here is not without its irony. For what in all Hardy's imaginative production most essentially parallels *Jude the Obscure* is Emma Lavinia Gifford's tremendous memorial in the *Poems of 1912-13*. Hardy's wife had died; as he sat at his desk the long years of disillusion and alienation vanished; the result was the recalling of a woman known long ago in terms so vivid and poignant as to rank with the greatest love poetry in English. We feel the presence of some similar evocation in the novel. Again, surely, there has been a death—whether Tryphena's or another's—and again there takes place a profound response in memory and passion recalled. What was to have been Jude's story becomes Sue's. This does not mean that we feel the story itself as chronicling a veridical course of events. On the contrary, much of it is rather obviously just a novelist's concoction. But no character in the Wessex novels is less a concoction than Sue Bridehead. She is the last and greatest of Hardy's gifts to fiction. Wherever she comes from, her reality is as unchallengeable as Emma Bovary's or Anna Karenina's.

13

The Dynasts

IN *MOMENTS OF VISION* THERE IS A POEM BEGINNING 'I LOOKED UP
from my writing' which describes a little colloquy with the moon.
The poet at his desk becomes aware of the moon peering in on him
and asks 'What are you doing there?' The moon replies that it has
been 'scanning pond and hole' for the body of a man who has
drowned himself out of sorrow for a son 'slain in brutish battle',
and adds:

> 'And now I am curious to look
>   Into the blinkered mind
> Of one who wants to write a book
>   In a world of such a kind.'

It is with a certain appositeness that the moon chooses the author
of *The Dynasts* for this scrutiny, since the world of that enormous
'Epic-Drama' is precisely of such a kind as to make the attempt
to write an epic-drama seem to many a wholly inept and forlorn
proposal.

Hardy's greatest hazard as an artist, it may be felt by those who
take this view, was his dogged determination to be what the age
called an 'advanced thinker'. Throughout his long and brooding
consideration of the historical masterpiece he was one day to
achieve there had steadily strengthened the persuasion that it must
constitute what he was eventually to define as 'the modern
expression of a modern outlook'. This outlook he called 'monistic',
and he came to it partly by way of the scientific determinism of the
age as instanced in Darwin's work on the origin of species, and
partly by way of whatever he managed to make of the philosophy
of Schopenhauer—a philosophy no easier than that of Kant, from
which it derives. Schopenhauer believed that the only reality is a
universal Will; that the notion of our own separateness from that
Will is an illusion; that what the Will generates is suffering;
that the more we will the more we suffer, and the more we know

the more we suffer; and that what is chiefly to be desiderated, therefore, is the extinction of the Will. With all this, moreover, the Will *is* will only in some mysterious sense, since it is without consciousness, and therefore cannot be willing anything in particular.

Having this speculative hinterland, *The Dynasts* is well defined, in its first act, as

This tale of Will
And Life's impulsion by Incognizance.

Yet the definition is imprecise, since 'Incognizance' may mean either Schopenhauer's Will or the Will of Schopenhauer's successor von Hartmann, whose own scrutiny of the cosmos hints at the possibility of a little cheerfulness eventually creeping in. Von Hartmann called his Will the Unconscious, and believed that since evolution appears to be a matter of the development of consciousness it is conceivable that the Unconscious itself may become conscious one day. When Hardy, in the highly Shelleyan last lines of *The Dynasts*, looks forward to 'Consciousness the Will informing, till It fashion all things fair!' he is undoubtedly getting this up-beat conclusion from von Hartmann.[1] But the exact philosophical provenance, status, and conceivable ultimate potential of Hardy's Immanent Will is of little importance. What is cardinal is his general sense of the postulates that would make his spectacle agreeable to what he called 'modern thinking minds'. Here and now, at least, the Will is mindless—and everything exhibited to us in the drama is part of the Will. The conception is magnificently expressed as, in the 'Fore Scene', the action's terrestrial theatre is revealed:

The nether sky opens, and Europe is disclosed as a prone and emaciated figure, the Alps shaping like a backbone, and the branching mountain-chains like ribs, the peninsular plateau of Spain forming a head. Broad and lengthy lowlands stretch from

---

[1] But actually von Hartmann sees the Will's coming to consciousness as desirable only in being a possible step towards annihilation, a consummation which Schopenhauer had already seen as devoutly to be wished. This manner of seeing the matter drifts into *The Dynasts* when (Part Second, IV, v) the Spirit Sinister says to the Spirit Ironic:

Come, Sprite, don't carry your ironies too far, or you may wake up the Unconscious Itself, and tempt it to let all the gory clock-work of the show run down to spite me!

the north of France across Russia like a grey-green garment
hemmed by the Ural mountains and the glistening Arctic Ocean.
    The point of view sinks downwards through space, and draws
near to the surface of the perturbed countries, where the peoples,
distressed by events which they did not cause, are seen writhing,
crawling, and vibrating in their various cities and nationalities.

And presently:

    A new and penetrating light descends on the spectacle, enduing
men and things with a seeming transparency, and exhibiting
as one organism the anatomy of life and movement in all
humanity and vitalized matter included in the display.

The 'new and penetrating light' here is nothing other than what
Hardy elsewhere calls 'the latest illumination of the time'. Turn
this upon the coronation of Napoleon in Milan Cathedral, and
'there is again beheld as it were the interior of a brain which seems
to manifest the volitions of a Universal Will, of whose tissues the
personages of the action form portion'. Turn it upon the Field of
Austerlitz and

    At once, as earlier, a preternatural clearness possesses the
atmosphere of the battle-field, in which the scene becomes
anatomized and the living masses of humanity transparent.
The controlling Immanent Will appears therein, as a brain-like
network of currents and ejections, twitching, interpenetrating,
entangling, and thrusting hither and thither the human forms.

That the 'human forms' are simply thrust 'hither and thither' is one
of the two main postulates of the drama. The other is that these
are sentient beings that are thus pushed around. We are confronted in our universe by a blind force which has contrived

the intolerable antilogy
Of making figments feel!

This has been a kind of primal disaster—as is expressed by the
Shade of the Earth in ironical understatement:

Yes; that they feel, and puppetry remain,
Is an owned flaw in her consistency
Men love to dub Dame Nature.

It is within this frame of reference, actually enclosing the action in the form of a massive and supernal choric commentary, that Hardy sets his 'three parts, nineteen acts, and one hundred and thirty scenes' exhibiting the war with Napoleon.

2

Even if we do not agree with those critics who view *The Dynasts* as patently absurd, we must admit that the persuasions with which Hardy had saddled himself set formidable difficulties in his path. It is perfectly justly that Howe describes the drama as 'dedicated to an idea of human helplessness, the idea that men are mere refractions of impersonal force'. How is *drama*, of all things, to be wrung from such a situation? 'Write a history of human automatism', Hardy had enjoined himself in one note; and in another: 'Mode for a historical Drama. Action mostly automatic; reflex movement, etc.' Here he is again being up to date. 'Coughing and sneezing are familiar instances of reflex actions', Darwin had written in 1872. But is it sensible to propose that we should be interested, moved, or edified by the spectacle of Napoleon and Nelson coughing and sneezing their way through the longest dramatic composition in English literature? And, again, the action is not only, as it were, automated; it is miniaturized or transistorized as well. Both in the tremendous panoramic effects which Hardy commands in those descriptive passages passing as 'dumb shows' and 'stage directions' (that, for instance, in which the allied forces are seen closing in upon France after the ruin of the Grand Army), and in the rapid interchange of scenes and multiplication of characters throughout, dwarfing processes are at work. Of similar effect and implication, too, is the almost complete disjunction maintained between world and overworld, mortal participants and disembodied commenting intelligences. The spirits do not agree among themselves, or show the slightest disposition to pay rational attention to one another's arguments. Yet at least they *are* spirits, and it is clearly expected that we should listen to them, even if they quite fail to listen to each other. But the mortal characters are unable to listen; they are unaware of the spirits' existence. This is as well for them, as little they might hear would be encouraging. But the result is that the mortals have nothing of that sort of additional dimension which comes to their fellows in epic and tragedy proper through some apprehension of a supersensible order. It is true that much great epic and tragedy—and saga and ballad—is heavy with fatality, and that Hardy's determinism, or something like it, relates itself to ways of

taking experience which have proved congruous with the production of much major poetry of one sort or another. But what is
lacking in *The Dynasts* is the slightest suggestion of anything like
an Affair with the Gods. In this martial panorama even the heroic
idea—Sarpedon to Glaucus, or Byrhtnoth at Maldon—is entirely
absent.

But there are really two overworlds in *The Dynasts*. In the first,
that of the abstract intelligences, we are constrained to watch
something like a losing battle fought by Hardy against the oppres-
siveness and obsessiveness of his philosophical presuppositions.
It is as if he *knows* the Intelligences are bores, but is nevertheless
under some deep emotional compulsion to bring them back, and
again back, to say just what they have said before. How did the
universe we know begin? *Something hidden urged the giving matter
motion.* How did it begin? *Cognizance . . . came unmeant, emerging with blind gropes from impercipience by listless sequence.* How
did it begin? It began with *an unreckoned incident of the all-urging
Will, raptly magnipotent.* What is the Will? *An unconscious planning, like a potter raptly panning!* What is to be said of It? *A fixed
foresightless dream is Its whole philosopheme.* Hardy works very
hard at drawing out, diversifying, and energizing this commentary.
The Phantoms are divided into various camps, each with an
attendant chorus: The Ancient Spirit of the Years, the Spirit of the
Pities, The Spirit of Rumour, Spirits Sinister and Ironic—with
Spirit-Messengers, Recording Angels, and the Shade of the Earth
thrown in. They speak now in blank verse and now in a wide
diversity of rhymed stanzas, most of these latter moving with a
nervous rapidity, and some—as when the Chorus Ironic responds
to the spectacle of King George's madness in Part III, Act VI,
Scene V—with a shattering quick-fire effect unique in English
verse.[1] They employ a syntax and vocabulary at least congruous
with disembodied spirits in the sense of being distinguishably alien
to mortal English speech: the years are *fineless* because they go on
and on; the Spirit of the Years points out that it is impossible to
swerve the pulsion of the Byss: all the Intelligences take particular
satisfaction in privative forms unknown to the *Oxford English
Dictionary*—as when we are told that in a reasonable universe we
should *inexist*, or of Napoleon's devoted troops that *his projects
they unknow, his grin unsee,* or, again, of *forms that now unbe.* They
operate at a very varying remove from the scenes they contem-
plate—sometimes with the largest effect of withdrawal and generality and sometimes in mere *reportage* of a deflationary sort, as
when we learn, on the eve of the Hundred Days, that

[1] The Spirits Sinister and Ironic commonly employ prose.

The guardian on behalf of the Allies
Absents himself from Elba. Slow surmise
Too vague to pen, too actual to ignore,
Have strained him hour by hour, and more and more.
He takes the sea to Florence, to declare
His doubt to Austria's ministrator there.

The Spirit of Rumour, we are bound to feel, has little future as a
poet—any more than has his attendant Chorus:

> Should the corvette return
> With the anxious Scotch colonel,
> Escape would be frustrate,
> Retention eternal.

This is mere patter. On the other hand, when the Intelligences
weigh in heavily, as the Spirit of the Years does in the Fore Scene
in reply to those 'young Compassionates', the Pities, it is to assert
with an inartistic explicitness the mechanical order of the spectacle
contemplated:

> Behoves it us to enter scene by scene,
> And watch the spectacle of Europe's moves
> In her embroil, as they were self-ordained,
> According to the naïve and liberal creed
> Of our great-hearted young Compassionates,
> Forgetting the Prime Mover of the gear,
> As puppet-watchers him who pulls the strings.
> You'll mark the twitchings of this Bonaparte
> As he with other figures foots his reel,
> Until he twitch him into his lonely grave:
> Also regard the frail ones that his flings
> Have made gyrate like animalcula
> In tepid pools.

Although already in Part One, indeed, the Chorus of the Years,
as if looking ahead to the note of meliorism it is to sound in the
closing lines of the drama, enjoins

> Nay, nay, nay;
> Your hasty judgments stay,
> Until the topmost cyme
> Have crowned the last entablature of Time.
> O heap not blame on that in-brooding Will;
> O pause, till all things all their days fulfil—

the whole burden of the supernal commentary, viewed overall, is essentially that human destiny can be neither tragic nor heroic, since it is meaningless.

But there is a second overworld in *The Dynasts*, which we may think of under the unassuming character of a balloon—although at times, indeed, it takes Hardy and ourselves, whether accompanied by Intelligences or not, to elevations not physically compassed until the coming of the artificial satellite. A French army in retreat from Moscow becomes a caterpillar; it 'creeps laboriously nearer, but instead of increasing in size by the rules of perspective, it gets more attenuated, and there are left upon the ground behind it minute parts of itself, which are speedily flaked over, and remain as white pimples by the wayside'. Or across a whole continent we see the armies of many nations converge, but at such a remove that it is only, as it were, by an intellectual effort that we are able to distinguish human volition at work:

> At first nothing—not even the river itself—seems to move in the panorama. But anon certain strange dark patches in the landscape, flexuous and riband-shaped, are discerned to be moving slowly. Only one moveable object on earth is large enough to be conspicuous herefrom, and that is an army. The moving shapes are armies. . . .
>
> All these dark and grey columns, converging westward by sure degrees, advance without opposition. They glide on as if by gravitation, in fluid figures, dictated by the conformation of the country, like water from a burst reservoir; mostly snake-shaped, but occasionally with batrachian and saurian outlines. In spite of the immensity of this human mechanism on its surface, the winter landscape wears an impassive look, as if nothing were happening.

The Dynasts contains many visual *tours de force* of this kind. They are highly imaginative, yet Hardy's command of them has its basis in his observing and recording power in the face of actual visual experience. Thus, more than twenty years before beginning to write the drama, he had taken his wife to view the Lord Mayor's Show 'from the upper windows of *Good Words* in Ludgate Hill'. Mrs Hardy thought that 'the surface of the crowd seemed like a boiling cauldron of porridge', and this Hardy thought worth recording. On his own account he wrote:

> As the crowd grows denser it loses its character of an aggregate of countless units, and becomes an organic whole, a

molluscous black creature having nothing in common with humanity, that takes the shape of the streets along which it has lain itself, and throws out horrid excrescences and limbs into neighbouring alleys; a creature whose voice exudes from its scaly coat, and who has an eye in every pore of its body. The balconies, stands, and railway-bridge are occupied by small detached shapes of the same tissue, but of gentler motion, as if they were the spawn of the monster in their midst.

The great aerial perspectives of *The Dynasts* are justly famous, but Hardy's extraordinary power of sharply evoking a scene extends itself over the entire work. When the French cavalry are manœuvring at a distance near Boulogne, we see 'their accoutrements flashing in the sun like a school of mackerel'; on the field of Waterloo at sunrise the English soldiers 'pipeclay from their cross-belts the red dye washed off their jackets by the rain'; there is rain, too, at Albuera:

The ghastly climax of the strife is reached; the combatants are seen to be firing grape and canister at speaking distance, and discharging musketry in each other's faces when so close that their complexions may be recognized. Hot corpses, their mouths blackened by cartridge-biting, and surrounded by castaway knapsacks, firelocks, hats, stocks, flint-boxes, and priming-horns, together with red and blue rags of clothing, gaiters, epaulettes, limbs, and viscera, accumulate on the slopes, increasing from twos and threes to half-dozens, and from half-dozens to heaps, which steam with their own warmth as the spring rain falls gently upon them.

3

With a description like this, and with similar prose evocations of carnage and misery during the Russian campaign, we may compare similar material as it is handled in the blank verse in which the greater part of the drama is composed. An excited midshipman brings the dying Nelson a report of the further progress of the Battle of Trafalgar:

Meanwhile the 'Achille' fought on,
Even while the ship was blazing, knowing well
The fire must reach their powder; which it did.
The spot is covered now with floating men,
Some whole, the main in parts; arms, legs, trunks, heads,

Bobbing with tons of timber on the waves,
And splinters looped with entrails of the crew.

Just before this, a surgeon, Dr Beatty, has given Nelson a tally
of the dead and wounded:

BEATTY. Besides poor Scott, my lord, and Charles Adair,
Lieutenant Ram, and Whipple, captain's clerk,
There's Smith, and Palmer, midshipmen, just killed,
And fifty odd of seamen and marines.
NELSON. Poor youngsters! Scarred old Nelson joins you soon.
BEATTY. And wounded: Bligh, lieutenant; Pasco, too,
And Reeves, and Peake, lieutenants of marines,
And Rivers, Westphall, Bulkeley, midshipmen,
With, of the crew, a hundred odd just now,
Unreckoning those late fallen not brought below.

We respect this as a roll of honour, but are bound to reflect that
it comes disconcertingly direct from Shakespeare. And here at
once we are in the presence of the cardinal weakness of *The
Dynasts*—of *The Dynasts* considered not as a philosophical but
as a poetic drama. Hardy has become one of a long line of poets
with whom, for this purpose, blank verse simply does not come
off.

He shows himself determined, from the start, to extract from it
a viable middle style. From a historical character we first hear it in
the second scene, when the French Minister of Marine reads aloud
to himself a letter from Napoleon beginning:

I am resolved that no wild dream of Ind,
And what we there might win; or of the West,
And bold re-conquest there of Surinam
And other Dutch retreats along those coasts,
Or British islands nigh, shall draw me now
From piercing into England through Boulogne
As lined in my first plan.

This is followed by a versifying, to the length of some three
hundred lines, of a full-dress debate in the House of Commons—
the opening speaker being Sheridan, thus:

The Bill I would have leave to introduce
Is framed, sir, to repeal last Session's Act,

> By party-scribes intituled a Provision
> For England's Proper Guard; but elsewhere known
> As Mr Pitt's new Patent Parish Pill.

The joke is, very properly, Sheridan's own, and Hardy is, in fact, boldly launching himself on that sort of verse-recension of existing English prose which we inevitably associate with Enobarbus's description of Cleopatra on the Cydnus and Volumnia's appeal to her son Coriolanus before the walls of Rome. And as we read this and other long stretches of undistinguished declamation we are likely to remind ourselves that Hardy is essentially a lyric poet. It is hardly surprising that there are places during these marathon performances in which he distinguishably tires. In the middle of Part Three there is another debate in the Commons, beginning with a stage-direction in which twenty-seven of those present are conscientiously named. Castlereagh speaks:

> At never a moment in my stressed career,
> Amid no memory-moving urgencies,
> Have I, sir, felt so gravely set on me
> The sudden, vast responsibility
> That I feel now. Few things conceivable
> Could more momentous to the future be
> Than what may spring from counsel here to-night
> On means to meet the plot unparalleled
> In full fierce play elsewhere. . . .

Castlereagh is doing better than Hardy, who has let slip in an awkward inversion, and a heroic couplet echoed and emphasized by the inverted 'be' a couple of lines later.

Yet it is obvious that we cannot justly judge this vast performance by its blemishes—nor (as Howe tends to do) think to strike a balance by rescuing from the whole drama a few isolated felicities. *The Dynasts* has very notable and pervasive strengths.

4

'From many casual critical references', Morrell writes, 'we might infer that *The Dynasts* has nothing to do with human beings at all.' This is to understate a case, since there are several formal and extended considerations of the drama which almost ignore the mundane part of it. Mr W. R. Rutland, one of Hardy's most learned and useful commentators, declares roundly that the Intelligences 'are the only real characters in *The Dynasts*'. And

Mr Samuel Hynes, although at least aware of Napoleon as a
figure in whom 'the paradox of human power and human helplessness, of will and necessity, emerges as a vast, cosmic irony',
declares that

> the spirit world has more reality, more specificity, than the
> human one. The major spirits . . . maintain their individuality
> throughout the piece, while men are submerged into the vast,
> blurring symbols of brain and nerves, which are intended to
> exhibit 'as one organism the anatomy of life and movement in
> all humanity and vitalised matter'.

The quoted words here are from the Fore Scene, and it is fair to
say that for this general view of *The Dynasts* Hardy himself is
responsible. As an amateur philosopher ('I do read *Mind* occasionally', he wrote to J. M. McTaggart) he had attached himself, as
we have seen, to the notion of a 'monistic' universe, and as early
as 1886 he was looking forward to those extraordinary stage-
directions in which the cosmos is revealed as a computer-like
mechanism, or a single brain with the lid off:

> The human race to be shown as one great network or tissue
> which quivers in every part when one point is shaken, like a
> spider's web if touched. Abstract realisms to be in the form of
> Spirits, Spectral figures, etc.
> The Realities to be the true Realities of life, hitherto called
> abstractions. The old material realities to be placed behind the
> former, as shadowy accessories.

The second paragraph of this note, which may reflect Schopenhauer's inversion of traditional philosophical categories, certainly
records a conception, a paradoxical way of handling the traditional relationship of heroic action and supernatural machinery in
epic, which was to remain in Hardy's mind while he was writing
The Dynasts. But it is Guerard who has pointed to the significance
of the earlier part of the note upon which both these paragraphs
succeed:

> Novel-writing as an art cannot go backward. Having reached
> the analytic stage it must transcend it by going still further in the
> same direction. Why not by rendering as visible essences,
> spectres, etc. the abstract thoughts of the analytic school?

Guerard may be stretching things a little far when he declares, on
the basis of this, that the Intelligences were 'originally conceived

as a technical means of transcending threadbare analytic realism in the novel'. Long before this note there are notes which show Hardy as working towards some means of displaying great historical events as 'automatism', and it is undeniable that his overworld is developed primarily in this interest. The fact is that, during the long period of time in which he was brooding over what he saw as his most serious and ambitious work, two quite distinct impulses were at play upon him. The first was the wish to bring in that 'modern expression of a modern outlook' which we have now, perhaps, sufficiently considered. The second—quite simply, and as expressed on the title-page of the completed work—was to write *An Epic-Drama of the War with Napoleon*.

Both these impulses are at play upon Hardy's Preface of September 1903. There is something about what 'the Monistic theory of the Universe forbade', and a suggestion that 'monotonic delivery of speeches, with dreamy conventional gestures' and the 'automatic style' adopted by the old Christmas mummers, would be apposite in any realizing or imagining of such a drama on a stage. But the Preface begins with something quite different:

The Spectacle here presented in the likeness of a Drama is concerned with the Great Historical Calamity, or Clash of Peoples, artificially brought about some hundred years ago.

The choice of such a subject was mainly due to three accidents of locality. It chanced that the writer was familiar with a part of England that lay within hail of the watering-place in which King George the Third had his favourite summer residence during the war with the first Napoléon, and where he was visited by ministers and others who bore the weight of English affairs on their more or less competent shoulders at that stressful time. Secondly, this district, being also near the coast which had echoed with rumours of invasion in their intensest form while the descent threatened, was formerly animated by memories and traditions of the desperate military preparations for that contingency. Thirdly, the same countryside happened to include the village which was the birthplace of Nelson's flag-captain at Trafalgar.

This statement, with its modest and local note, is sometimes dismissed as not really authentic to the inspiration of the drama. Captain Hardy does not figure in any of Hardy's periodic brief considerations of his subject, nor does Dorset threatened by invasion. And the imaginative excitement which 'traditionary' matter relating to the Napoleonic wars is said to have engendered in Hardy is also a doubtful quantity. It had produced *The Trumpet-Major*, a very minor novel, and such a thoroughly poor short story as 'A Tradition of 1804'. In the popular mind, immemorial Wessex was his stock-in-trade; it had become his habit to bring it forward as constituting the main region of his song. But what he really sought was Aeschylean success with matter of the broadest philosophical generality. Aeschylus actually turns up in the Preface. So does Shelley, with a quotation from *Hellas*. And Shelley, for that matter, was probably a more direct influence than any ancient dramatist. The pervasively disembodied effects and hypertrophied choric performances of *Prometheus Unbound* indicate the direction in which Hardy wanted to go.

But a mere count of pages in *The Dynasts* should prevent us from getting the emphasis of Hardy's intention wrong. What we find deployed in the work, far more copiously than anything else, is a widely ranging and densely populated chronicle play turning upon the career of Napoleon Bonaparte. As the great project forms itself Napoleon is early at the centre of the design—and once (in 1887) in sketched supernatural settings oddly remote from the overworld eventually to be set commenting on him, thus:

> Another outline scheme for *The Dynasts* was shaped in November, in which Napoleon was represented as haunted by an Evil Genius or Familiar, whose existence he has to confess to his wives. This was abandoned, and another tried in which Napoleon by means of necromancy becomes possessed of an insight, enabling him to see the thoughts of opposing generals. This does not seem to have come to anything either.

It would have been surprising if it had! But what we have to notice is that the scheme for a historical drama on a vast scale was firmly established in Hardy's mind before he was at all sure of the particular sort of further and philosophical dimension that might be added to it. And, to the end, the overworld *is* an addition, a vast embellishment most fairly to be described as impressive and tedious by turns. And we best indicate the true character and proportions of the work by saying that Part I begins with England preparing to resist invasion, rises to the two great set pieces of Austerlitz and Trafalgar, and ends with the death of Pitt; that Part II is about Napoleon at his zenith, an established Dynast on whose horizon begins to hover a small cloud called Wellington; and that in Part III the Emperor's fortunes are traced from the Niemen to Moscow, and from Moscow to Waterloo. The spectacle comprehends alike the councils of princes and statesmen, the common peoples of Europe 'distressed by events which they did not cause', and battle-pieces of a terrifying and austere authenticity, scenes of rout, carnage and misery such as challenge comparison with kindred places in the greatest of all imaginative treatments of history, *War and Peace.*

It is, of course, idle to imagine what *The Dynasts* would be like without its overworld. Certainly it would be notably impoverished in many places:

> The mole's tunnelled chambers are crushed by wheels,
> The lark's eggs scattered, their owners fled;
> And the hedgehog's household the sapper unseals. . . .

Had Hardy's Chorus of the Years not disclosed this aspect of the Battle of Waterloo we may be sure that it would remain undisclosed today. Nevertheless, as soon as we bring Tolstoi into the comparison we are likely to feel that in Hardy's presentation of 'the Great Historical Calamity' there is a dimension lacking—a dimension of historical reflection by no means compensated for by the insistent cosmic reflection that the Intelligences provide. Tolstoi has thought deeply about the enigmatic spectacle of hundreds of thousands of men surging hither and thither across Europe at the command—although this, he sees, cannot be the true explanation—of supposedly great men. For Tolstoi 'the movement of nations' is caused 'by the activity of *all* the people who participate in the event'; and it really follows from this, he says, that 'the concept of a cause is not applicable to the phenomenon we are examining'. Do the Tsar and Kutuzov move the Russian people? Certainly no more than the Russian people move them. 'In the last analysis we reach an endless circle.' Tolstoi's sense of Napoleon's invasion of Russia and its repulse as essentially events within the soul of the Russian people may be logically somewhat elusive. But it does enable him to evoke a powerful national, or folk, experience. And this *The Dynasts* surely fails to do. The Dynasts themselves may be puppets, but Hardy is a little sold on them, all the same. Like another great writer of peasant origin, Carlyle, he has a fancy for great men. Common people have the same roles in *The Dynasts* as in Shakespeare's history plays; they huzza, or they misbehave themselves, or they are quaintly or robustly humorous—as when they tell each other how Nelson's body was pickled in grog and how the thirsty crew of the *Victory* 'broached the Adm'l'. It is Tolstoi, the aristocrat, who treats simple people seriously.

One sometimes reads that Hardy's principal historical characters

218   'THE DYNASTS'

in the drama are 'flat' because creating them flat was the best
way of suggesting that they are puppets in a last analysis. Yet
equally flat, in this particular sense, are Tolstoi's Dynasts:

> The deeds of Napoleon and Alexander, on whose fiat the
> whole question of war or no war apparently depended, were as
> little spontaneous and free as the actions of every common
> soldier drawn into the campaign by lot or by conscription.
> This could not be otherwise, for in order that the will of
> Napoleon and Alexander (the people on whom the whole
> decision appeared to rest) should be effected a combination of
> innumerable circumstances was essential, without any one of
> which the event could not have taken place. It was necessary
> that millions of men in whose hands the real power lay—the
> soldiers who fired the guns or transported provisions and
> cannon—should consent to carry out the will of those weak
> individuals, and should have been induced to do so by an infinite
> number of diverse and complex causes.

This is not far from Hardy's vision of the human race as 'one great
network or tissue'. Yet, considered more at large, Tolstoi's
historical characters (who are, of course, only of the second order
of characters in his novel) remain far more in the round than
Hardy's. It is no doubt reasonable to account for this merely in
terms of disparity of genius—and to reflect, too, that the novel
rather than the drama is the natural home of the round character.
Nevertheless, we may wonder whether the fulness and vitality of
The Dynasts as a historical drama (which is what it was intended to
be and essentially is) have not been attenuated as a consequence of
Hardy's persuasion that he had much to say about the Immanent
Will and Its designs.

14
Hardy's Major Poetry

IT MIGHT BE ARGUED THAT HARDY WAS LUCKY IN HAVING FOR SO
long to accommodate himself to the sheer brute length of the
Victorian novel. A writer's first need in confronting such a form is
simply that of 'keeping it up', and to this end he must tip in a
diversity of characters and incidents, describe a variety of scenes, and
in general set his central action—however much it command him—
moving amid some more or less balanced exhibition of the common
transactions of life. This condition extends, indeed, far beyond the
limits of Victoria's reign. From *Clarissa* to *Ulysses* the traditional
canons of representative fiction may be viewed as mitigating and
controlling what was potentially obsessional of one sort or another
in many of our major novelists. It was Hardy's good fortune to
establish himself fairly early as a great 'regional' writer, alike the
natural historian and the social historian of Wessex, abundantly
spreading powers of observation and humour and memory, as
well as of pathos and tragedy, over a field very reasonably full of a
diversity of folk. He sometimes chafed at having been 'typed' in
this way, and his failures are for the most part the consequence of
ill-considered bolts towards other territories. But in fact the extent
of the terrain he did command, broad yet sharply defined in point
both of actual scene and of men in their classes and occupations,
was just right for enabling him to meet the traditional (which are
thereby the sustaining) requirements of the novel. He had contracted to be Hardy of Wessex, and the contract preserved him
from at least any oppressive degree of temperamental expatiation.

Hardy published fourteen novels, but over nine hundred short
poems. It is significant that he called the first collection *Wessex
Poems*, since the title acknowledged that, in his new character before
the public, he was to be very much Hardy of Wessex still. We
cannot quite say—since the novels themselves are so poetic—that
the poems add a new dimension to Wessex, but they do deepen and
enrich it as a country of the mind. Had Hardy, who delayed so
long, resigned himself to *never* facing posterity as a lyric poet, our

H

loss would have been great. And his eventual achievement as a poet, his stature as we now acknowledge it to be, is the more impressive as having been achieved from a position of great hazard.

What that hazard was, we begin to be aware of as soon as we have taken up the *Collected Poems*, begun at the beginning, and for some hours read doggedly on. Of course we must not be too professional. Professor Lionel Trilling, once faced with the similarly assembled poems of Kipling, took comfort from the calculation that they could be read through 'in two evenings, or even in a single very long one'. Kipling did not, presumably, labour to be ingested under these conditions; nor did Hardy. And when we study a poet's output intensively and against the clock (which is what we may be constrained to do, if we are university students) we ought to remember that we are creating a reading-situation such as never entered the poet's head. Nevertheless some significance must attach to impressions gathered in this way. And even a judiciously compiled volume of selections from Hardy's poems (such as that by G. M. Young, or John Crowe Ransom, or John Wain, or Donald Morrison) quickly persuades us of Hardy's risky situation. What he has been chiefly aware of during an exhausting career of novel-writing has been the indignity of churning out endless long popular entertainments under the eye (or indeed the birch, as we may say of one so sensitive as Hardy) of Mrs Grundy. Now, at last, he can please himself and be himself. Hardy of Wessex, yes. But, essentially, Thomas Hardy.

We must not exaggerate this sense of being on his own. He had the largely self-educated man's respect for authority. He mugged up prosody; he was soaked in Shelley; he brooded over the 'optimism' of Browning. But essentially he was going to look in his heart and write. Fulfilling this programme in short poems by the hundred was at least to incur the possibility of being judged monotonous and confined within a narrow range of thought and sensibility. Indeed, only an exceptional responsiveness to a wide range of human feeling, a power of tentative engagement with a diversity of ideas, a conduct of the personality very much in terms of Keats's conception of 'negative capability' would have constituted much insurance in this regard. As it is, a great deal of Hardy's poetry appears constricted and personal in a disabling sense. It revolves around a small number of *idées fixes*. The oddity of his diction—always the same oddities, diversely applied—reflects this. His laborious contriving of new stanza-forms merely accents it. He is an obsessional poet.

2

The obsessions are with topics that a reader coming from the novels might expect, but their comparative incidence is perhaps surprising. There are plenty of poems the burden of which is indignant reproach to God for venturing not to exist; plenty commiserating with man for having been dragged into sentience; and plenty commiserating with him, too, because his sentience must one day leave him, since he is

> but a thing of flesh and bone
> Speeding on to its cleft in the clay.

But these matters of cosmic concern—which of course achieve their major stamping-ground in *The Dynasts*—are less prominent than is the theme of disastrous or frustrated or betrayed or merely boring sexual relationships. Alike in love and marriage, the characters of Hardy's poems are perpetually getting themselves into luckless situations of which the best that can sometimes be said is that they are presented to us with ingenious economy. A fair example is 'The Memorial Brass: 186–', in which the appended date would appear designed to suggest that it is based on some experience of Hardy's as a young man. It begins:

> 'Why do you weep there, O sweet lady,
>   Why do you weep before that brass?—
> (I'm a mere student sketching the mediaeval)
>   Is some late death lined there, alas?—
> Your father's?... Well, all pay the debt that paid he!'

To these, as we may think, somewhat impertinent enquiries the lady (who is obviously Hardy's standard lady of the manor) replies with the information that the memorial is her late husband's, and that she has caused the fact of her own death, too, to be recorded on it, bating only the date, together with an assertion of her undying fidelity. The student says that he is surprised the lady is a widow—this perhaps by way of complimenting her on a youthful and blooming appearance. She rejoins that in fact she has just married again, must bring her second husband to the church 'next Sunday morning', and is in a panic because he is a Bad-tempered man who may make a scene when he reads the inscription. 'O dear, O dear!' she says. And the student says, 'Madam, I swear your beauty will disarm him!'

Many of the poems of this kind, particularly those in *Satires of Circumstance*, are so trivial in their occasions that it was possible for Hardy to claim that they had been written with no other aim than to provide light amusement. Thus 'At a Watering-Place' is a twelve-line poem which concludes:

> 'That smart proud pair,' says the man to his friend,
> 'Are to marry next week. . . . How little he thinks
> That dozens of days and nights on end
> I have stroked her neck, unhooked the links
> Of her sleeve to get at her upper arm. . . .
> Well, bliss is in ignorance: what's the harm!'

There is a number of these 'ignorance is bliss' poems—

> And the happy young housewife does not know
> That the woman beside her was first his choice—

and a great many more which concern shocking discoveries, many of them brought about through that peeping or eavesdropping which is so disconcertingly prevalent in Hardy's world. In one a dying man lurks at the back of a draper's shop and detects his wife in buying fashionable mourning. In another a lover returns for a forgotten walking-stick, and

> sees within that the girl of his choice
> Stands rating her mother with eyes aglare
> For something said while he was there.

He 'steals off', and decides to think better of his engagement. Another peeping poem is 'Seen by the Waits':

> Through snowy woods and shady
>   We went to play a tune
> To the lonely manor-lady
>   By the light of the Christmas moon.
>
> We violed till, upward glancing
>   To where a mirror leaned,
> It showed her airily dancing,
>   Deeming her movements screened;
>
> Dancing alone in the room there,
>   Thin-draped in her robe of night;
> Her postures, glassed in the gloom there,
>   Were a strange phantasmal sight.

> She had learnt (we heard when homing)
> That her roving spouse was dead:
> Why she had danced in the gloaming
> We thought, but never said.

R. P. Blackmur, in a penetrating essay on Hardy's shorter poems,
has a good many hard words for this as 'bad writing'. It is true
that 'robe of night' for 'night-dress' brings vaguely in some image
not intended, and that it is the waits and not the lady who are 'in
the gloaming'. We may add that it is only because of the 'manor-
lady' that the woods are '*shady*', since it is shadow and not shade
that is cast by moonlight, and 'shady' even suggests a refuge from
heat entirely inapposite in a snow-scene. But as total appraisal this
will not quite do, since these oddities of diction are as nothing
compared with the virtuosity exhibited in compressing the episode
into sixteen short, easy-flowing, and uncrowded lines. These poems
are some of them petty—as when, peeping again, we see a clergyman

> re-enact at the vestry-glass
> Each pulpit gesture in deft dumb-show
> That had moved the congregation so—

and they are sometimes cruel, but the writing can commonly be
faulted only upon some narrow principle of taste. The cruelty may
be alarming, but nothing less is intended—as, for example, in 'In
the Nuptial Chamber':

> 'O that mastering tune!' And up in the bed
> Like a lace-robed phantom springs the bride. . . .

The tune—a rustic marriage-salute—recalls to the bride her former
lover. And she hurls the fact at the man (who has just possessed
her or been about to possess her) in six lines which conclude:

> 'And he dominates me and thrills me through,
> And it's he I embrace while embracing you!'

Concomitant with the violence in many of these poems is a
certain ruthless mechanical ingenuity which often suggests that the
poet is merely versifying a short story of a somewhat unassuming
sort. 'The Contretemps' is at least well-named, since it concerns a
man who, about to board a packet-boat with another man's wife,
embraces in the dark not merely the wrong woman but one who

happens herself to be proposing elopement with another woman's husband. The main trouble about all these ingenuities is simply that there are too many of them; each is in a sense given away by the others, as with a bunch of detective stories; and we come to question rather radically the motives prompting Hardy to address himself again and again, and with unflagging technical skill, to these tired ironies and over-transparent formulas. There is, as Blackmur somewhat scholastically says, nothing heuristic about this body of verse. There is nothing of an ever-renewed exploring and questioning of experience. We are in the presence of a melancholic temperament, which has perhaps elected experiences compatible with that temperament, and which has certainly equipped itself with a stock of ideas grateful to it. And the poet has then looked round, peeped round, peered inside his own head, for material upon which a resulting emotional state may be projected to some rather privately cathartic end.

3

Next in bulk after the sex poems come the death poems, and perhaps it is a sign of their greater merit that, when we think back to Hardy's poetry without a fresh reading of it, it is the death poems that we imagine as taking the greater space. The term, of course, has to be received broadly. Yet the point is, perhaps, precisely that Hardy here narrows a vast theme down—down to the 'cleft in the clay', to 'this close bin with earthen sides'. The process may be made apparent by quoting in full a very powerful poem, 'During Wind and Rain'. It seems to have been prompted not by memories of Hardy's own but by recollections recorded by his first wife and read by him after her death:

> They sing their dearest songs—
> He, she, all of them—yea,
> Treble and tenor and bass,
>   And one to play;
> With the candles mooning each face. . . .
>   Ah, no; the years O!
> How the sick leaves reel down in throngs!
>
> They clear the creeping moss—
> Elders and juniors—aye,
> Making the pathways neat
>   And the garden gay;

And they build a shady seat. . . .
    Ah, no; the years, the years;
See, the white storm-birds wing across!

They are blithely breakfasting all—
Men and maidens—yea,
Under the summer tree,
    With a glimpse of the bay,
While pet fowl come to the knee. . . .
    Ah, no; the years O!
And the rotten rose is ript from the wall.

They change to a high new house,
He, she, all of them—aye,
Clocks and carpets and chairs
    On the lawn all day,
And brightest things that are theirs. . . .
    Ah, no; the years, the years;
Down their carved names the rain-drop ploughs.

Here we come at once upon the transforming factor in Hardy's
verse: the great divide between its immense inventiveness, vigour,
emotional plenitude on the one hand—all impressive but not
precious things—and on the other its declared voice as poetry, and
sometimes major poetry. There are various ways of approaching
a definition of this divide, but the only observation upon which
most readers are likely to agree is that it has to do with something
happening to the rhythm. Yet this takes us not very far, since we
have to admit that we are using 'rhythm' to describe something
inaccessible to the most subtle prosodic analysis. And it may,
after all, be more useful to speak in larger and vaguer terms,
hazarding that this different quality of utterance is the consequence
of something coming to, rather than proceeding from, the poet.
He is no longer grabbing a promising situation—preferably a
'contretemps'—and forcing it with the feelings which daily burden
the man Hardy. He is receiving, accepting, and declaring something. He is doing this, here in 'During Wind and Rain', until he
takes that final hop from the pet fowl, the rotten rose on the wall,
the clocks and carpets and chairs on the lawn to the churchyard
which in his last line conveniently bobs up near by: 'Down their
carved names the rain-drop ploughs'. Up to this point the elegiac
vision has been realized in images of marked freshness and specifi-
city, but the trouble about the tombstones in the rain is less that
they are intrusively emblematic than that we view them with a

consciousness that Hardy has trundled them too frequently on-stage before. The formulaic has taken hold again.

The theme of mortality is one on which Hardy comes to write as a great poet should, but it is not without having to purge himself from that species of facile indulgence in mortuary feeling which must be counted among the simple pleasures of English rustic life. He was liable, moreover, to run together death (in its under-taker's aspect, we may say) and sex (as virtually synonymous with infidelity whether in act or thought) in 'ironic' poems which move as predictably as a coin-in-the-slot machine delivering a ticket. Thus in 'The Workbox' a joiner gives his wife a present made from bits and pieces left over, as he explains, from 'poor John Wayward's coffin'. He is nothing if not explicit about this:

> 'The shingled pattern that seems to cease
>   Against your box's rim
> Continues right on in the piece
>   That's underground with him.'

But the reason why this information turns the joiner's wife 'limp and wan' is not its disagreeableness in a general sense. Between John Wayward and herself there has been a secret, and she knows 'of what he died'.

We are back with the trivial again in such a poem as this—and it must show, too, as almost touchingly old-fashioned, like one of those minor Pre-Raphaelite paintings in which are exhibited moments of aroused conscience, or guilts unmasked, or chickens coming home to roost. But the point of significance is that here is Hardy hard at work producing a mishmash of obsessional themes compelled upon him by personal experience to which we are unable to penetrate, and which would certainly be more painful than critically useful if we could. He cannot get away from a universe the 'ghastliness' of which he is determined to view as having been demonstrated by that 'latest illumination of the time'. He cannot get away from the grave and 'the worms waggling under the grass'. He cannot get away from a scene in which the domestic affections are beaten down, and again beaten down, by competing infideli-ties. Page after page as we read, it is the poetry of nervous traumata that is before us. So at this stage it looks as if we must be on the verge of giving him up to the verdict of T. S. Eliot, arrived at—as we have seen—on the basis of 'Barbara of the House of Grebe'. Here is a man writing 'as nearly for the sake of "self-expression" as a man well can'; and the self is not a wholesome self. Or, as Blackmur puts it in more general terms, Hardy—through 'a life-

time of devoted bad or inadequate practice'—can celebrate felt
reality only for 'the sake of the act of feeling'; he is incapable of
any 'celebration of the feeling of things for their own sake'. Hence
all this morbid expatiation.

4

But we have been considering hazards—the hazards attending
imaginative creation on the basis of intimate personal experience
and powerful temperamental response to such experience; we have
been considering hazards and not disablements. Hardy arrives at a
body, if a small body, of great poetry, after all. And he does so not
through that 'escape from personality' which T. S. Eliot, in a
celebrated if mysterious place, offers as an actual definition of
poetry. Nor does he arrive at a clarification and enhancement and
enrichment of his art through processes of intellectual analysis,
such as one might find in Gide or Joyce. Hardy was not an
intellectual man, and his critical formulations often seem to belong
with the dogmatic and opinionative side of him which as an artist
was his great liability. But he was honest and courageous; he was
meditative; he was capable of moments of vision in which the
personality, still powerfully operative, was yet a purged and
chastened personality. It no longer erected any barrier between
his sensibility and his experience, nor impressed upon that experience any philosophic presuppositions, whether traditional or
'advanced'. Indeed, in some of his finest poems the effect is almost
of our watching Hardy learning to feel and think anew, acknowledging intimations momentarily perceived, advancing (often with
a moving hesitancy and tentativeness) upon fresh interpretations
and evaluations of old sorrows and old joys.

One can go further. Hardy is often least 'personal'—in the
disabling sense of unloading his own opinions and appraisals of
the matter in hand—when he is writing most directly about himself. He was a man with whom honesty began at home. Consider
the group of poems which includes 'The Oxen', 'The Darkling
Thrush', and 'The Impercipient'. The last of these is subtitled 'At
a Cathedral Service', and begins:

> That with this bright believing band
>   I have no claim to be,
> That faiths by which my comrades stand
>   Seem fantasies to me,
> And mirage-mists their Shining Land,
>   Is a strange destiny.

> Why thus my soul should be consigned
> To infelicity. . . .

These poems have become popular anthology pieces partly because they have been taken to show that religious scepticism makes
people unhappy and regretful, and that Hardy was almost prepared to 'come round' to Christianity. And some readers of more
literary sophistication may react against this approval by asserting
that these are inferior poems, not untouched by sentimentality
and self-pity. Neither judgement is valid. Hardy is not wavering
in his mind. What he believes and will continue to believe is
implicit in the poems. Only his belief has been, in Howe's phrase,
'freed from the distempers of egotism'. And with that emanci-
pation has come an extraordinary sensitiveness to, and honesty
about, what is alike his situation and representative modern
man's.

Yet more remarkable is 'Afterwards', the poem which closes
the volume *Moments of Vision*. Some may think this Hardy's
finest poem, and it is very simply about himself:

> When the Present has latched its postern behind my tremu-
>   lous stay,
>   And the May month flaps its glad green leaves like wings,
> Delicate-filmed as new-spun silk, will the neighbours say,
>   'He was a man who used to notice such things'?
>
> If it be in the dusk when, like an eyelid's soundless blink,
>   The dewfall-hawk comes crossing the shades to alight
> Upon the wind-warped upland thorn, a gazer may think,
>   'To him this must have been a familiar sight.'
>
> If I pass during some nocturnal blackness, mothy and warm,
>   When the hedgehog travels furtively over the lawn,
> One may say, 'He strove that such innocent creatures should
>   come to no harm,
>   But he could do little for them; and now he is gone.'
>
> If, when hearing that I have been stilled at last, they stand at
>   the door,
>   Watching the full-starred heavens that winter sees,
> Will this thought rise on those who will meet my face no more,
>   'He was one who had an eye for such mysteries'?

And will any say when my bell of quittance is heard in the
   gloom,
  And a crossing breeze cuts a pause in its outrollings,
Till they rise again, as they were a new bell's boom,
  'He hears it not now, but used to notice such things'?

'Afterwards', too, has achieved wide popularity—and among
readers who will not pause to discuss the odd rhymes and asson-
ances in the third stanza. And again one may be critical. Did the
eminent Mr Hardy of Max Gate really feel like that about his
neighbours? Is it poetically respectable to proclaim one's kindness to hedgehogs? Are the modesty, the gentleness, the sensitiveness, the decorum a little too obtrusive? But these questions are,
of course, nonsense. For here is poetry—which is perception
authenticated by a certain manner in which words with their
meanings and cadences, their textures and tones, have been
assembled together. The Hardy of the poem is no doubt Hardy in
his poetic, in his ideal, character. It may be in reference to this
Hardy that the poem is delicately yet majestically exploratory, or
is 'sincere'. But here again, surely, is an egotism purged. Compare
'Afterwards' with 'In Death Divided', one of the poems supposed
to have been addressed to Mrs Henniker:

   I shall rot here, with those whom in their day
     You never knew,
   And alien ones who, ere they chilled to clay,
     Met not my view,
  Will in your distant grave-place ever neighbour you. . . .

'In Death Divided' is a moving poem. It is very far from having
the purity of 'Afterwards'.

5

Wessex Poems, published in 1898, contains work dating back to
the mid-1860s, and in subsequent volumes Hardy continued to
include verse written long before these volumes' several dates of
publication, so that any comprehensive chronological order would
be hard to establish. But in fact Hardy's poetry does not develop
very much. Of course, he gained in technical expertness when the
distraction of producing prose was behind him; and towards the
end of his career, not very surprisingly, his work ceases to be of
great interest. On the whole, however, the impression of anyone
who manages to read through the *Collected Poems* is likely to be

that good poems occur among indifferent ones (the indifferent greatly preponderating) in a ratio that is fairly constant through the several collections. Hardy at no time enjoyed anything like a settled command of excellence in verse.

This appears strikingly in the compilation which Weber has called *Hardy's Love Poems*. It contains 116 poems which Weber supposes to be more or less directly associated with Emma Hardy, and although the association must in some cases appear conjectural there can be no question about the great majority. They were nearly all written after Mrs Hardy's death, and a great many of them quite shortly after her death. Writing poems about his dead wife became, in fact, an important part of Hardy's *post mortem* obsession with her. 'Almost as soon as Emma was buried,' Weber tells us, 'the poet began making sentimental pilgrimages to spots associated with her'; and to her grave at Stinsford his visits were so constant that his secretary Florence Dugdale (soon to be the second Mrs Hardy) permitted herself in a letter to refer tartly to Emma as 'the late espoused saint'. We do not know how Milton treated the wife to whom in his sonnet he so referred, but it may well have been not too kindly. Hardy was very clear that he had not treated Emma kindly; her impossible side had been too much for him, and he knew that their long wedded estrangement had been as much his fault as hers. At her death, he told Edmund Gosse, the scales had fallen from his eyes. Arthur Quiller-Couch was of the opinion that Hardy in his seventies had constructed 'a pure fairy-tale' out of his long-distant courtship.

There is nothing remarkable in the fact that a highly sensitive man, after an unhappy marriage has been closed by death, should be overwhelmed by feelings of love and remorse, and that his memories should assume for a time great poignancy and vividness. But Hardy's experience of bereavement was accompanied by this very special circumstance: that the habitual bent of his temperament was such that mourning and sorrowful retrospection had been master themes with him almost since he began to write. Now, in this kind, a supremely personal occasion challenged him. How often he thought to meet it, Weber's gathering brings home to us. But Hardy was without capacity for a *sustained* response at a high level; for anything like the long sequence of elegiac meditations, for example, achieved by Tennyson in *In Memoriam*. Dr Leavis, a critic with a fondness for sharply delimiting what is of the first excellence in the body of a poet's achievement, asserted long ago that Hardy's 'rank as a major poet rests upon a dozen poems', and this, if an exaggeration, is not a foolish one. There are twenty-one poems in *Poems of 1912-13*; by no means all of them are outstanding; even so, they contain perhaps the greater part of such utterance as Hardy achieved as a major poet.

When these memorial poems depart from excellence we may feel Blackmur's 'lifetime of devoted bad or inadequate practice' to be at work. The sheerly mortuary makes in places too facile, almost tripping, an entrance, as when we find on the same opening:

> She will never be stirred
> In her loamy cell
> By the waves long heard
> And loved so well. . . .

and

> She is shut, she is shut
> From friendship's spell
> In the jailing shell
> Of her tiny cell.

On the previous page is 'her mound' and on the succeeding page 'her yew-arched bed'. What disturbs us here, if we are familiar with the body of Hardy's verse, is again the sense of something too familiar being laid on. In other poems we meet once more that facile reaching after small ironies which has been another routine resource—as when, in 'A Circular', the poet opens an advertisement for 'charming ball-dresses, millinery' sent through the post to

> Her who before last year ebbed out
> Was costumed in a shroud.

Yet again, the habit of jogtrot versifying breaks in—for example, in a curious poem called 'His Visitor', which appears to have been prompted by certain redecorations carried out at Max Gate shortly after Mrs Hardy's death, and in which the dead woman speaks:

> The change I notice in my once own quarters!
> A formal-fashioned border where the daisies used to be,
> The rooms new painted, and the pictures altered,
> And other cups and saucers, and no cosy nook for tea
>   As with me. . . .
> So I don't want to linger in this re-decked dwelling,
> I feel too uneasy at the contrasts I behold. . . .

On the other hand, some of the most wonderful of these poems delicately exploit small metrical equivalences in the midst of the insistent rhythms. Leavis has pointed out how 'The Voice' (which is a love poem as great as any in English) 'seems to start dangerously with a crude popular lilt' but modulates, under the burden of its statement, into something quite different. Or one may cite here the final lines of the opening stanza of the poem called 'Beeny Cliff: March 1870–March 1913':

> O the opal and the sapphire of that wandering western sea,
> And the woman riding high above with bright hair flapping
>   free—
> The woman whom I loved so, and who loyally loved me.

It is another characteristic of the finest of the poems that their diction is, for Hardy, singularly pure. 'The Walk', 'The Haunter', 'The Voice', 'After a Journey', 'A Death Day Recalled', 'Beeny Cliff', 'At Castle Boterel', 'The Phantom Horsewoman': one can read them through (and to do so is one of the most moving experiences poetry affords) with scarcely a consciousness of an odd expression or word:

> They say he sees as an instant thing. . . .
>   What his back years bring—
> A phantom of his own figuring.

This in 'The Phantom Horsewoman' is, with one exception, as near to Hardyese as we are brought. The exception is interesting. As originally published, the third stanza of 'The Voice' reads:

> Or is it only the breeze, in its listlessness
> Travelling across the wet mead to me here,
> You being ever dissolved to existlessness,
> Heard no more again far or near?

Hardy later changed this to:

> Or is it only the breeze, in its listlessness
> Travelling across the wet mead to me here,
> You being ever dissolved to wan wistlessness,
> Heard no more again far or near?

'Existlessness' is certainly a nonce-word of Hardy's. But even 'existless' has no recorded currency in English, whereas of 'wistlessness' at least 'wistless' is in the dictionary as an obsolete or archaic word used by Cary in his translation of Dante's *Paradiso* (which it is very probable that Hardy had read). Hardy is thus found excising the only really bizarre (yet quite characteristic) word in the whole group of poems and substituting one which is no more than a shade poetic or literary in flavour. The general avoidance of an idiosyncratic vocabulary in *Poems of 1912-13* is greatly to their advantage as a whole. One may regret the disappearance of the strong 'existlessness', all the same.

Hardy published these, his greatest poems, as a section of a volume called *Satires of Circumstance*, and 'Satires of Circumstance' is actually the running title under which they still appear in the *Collected Poems*. The fifteen satires themselves are, as we have glimpsed, his most extreme expressions of sexual disenchantment. To Edmund Gosse, who had reviewed the book, he wrote that 'the little group of satires cost.me much sadness in having to reprint them in the volume'. This is patently disingenuous; there was no reason why the satires (eleven of which had been printed in the *Fortnightly Review*) should be collected at all, if their author had ceased to care for them. Their having appeared in the company they did is a final instance of the power of the incongruous over Hardy's art. It has been said that his was a Gothic imagination. Certainly his earliest professional employment had lain in restoring Gothic churches, and we may be sure that the gargoyle and the tomb had appealed to him quite as much as the arch, the flying buttress, and the spire. When Sergeant Troy in *Far from the Madding Crowd* plants Fanny Robin's grave with flowers, we are told that he had 'in his prostration at this time . . . no perception that in the futility of these romantic doings, dictated by a remorseful reaction from previous indifference, there was any element of absurdity'. And it is a gargoyle, a 'horrible stone entity', that demonstrates the 'absurdity' by directing its obliterating vomit upon Troy's vain memorial. We may think of the *Satires of Circumstance* as being in something like this relationship to *Poems of 1912-13*. That Hardy should think of these great poems as themselves 'romantic doings, dictated by a remorseful reaction from previous indifference' is likely enough. That he should intimate his sense of this by setting the *Satires of Circumstance* where he did is congruous with the whole sombre cast of his mind.

Chronology

1840   T. H. born on 2 June at Higher Bockhampton, Dorset.

1849   Goes to school in Dorchester and learns Latin.

1856-61 Articled to John Hicks, Dorchester architect and church-restorer. Studies Greek with the assistance of Horace Moule of Trinity College, Oxford and Queen's College, Cambridge, Hardy's senior by eight years. Writes poetry.

1862   Removes to London and enters the office of Arthur Blomfield, restorer and designer of churches. Reads extensively and becomes aware of the 'advanced thinking' of the age; discusses philosophical and theological problems with his fellow students.

1865   *How I Built Myself a House* (Chambers's Journal).

1866   Writes 'Hap' (*Wessex Poems*).

1867   Returns to Dorchester to assist Hicks.

1868-70 Completes *The Poor Man and the Lady* (unpublished). Begins *Desperate Remedies*, a sensation novel in the manner of Wilkie Collins. Possibly in love with his cousin, Tryphena Sparks (born 1851).

1870   Professional visit to St Juliot in Cornwall. Meets Emma Lavinia Gifford.

1871   *Desperate Remedies.* Frequently in Cornwall, where he writes most of *Under the Greenwood Tree* and begins making notes for *A Pair of Blue Eyes.*

1872   *Under the Greenwood Tree.*

1873   Begins *Far from the Madding Crowd. A Pair of Blue Eyes.* Suicide of Horace Moule.

1874   *Far from the Madding Crowd.* Marries Miss Gifford, despite opposition from her family. Wedding journey on the Continent.

1876   A second continental tour, and residence at Sturminster Newton. *The Hand of Ethelberta.*

1878   *The Return of the Native.* Residence in London. Joins the Savile Club.

1880   *The Trumpet-Major.* Begins *A Laodicean,* and with his wife makes a tour of Normandy. Dictates the greater part of *A Laodicean* while immobilized by serious illness.

1881   Convalescence in Scotland. *A Laodicean.*

1882   With his wife visits Paris. *Two on a Tower.*

1883   Forms an attachment to social life in London, and hereafter resides there fairly regularly for some months of the year. Designs a house to be built outside Dorchester.

1884   *The Dorset Farm Labourer: Past and Present.*

1885   Moves into new house, Max Gate.

1886   *The Mayor of Casterbridge.*

1887   *The Woodlanders.* The Hardys tour Italy and spend some months in London.

1888   A further visit to Paris. *Wessex Tales.* Work begun on *Tess of the d'Urbervilles* under the projected title *Too Late Beloved.*

1889   The novel, when half completed, rejected first by Tillotson's and then by two magazines. Hardy bowdlerizes the text for English and American serial publication.

1891   *A Group of Noble Dames. Tess of the d'Urbervilles.*

1892   Death of Hardy's father. Beginning of work on *Jude the Obscure.*

1893   The Hardys visit Viceregal Lodge, Dublin, at the invitation of Mrs Henniker, for whom Hardy has been thought to have formed an attachment. Mrs Hardy shows symptoms of increasing eccentricity.

1894   *Life's Little Ironies.*

1895   *Jude the Obscure.* The novel is widely condemned, and Mrs Hardy is among its most severe critics. But shortly after its publication in book form the Hardys visit Belgium together, and Hardy surveys the field of Waterloo. He has resolved to write no more prose fiction.

1897   *The Well-Beloved.* This *novella* was written between *Tess of the d'Urbervilles* and *Jude the Obscure.*

1898   *Wessex Poems and Other Verses.*

1902   *Poems of the Past and Present.* Work begun on *The Dynasts.*

1904   Death of Hardy's mother. *The Dynasts, Part I.*

1905   Honorary degree of LL.D. from the University of Aberdeen.

1906   *The Dynasts, Part II.*

1908   *The Dynasts, Part III.*

1909   Hardy succeeds Meredith as President of the Society of Authors. *Time's Laughingstocks and Other Verses.*

1910   Order of Merit. Freedom of Dorchester.

1912   Gold Medal of the Royal Society of Literature. Emma Lavinia Hardy dies on 27 November at Max Gate, Dorchester.

1913   Hardy visits St Juliot. Honorary degree of Litt.D. from the University of Cambridge. *A Changed Man and Other Tales.*

1914   Hardy marries Miss Florence Dugdale. *Satires of Circumstance* (including 'Poems of 1912-1913').

1915   Death of Hardy's sister Mary.

1917   *Moments of Vision.*

1920   Honorary Degree of D.Litt. from the University of Oxford.

1922   *Late Lyrics and Earlier.*

1925   *Human Shows.*

1926   On 1 November Hardy visits his birthplace at Higher Bock-
        hampton for the last time.
1927   The *Iphigenia in Aulis* of Euripides played before Hardy at
        Max Gate by undergraduates of Balliol College, Oxford.
        Hardy lays the foundation-stone of a new building at Dorchester
        Grammar School.
1928   T. H. dies on 11 January at Max Gate, Dorchester. Posthumous
        publication of *Winter Words*.

Bibliography

ABERCROMBIE, L. *Thomas Hardy: A Critical Study*. London, 1912; reissued New York, 1964.

BAILEY, J. O. *Thomas Hardy and the Cosmic Mind: A New Reading of 'The Dynasts'*. Chapel Hill, 1956.

—— *The Poetry of Thomas Hardy*. Chapel Hill, 1970.

BARBER, D. F. (ed.). *Concerning Thomas Hardy*. London, 1968.

BEACH, J. W. *The Technique of Thomas Hardy*. Chicago, 1922; reissued New York, 1962.

BEATTY, C. J. P. (ed.). *The Architectural Notebook of Thomas Hardy*. Dorchester, 1966.

BLACKMUR, R. P. *Language as Gesture*. New York, 1952.

BLUNDEN, E. *Thomas Hardy*. London, 1942.

BOWRA, C. M. *The Lyrical Poetry of Thomas Hardy*. Nottingham, 1947; reprinted in *Inspiration and Poetry*, London, 1955.

BRENNECKE, E. *Thomas Hardy's Universe: A Study of a Poet's Mind* Boston, 1924.

—— *The Life of Thomas Hardy*. New York, 1925.

BROWN, D. *Thomas Hardy*. London, 1954; revised 1961.

CAZAMIAN, M. L. *Le Roman et les idées en Angleterre*. Strasbourg, 1923.

CECIL, LORD DAVID. *Hardy the Novelist*. London, 1943.

CHAKRAVARTY, A. *'The Dynasts' and the Post-War Age in Poetry*. Oxford, 1938.

CHAPMAN, F. 'Revaluations IV: Hardy the Novelist', *Scrutiny*, III, 1934.

CHASE, M. E. *Thomas Hardy from Serial to Novel*. Minneapolis, 1927.

CHEW, S. C. *Thomas Hardy: Poet and Novelist*. New York, 1921.

CHILD, H. *Thomas Hardy*. New York, 1916.

COLLINS, V. H. *Talks with Thomas Hardy*. London, 1928.

DAY LEWIS, C. 'The Lyrical Poetry of Thomas Hardy', *Proceedings of the British Academy*, XXXVII, 1951.

DEACON, L. AND COLEMAN, T. *Providence and Mr Hardy*. London, 1966.

D'EXIDEUIL, P. *The Human Pair in the Works of Thomas Hardy*. London, 1930.

DOBRÉE, B. 'Thomas Hardy', *The Lamp and the Lute*. Oxford, 1929.

—— *'The Dynasts'*, *Southern Review*, VI, 1940.

DUFFIN, H. C. *Thomas Hardy: A Study of the Wessex Novels*. Manchester, 1916; augmented edition, London, 1937.

ELIOT, T. S. *After Strange Gods*. London, 1934.

FIROR, R. A. *Folkways in Thomas Hardy*. Philadelphia, 1931; reissued New York, 1962.

GARWOOD, H. *Thomas Hardy: An Illustration of the Philosophy of Schopenhauer*. Philadelphia, 1911.

GREGOR, I. AND NICHOLAS, B. *The Moral and the Story*. London, 1962.

GRIMSDITCH, H. B. *Character and Environment in the Novels of Thomas Hardy*. London, 1925; New York, 1962.

GUERARD, A. J. *Thomas Hardy*. Harvard, 1949; augmented edition, New York, 1964.

—— (ed.). *Hardy: A Collection of Critical Essays*. Englewood Cliffs, 1963.

HARDY, B. *The Appropriate Form*. London, 1964.

HARDY, E. *Thomas Hardy: A Critical Biography*. London, 1954.

—— *Thomas Hardy's Notebooks, and Some Letters from Julia Augusta Martin*. London, 1955.

HARDY, E., AND GITTINGS, R. *Some Recollections by Emma Hardy*. Oxford, 1961.

HARDY, F. E. *The Early Life of Thomas Hardy*. London, 1928.

—— *The Later Years of Thomas Hardy*. London, 1930.

HAWKINS, D. *Hardy the Novelist*. London, 1950.

HEILMAN, R. B. 'Hardy's Sue Bridehead', *Nineteenth-Century Fiction*, 20, 1966.

HOLLOWAY, J. *The Victorian Sage: Studies in Argument*. London, 1953.

HOWE, I. *Thomas Hardy*. New York, 1967.

HYNES, S. L. *The Pattern of Hardy's Poetry*. Chapel Hill, 1961.

JAMES, H. *The House of Fiction* (ed. L. Edel). London, 1957.

JOHNSON, L. *The Art of Thomas Hardy*. London, 1894; augmented edition, 1923.

KING, R. W. 'Verse and Prose Parallels in the Works of Thomas Hardy', *Review of English Studies*, XIII, 1962.

LAWRENCE, D. H. *Phoenix*. London, 1936.

LEA, H. *Thomas Hardy's Wessex*. London, 1913.

LEAVIS, F. R. *New Bearings in English Poetry*. London, 1932.

—— 'Hardy the Poet', *Southern Review*, VI, 1940.

—— 'Reality and Sincerity', *Scrutiny*, XIX, 1952.

LEAVIS, Q. D. 'Thomas Hardy and Criticism', *Scrutiny*, XI, 1943.

LERNER, L. AND HOLMSTROM, J. *Thomas Hardy and his Readers*. London, 1968.

MACDOWELL, A. *Thomas Hardy: A Critical Study*. London, 1931.

MARSDEN, K. *The Poems of Thomas Hardy: A Critical Introduction*. London, 1969.

MORRELL, R. *Thomas Hardy: The Will and the Way*. Malaya, 1965.

MUIR, E. *Essays on Literature and Society*. London, 1949.

MURRY, J. M. *Aspects of Literature*. London, 1920.

OREL, H. *Thomas Hardy's Personal Writings*. Kansas, 1966.

PATERSON, J. 'The Mayor of Casterbridge as a Tragedy', *Victorian Studies*, III, 1959.

—— *The Making of 'The Return of the Native'*. Berkeley, 1960.

PINION, F. B. *A Hardy Companion*. London and New York, 1968.

PURDY, R. L. *Thomas Hardy: A Bibliographical Study*. Oxford, 1954.

RANSOM, J. C. 'Honey and Gall', *Southern Review*, VI, 1940.

—— 'Thomas Hardy's Poems', *Kenyon Review*, XXII, 1960.

RICHARDS, I. A. *Science and Poetry*. London, 1926.

ROPPEN, G. *Evolution and Poetic Belief*. Oxford, 1957.

RUTLAND, W. R. *Thomas Hardy: A Study of his Writings and their Background*. Oxford, 1938; reprinted New York, 1962.

SANKEY, B. *The Major Novels of Thomas Hardy*. Denver, 1965.

SOUTHERINGTON, F. R. *Hardy's Vision of Man*. London, 1971.

SOUTHWORTH, J. G. *The Poetry of Thomas Hardy*. New York, 1947.

STEVENSON, L. *Darwin among the Poets*. Chicago, 1932.

STEWART, J. I. M. 'The Integrity of Hardy', *Essays and Studies*, 1948.

—— *Eight Modern Writers*. Oxford, 1963.

TATE, A. 'Hardy's Philosophic Metaphors', *Southern Review*, VI, 1940.

VAN GHENT, D. *The English Novel: Form and Function*. New York, 1935.

WEBER, C. J. *Hardy of Wessex: His Life and Literary Career*. New York, 1940; revised edition, London, 1965.

—— *Hardy and the Lady from Madison Square*. Waterville, Maine, 1952.

—— (ed.). *The Letters of Thomas Hardy*. Waterville, Maine, 1954.

—— (ed.). *Hardy's Love Poems*. London, 1963.

—— *'Dearest Emmie': Hardy's Letters to his First Wife*. New York, 1963.

WEBSTER, H. C. *On a Darkling Plain*. Chicago, 1947; London, 1964.

WHEELER, O. B. 'Four Versions of "The Return of the Native"', *Nineteenth-Century Fiction*, XIV, 1959.

WOOLF, V. *The Common Reader: Second Series*. London, 1932.

—— *A Writer's Diary*. London, 1953.

ZABEL, M. D. *Craft and Character in Modern Fiction*. New York, 1957.

ZACHRISSON, R. E. *Thomas Hardy's Twilight View of Life*. Stockholm, 1931.

Index

Abercrombie, Lascelles, 70, 71, 81

Aeschylus, 93, 99, 100, 112, 119, 128, 216

Ainsworth, William Harrison, *Rookwood*, 84

Aldclyffe, Miss (in *Desperate Remedies*), 51, 53-55, 145

Alexander, I, Tsar, 217, 218

Allamont, Miss (in *The Poor Man and the Lady*), 47-48

Allenville, Miss (in 'An Indiscretion in the Life of an Heiress'), 49

Alvarez, Alfred, 188, 196

Archer, William, 42

Aristotle, 106, 121

Arnold, Matthew, 2, 18, 34

Aspent, Car'line (in 'The Fiddler of the Reels'), 152

Bailey, J. O., 154

Baker, J. E., *The Novel and the Oxford Movement*, 31

Balla, Giacomo, 86

Barnes, William, 188

Barnet, Mr and Mrs (in 'Fellow-Townsmen'), 149

Beach, Joseph, 76, 95, 139, 161

Beatty, Dr (in *The Dynasts*), 212

Bellini, Giovanni, 5

Bennett, Arnold, 132, 189

Besant, Walter, 162, 168

Blackmur, R. P., 223, 224, 226-227, 231

Blunden, Edmund, 70, 196

Boldwood, William (in *Far from the Madding Crowd*), 75n, 76-77, 79-80, 84, 90

Boswell, James, 3

Bow Church, Cheapside, 9

Bradley, Andrew Cecil, *Shakespearean Tragedy*, 121

Bridehead, Sue (in *Jude the Obscure*), 10, 18, 24, 29, 70, 114, 185, 186n, 187-188, 190-203

British Quarterly Review, 163

Bromell, Mrs (daughter of Tryphena Sparks), 18, 19

Brontë, Charlotte, *Jane Eyre*, 82

Brown, Douglas, 44, 88, 118, 139, 168

Browning, Robert, 188, 220

Byron, Lord, 125-126

Cambridge, 9, 184, 185, 188

Campbell, George, *Philosophy of Rhetoric*, 39

Caravaggio, Michelangelo Merisi da, 71, 86

Carlyle, Thomas, 217

Caro, Avice (in *The Well-Beloved*), 160

Cary, Henry Francis, 233

Castlereagh, Robert, 2nd Viscount (in *The Dynasts*), 213

Cazamian, M. L., 31

Cecil, Lord David, 98, 156-157

Changed Man, A, 151; 'The Romantic Adventures of a Milkmaid', 151

Chapman, Frederick, 50

Chapman and Hall (publishers), 50

Charmond, Mrs (in *The Woodlanders*), 128n, 133, 134n, 138, 139, 141, 143-145

Chaucer, Geoffrey, 72

Clare, Angel (in *Tess of the d'Urbervilles*), 165n, 166-167, 170-173, 176-177, 179-180

Coleman, Terry, *Providence and Mr Hardy*, 19

Coleridge, Samuel Taylor, 147

Colin Clout, 76

Collins, Wilkie, 54; *The Moonstone*, 53; *The Woman in White*, 53

Conrad, Joseph, 82, 130, 132; *The Secret Agent*, 176; *Under Western Eyes*, 121

Constantine, Lady (in *Two on a Tower*), 94, 157

Cornhill Magazine, The, 74, 89, 93, 155, 163

Correggio, Antonio, 53

Cowper, William, *Apocryphal Gospels*, 192

Crivelli, Carlo, 5, 53

Curzon, Lord, 7

Damson, Suke (in *The Woodlanders*), 133, 140, 144, 145, 178

Dante Alighieri, *Paradiso*, 233

Dare, William (in *A Laodicean*), 154

Darwin Charles, 10, 31, 35, 129, 204, 207; *The Origin of the Species*, 10

Day, Fancy (in *Under the Greenwood Tree*), 18, 58, 61-62, 72

Deacon, Lois, *Providence and Mr Hardy*, 19

de la Mare, Walter, 12

Derriman, Festus (in *The Trumpet-Major*), 156

Desperate Remedies, 23, 39, 40, 50-56, 72, 89, 106, 110, 154

Dewy, Dick (in *Under the Greenwood Tree*), 57-59, 61, 62, 72

Dickens, Charles, 82, 176

Donn, Arabella (in *Jude the Obscure*), 186-187, 194-197

Dorchester, 8

Dostoevsky, Feodor Michaelovich, 121

Downe, Mr and Mrs (in 'Fellow-Townsmen'), 149

Drayton, Michael, 188

Dublin, 29

Duchamp, Marcel, 86

Dugdale, Florence Emily, *see* Hardy, Florence Emily

d'Urberville, Alec (in *Tess of the d'Urbervilles*), 165n, 166, 169, 177, 178-179

Durbeyfield, John (in *Tess of the d'Urbervilles*), 165n, 169

Durbeyfield, Tess (in *Tess of the d'Urbervilles*), 165n, 166-183

Dynasts, The, 11, 15, 29, 32-33, 35, 42, 122, 148, 155, 204-218, 221

Eliot, George, 33, 44, 58, 75, 81, 90; *Adam Bede*, 57; *Middlemarch*, 56, 122, 123-124

Eliot, T. S., 31, 227; *After Strange Gods*, 37, 38, 40, 41, 147, 226

Encyclopaedia Britannica, The, 35

Essays and Reviews, 10

Everdene, Bathsheba (in *Far from the Madding Crowd*), 74n, 77-80, 84-87, 90, 93

Far from the Madding Crowd, 26, 33, 45, 74-90, 94, 97

Farfrae, Donald (in *The Mayor of Casterbridge*), 108n, 115, 117-119, 170

Father Time (in *Jude the Obscure*), 186n, 189, 201

Faust, 120

Fawley, Jude (in *Jude the Obscure*), 24, 70, 114, 186-203

Fielding, Henry, 76

Fitzpiers, Edred (in *The Woodlanders*), 128n, 133-134, 137-142, 144-145

Flaubert, Gustave, *Madame Bovary,* 203

Forster, E. M., 153; *A Room with a View,* 140

Fortnightly Review, The, 166, 167, 233

Gale, Charles, 17, 18, 20

Galsworthy, Mr and Mrs John, 6

Garland, Anne (in *The Trumpet-Major*), 156

Garnett, Richard, 26, 202

Garwood, Helen, *Thomas Hardy: An Illustration of the Philosophy of Schopenhauer,* 31

George III (in *The Dynasts*), 208, 215

George, Frank (cousin of Hardy), 13

Gibbon, Edward, 192

Gide, André, 227

Gifford, Emma Lavinia, *see* Hardy, Emma Lavinia

Good Words (periodical), 156

Goodenough, Mrs (in *The Mayor of Casterbridge*), 113, 124

Gosse, Edmund, 35, 47, 135, 188, 197, 201, 230, 233

Graphic, The, 108, 119, 150, 166, 167

Graye, Cytherea (in *Desperate Remedies*), 51-55, 61, 145

Great Exhibition of 1851, The, 152

Green, T. H., *An Estimate of the Value and Influence of Works of Fiction in Modern Times,* 31

Greuze, Jean Baptiste, 53

Grosart, A. B., 14-15

Group of Noble Dames, A, 149-150; 'Barbara of the House of Grebe', 37, 150, 226; 'Squire Petrick's Lady', 150

Guerard, Albert J., 72, 88-89, 137, 154, 155, 157, 158, 161, 178, 214-215

Haggard, Rider, 45, 46

Hand, Jemima, *see* Hardy, Jemima

Hand of Ethelberta, The, 75, 147, 153-154, 163

Hardy, Emma Lavinia, (1st wife), 3, 8, 10, 12, 16, 20, 22-27, 38, 154, 202-203, 210, 230

Hardy, Florence Emily (2nd wife), 1, 26, 29, 230

Hardy, Henry (brother), 18

Hardy, Jemima (mother), 19, 45, 153

Hardy, Mary (sister), 18, 184

Hardy, Thomas (father), 8, 153

Hardy, Thomas: origins, 4, 131, 153; as a child, 8, 13; and Tryphena Sparks, 17-22; possible son by Tryphena Sparks, 3, 18-19; and Emma Gifford, 16, 22-27, 203, 224; and Florence Henniker, 29-30; and Florence Dugdale, 29; illness, 154; aims as a writer, 5, 33-34, 112, 128; and the agricultural way of life, 44-46, 88, 131-132, 169-170; and agnosticism, 8, 10, 15, 44, 88; and the Anglican Church, 8-13; and philosophy, 15, 31-44, 204-210, 214; has to make concessions to popular taste, 92-95, 126, 149, 156, 163-164, 166-167, 189; interest in painting, 5, 53, 83, 86, 115, 122, 144; treatment of Lesbianism, 55; uses his own experiences, 16, 38, 131, 188, 202

Writings: article, 'The Dorsetshire Labourer', 46, 89, 170: autobiography, *The Early Life of Thomas Hardy* and *The Later Years of Thomas Hardy*, 1-15; drama, *see The Dynasts*; novels and short stories, *see* individual titles; poetry, *Lyrics and Reveries*, 30; *Moments of Vision*, 159, 204, 228; *Poems 1912-13*, 29, 203, 230-231, 233; *Satires of Circumstance*, 222, 233; *Wessex Poems*, 219, 229; 'After a Journey', 232; 'Afterwards', 228-229; 'At a Lunar Eclipse', 157; 'At a Waterfall', 222; 'At an Inn', 27-29; 'At Castle Boterel', 232; 'Beeny Cliff: March 1870-March 1913', 232; 'The Breaking of Nations', 16; 'A Broken Appointment', 29; 'The Christening', 21; 'A Circular', 231; 'The Contretemps', 223; 'The Convergence of the Twain', 56; 'The Darkling Thrush', 26, 227; 'A Death Day Recalled', 232; 'The Division', 28-29; 'During Wind and Rain', 224-225; 'Hap', 36; 'The Haunter', 232; 'Heredity', 159; 'His Visitor', 231; 'A Hurried Meeting', 21; 'I looked up from my writing', 204; 'The Impercipient', 227-228; 'In a Wood', 132n; 'In Death Divided', 29, 229; 'In the Nuptial Chamber', 223; 'In Vision I Roamed', 157; 'Last Love-Word', 29; 'The Memorial Brass 186-', 221; 'Midnight on the Great Western', 189; 'On a Heath', 21-22; 'The Oxen', 227; 'The Phantom Horsewoman', 232; 'The Pine Planters', 132n; 'Seen by the Waits', 222; 'The Stranger's Song', 147-148; 'Thoughts of Phena at News of her Death', 17; 'A Thunderstorm in Town', 30; 'The Torn Letter', 30; 'The Voice', 232; 'The Walk', 232; 'When I set out for Lyonnesse', 23; 'The Workbox', 226; 'You Were the Sort that Men Forgot', 25

Harper's Weekly, 108
Harris, Frank, 2
Hartmann, Eduard von, 32, 205
Hedgcock, F. A., *Thomas Hardy*; *Penseur et Artiste*, 31
Hegel, Georg Wilhelm Friedrich, 121

Henchard, Elizabeth-Jane (in *The Mayor of Casterbridge*), 108n, 110-111, 116, 119, 123

Henchard, Michael (in *The Mayor of Casterbridge*), 108n, 110-121, 123-126, 136

Henchard, Susan (in *The Mayor of Casterbridge*), 108n, 110-114, 118, 123

Henniker, Florence, 29-30

Henniker-Major, Major the Hon. Arthur Henry, 29

Hipcroft, Ned (in 'The Fiddler of the Reels'), 152

Hobbema, Meindert, 83, 86

Holloway, John, 36, 168

Hooker, Richard, *Ecclesiastical Polity*, 9

Houghton, 1st Lord, *see* Milnes, Richard Monckton

Houghton, 2nd Lord (later Marquess of Crewe), 29

Howe, Irving, 70, 105, 123, 128, 141, 155, 179, 207, 213

Humboldt, Alexander von, 190

Hume, David, 31

Hutchins, John, *The History and Antiquities of the County of Dorset*, 150

Huxley, Thomas Henry, 31, 35

Hynes, Samuel, 214

Ibsen, Henrik, 184-185, 197; *The Master Builder*, 53, 185

Impressionists, The, 86, 144

'Indiscretion in the Life of an Heiress, An', short story, 49-50, 54n

James, Henry, 82, 93, 115, 132; *The Ambassadors*, 193; *The Bostonians*, 55; *The Turn of the Screw*, 151

Jethway, Felix (in *A Pair of Blue Eyes*), 65-67

Johnson, Lionel, *The Art of Thomas Hardy*, 44, 169

Johnson, Samuel, 3; *Rasselas*, 34

Joyce, James, 227; *Ulysses*, 219

Jude the Obscure, 10, 30, 47, 95, 121, 151, 164, 184-203

Keats, John, 34, 168, 177, 220

Kipling, Rudyard, 2-3, 220

Knight, Henry (in *A Pair of Blue Eyes*), 9, 63n, 64-70, 72, 73, 179

Kutuzov, Mikhail Ilarionovich, 217

Laodicean, A, 147, 154-155, 157

La Tour, Georges de, 71, 86

Lawrence, D. H., 97, 175, 176, 202; *Lady Chatterley's Lover*, 139; *The Rainbow*, 196; *Sons and Lovers*, 38; *Women in Love*, 196

Lea, Hermann, 29

Leavis, F. R., 230, 232

Lee, Vernon, 182

Le Nains (painters), 71

Le Sueur, Lucetta (in *The Mayor of Casterbridge*), 108n, 115-116

Life's Little Ironies, 151; 'The Fiddler of the Reels', 151-152; 'The Son's Veto', 151, 153; 'A Tragedy of Two Ambitions', 151, 153

Linton, Lynn, 162, 163

London, 47

Longman's Magazine, 46

Loveday, John (in *The Trumpet-Major*), 156

Loveday, Robert (in *The Trumpet-Major*), 156

Luxellian, Lord (in *A Pair of Blue Eyes*), 63n, 64, 69
Lydgate, Tertius (in *Middlemarch*), 99

Macleod, Dr Donald, 156
Macmillan (publishers), 50, 132, 164
Macmillan, Alexander, 47, 48-49
Macmillan's Magazine, 166
McTaggart, J. M., 214
Manston, Charles (in *Desperate Remedies*), 51-55
Max Gate, 4-5, 27, 29, 132, 231
Maybold, Mr (in *Under the Greenwood Tree*), 72
Mayne, Egbert (in 'An Indiscretion in the Life of an Heiress'), 49
Mayor of Casterbridge, The, 108-126, 127, 136, 143, 149
Melbury, George (in *The Woodlanders*), 128n, 131, 137-138
Melbury, Grace (in *The Woodlanders*), 84, 128n, 133-142, 144-145
Mellstock Quire, The (in *Under the Greenwood Tree*), 9, 58-60
Meredith, George, 50, 51; *The Adventures of Harry Richmond*, 56; *Evan Harrington*, 153
Mill, John Stuart, 31, 42, 190; *System of Logic*, 42
Milnes, Richard Monckton, 29
Milton, John, 135; *Samson Agonistes*, 189
Mind, 214
Moore, George, 171, 182
Morley, John, 49, 58
Morrell, Roy, *Thomas Hardy: the Will and the Way*, 41-44, 87, 161, 213

Morrison, Donald, 220
Moule, Horace, 9, 32
Murray's Magazine, 166

Napoleon (in *The Dynasts*), 148, 155, 206, 207, 214, 215, 216
National Observer, The, 166, 167
Nelson, Horatio, Lord (in *The Dynasts*), 207, 212
New Quarterly Magazine, The, 49
New Review, The, 162
Newman, John Henry, *Apologia*, 9
Newson (in The *Mayor of Casterbridge*), 108n, 111
Nicolson, Sir Harold, 161n
Nietzsche, Friedrich Wilhelm, 42
Noyes, Alfred, 39

Oak, Gabriel (in *Far from the Madding Crowd*), 41, 74n, 76-79, 81, 82, 84, 86, 90, 93, 96
O'Connor, T. P., 27
Ollamoor, Wat (in 'The Fiddler of the Reels'), 152
Owen, Rebekah, 139
Oxford, 184, 188

Pair of Blue Eyes, A, 23, 26, 37-38, 49, 63-73, 74, 89, 105, 134, 157
Paterson, John, 96, 97-98, 115n, 124-125
Patmore, Coventry, 71, 161n
Peacock, Thomas Love, 119, 161
Pennsylvania, University of, 31
Petrick, Squire (in 'Squire Petrick's Lady'), 150
Phillotson, Richard (in *Jude the Obscure*), 185, 186n, 200

Pierston, Jocelyn (in *The Well-Beloved*), 159-160

Pinion, F. B., *A Hardy Companion*, 95

Pitt, William (in *The Dynasts*), 213, 216

Plymouth Public Free School, 18

Podsnap, Mr (in *Our Mutual Friend*), 162

Poor Man and the Lady, The, 7, 10, 23, 38, 47-50, 51, 54n, 58, 153, 154

Portsmouth, Lord, 6

Power, Paula (in *A Laodicean*), 154

Proust, Marcel, 161

Purdy, R. L., 1, 3, 29, 165

Quiller-Couch, Sir Arthur, 230

Randolph (possible son of Tryphena Sparks and Hardy), 18-19

Ransom, John Crowe, 220

Rationalist Press Association, 43-44

Return of the Native, The, 26, 53, 78, 81, 91-017, 132, 148, 149, 170

Richardson, Samuel, *Clarissa*, 183, 219

Robin, Fanny (in *Far from the Madding Crowd*), 75n, 79-80, 94

Rousseau, Jean-Jacques, 103, 136

Rutland, W, R., 213

Ruysdael, Jacob van, 83, 86

St Cleeve, Swithin (in *Two on a Tower*), 157

St George's, Hanover Square, 9

St Juliot, 23, 26

St Mary Abbots, Kensington, 11-12

Salisbury, 8, 9-10, 29

Sappho, 103

Savile Club, 168

Savile, Lucy (in 'Fellow-Townsmen'), 149

Schopenhauer, Arthur, 31-32, 204-205, 214; *On the Fourfold Root of the Principle of Sufficient Reason*, 32

Scott, Sir Walter, 58

Scribner's Magazine, 152

Shaftesbury, 5th Earl, 150

Shakespeare, William, 58, 76, 111-112, 119, 131, 175, 217; *Antony and Cleopatra*, 213; *Coriolanus*, 213; *Hamlet*, 13, 124; *Love's Labour's Lost*, 157; *Macbeth*, 14; *Measure for Measure*, 124; *Venus and Adonis*, 157

Shaw, George Bernard, 136, 197; *You Never Can Tell*, 154

Shelley, Percy Bysshe, 41, 220; *Hellas*, 216; *Prometheus Unbound*, 216

Sheridan, Richard (in *The Dynasts*), 212-213

Siddons, Mrs, 103

Sloper, Dr (in *Washington Square*), 137

Smith, Elder (publishers), 123

Smith, Stephen (in *A Pair of Blue Eyes*), 9, 63n, 64-69, 72, 73, 94

Sophocles, 81, 93, 164, 175; *Oedipus Rex*, 112, 121

South, Marty (in *The Woodlanders*), 128n, 137, 141, 142-143, 145, 169, 178

Southsea, 29

Sparks, James, 19

Sparks, Maria (aunt of Hardy), 19

Sparks, Rebecca, 19, 142

Sparks, Tryphena, 17-22, 142, 180, 185, 188, 202, 203

Spectator, The, 33, 51, 75, 163

Spencer, Herbert, 15, 31

Spenser, Edmund, 76

Stephen, Leslie, 10, 74, 92, 93, 94, 156, 163, 164

Stevenson, Robert Louis, 132

Stinsford Church, 12, 58, 230

Stockwell College, Clapham, 18, 202

Strong, Will (in *The Poor Man and the Lady*), 47-48

Swancourt, Elfride (in *A Pair of Blue Eyes*), 26, 38, 63n, 64-69, 72-73, 94, 105, 113, 134, 176

Swancourt, Mr (in *A Pair of Blue Eyes*), 63-64

Swinburne, Algernon Charles, 188, 192

Symons, Arthur, 35

Tennyson, Alfred, Lord, 38, 71, 161n; *In Memoriam,* 230

Tess of the d'Urbervilles, 70, 92, 94, 115, 128, 148, 158, 165-183, 191, 198

Thackeray, William Makepeace, 48, 74, 93; *Vanity Fair,* 94, 95

Thomson, James, 41

Tillotson, W. F., 165-166

Tillotson & Son (publishers), 158, 164, 165-166

Times, The, 47

Tinsley, William, 50

Tinsley's Magazine, 63

Titian, 115

Tolstoi, Leo, 175, 217-218; *Anna Karenina,* 203

Toobad, Mr (in *Nightmare Abbey*), 41

Trevelyan, G. M., *The Poetry and Philosophy of George Meredith,* 31

Trilling, Lionel, 220

Trollope, Anthony, 156

Troy, Sergeant (in *Far from the Madding Crowd*), 75n, 79-81, 83, 84-87, 94, 233

Trumpet-Major, The, 147, 155-156, 163, 216

Turner, J. M. W., 5

Two on a Tower, 40, 147, 155, 156-157

Under the Greenwood Tree, 49, 57-62, 72, 74, 88, 89, 97, 129

Uplandtowers, Lady (in 'Barbara of the House of Grebe'), 150

Venn, Diggory (in *The Return of the Native*), 78, 91n, 92, 93, 96, 97, 104, 106

Voss, T., 6

Vye, Eustacia (in *The Return of the Native*), 91n, 95, 98, 100-105

Wagner, Richard, 5

Wain, John, 220

Weber, Carl J., 25, 27, 49, 132, 156, 184, 198, 230

Webster, H. C., 115n

Well-Beloved, The, 147, 158-161

Wellington, Duke of (in *The Dynasts*), 216

Wessex Tales, 147; 'The Distracted Preacher', 149; 'Fellow-Townsmen', 149; 'Interlopers at the Knap', 148-149; 'The Melancholy Hussar', 148; 'The Three Strangers', 147-148; 'A Tradition of

Eighteen Hundred and Four',
148, 216; 'The Withered Arm'
148, 149
Westminster Abbey, 9, 10, 18
Whittle (in *The Mayor of Caster-
bridge*), 112, 118-119
Wildeve, Damon (in *The Return
of the Native*), 91n, 94, 95,
100, 101, 103-105
Winchester, 29
Winterborne, Giles (in *The
Woodlanders*), 128n, 137-144
Woodlanders, The, 75, 81, 127-
146, 164, 178, 193
Woolf, Virginia, 127
Wordsworth, William, 16, 34;

'Resolution and Independ-
ence', 13
Wouvermans, Philips, 144

Yeats, W. B., 2, 31
Yeobright, Clym (in *The Return
of the Native*), 91n, 97, 99-102,
104, 105, 106, 126
Yeobright, Mrs (in *The Return
of the Native*), 91n, 95, 97,
100, 103, 105-107, 171
Yeobright, Thomasin (in *The
Return of the Native*), 91n, 92,
93, 94, 98, 100, 104
Young, G. M., 220